SECOND EDITION

IN CHARGE 1
TEACHER'S GUIDE

An Integrated Skills Course for High-Level Students

Evelina Dimitrova-Galaczi
Árpád Galaczi

Consulting authors
James E. Purpura
Diane Pinkley

Teacher's Guide by
Thomas Impola

LONGMAN ON THE **WEB**

Longman.com offers online resources for teachers
and students. Access our Companion Websites, our
online catalog, and our local offices around the world.

Longman English Success offers online courses
to give learners flexible study options. Courses cover
General English, Business English, and Exam Preparation.

Visit us at **longman.com** and **englishsuccess.com**.

Longman

In Charge 1, Teacher's Guide, Second Edition

Pearson Education, 10 Bank Street, White Plains, NY 10606

Vice president, instructional design: Allen Ascher
Editorial manager: Pam Fishman
Project manager: Margaret Grant
Assistant editor: Jennifer McAliney
Vice president, director of design and production: Rhea Banker
Executive managing editor: Linda Moser
Production manager: Liza Pleva
Production coordinator: Melissa Leyva
Production editor: Kathleen Silloway
Director of manufacturing: Patrice Fraccio
Senior manufacturing buyer: Edith Pullman
Cover design: Tracey Cataldo
Text composition: Design 5 Creatives
Text font: 10.5/13 Palatino

ISBN: 0-13-094265-0

Printed in the United States of America
1 2 3 4 5 6 7 8 9 10-TCS-07 06 05 04 03 02

CONTENTS

Introduction to *In Charge,*

Second Edition

This new edition of *In Charge* is a theme-based, integrated-skills series for secondary and adult students. It is a unique and flexible program with multiple entry levels. The components can be used together as a comprehensive two-level course or used individually as separate mini-courses.

Key Features of the First Edition

The second edition of *In Charge* maintains and builds on the key features of the successful and popular first edition.

- **An integrated syllabus** presents the communication skills—listening, speaking, reading, writing—together with functions, notions, and grammar.
- **Thematic units** teach English through a variety of high-interest topics and content.
- **A learner-centered approach** makes students active participants in every lesson by activating their prior knowledge of the topics and encouraging them to share and express their personal experiences, ideas, and opinions in English.
- **The development of critical-thinking skills** such as classifying, sequencing, making inferences, and drawing conclusions helps students learn more effectively and retain learned material longer.
- **The application of learning strategies** such as applying prior knowledge, scanning for specific information, skimming for main ideas, and getting meaning from context helps students take responsibility for their own learning and become more effective, independent learners.

New Features of the Second Edition

The second edition incorporates many ideas and improvements suggested by teachers from around the world.

- **Revised and updated content** includes new conversations, listening activities, and readings.

- **Scope and sequence** charts highlight the new unit organization and identify and summarize key language skills, strategies, and topics in each unit.
- **Grammar presentations and practice** allow students to focus on form, meaning, and use. Many new and revised grammar presentations provide clear explanations and examples. New exercises and activities offer a balance of controlled and communicative practice.
- **Learning strategies** are now highlighted in all levels with the symbol ➡. Many new strategies have been added to promote effective, independent learning, and academic success.
- **Progress Checks** have been added every three units to recycle and reinforce grammar, key vocabulary, and writing. Test-taking strategies have been incorporated into each Progress Check.
- **Teacher's Guides** are easier to use, with unit objectives, audioscripts, and answers to exercises clearly identified and highlighted.
- **Achievement tests** allow teachers and students to assess progress after each unit.
- **The audio program** is now available in two formats: audiocassettes and audio CDs.

About the Authors

Evelina Dimitrova-Galaczi is currently pursuing her doctoral degree in Applied Linguistics at Teachers College, Columbia University, in New York City and is working as a Teaching Associate at the American Language Program, Columbia University. She holds a B.A. in English Philology from Sofia University, Bulgaria, and an M.A. in TESOL from Teachers College, Columbia University.

Ms. Dimitrova-Galaczi has been an EFL/ESL teacher for the past twelve years, with a current focus on academic writing and discussion skills. In addition, she has been involved in teacher education and the teaching of ESL practica in New York City.

Árpád Galaczi is the Coordinator of the Community English Program at Teachers College, Columbia University, in New York City. He holds a B.A. in English Literature and Linguistics from the Babeş-Bolyai University in Cluj-Napoca, Romania, an M.A. in TESOL and an Ed.M. in Applied Linguistics from Teachers College, Columbia University. He is currently pursuing his doctoral studies in Applied Linguistics at Teachers College.

Mr. Galaczi has been teaching EFL and ESL for the past ten years, working with all age groups and all proficiency levels. He has also been involved in teacher training, taught undergraduate practical courses, and acted as consultant for the development of an EFL educational CD-ROM in his native Romania.

Components of the Program

Each level of *In Charge*, Second Edition, contains these components.

Student Book

Each Student Book contains twelve thematic units. A new Scope and Sequence chart following the Contents page highlights and summarizes the important language skills, learning strategies, and teaching points in each unit. New Progress Checks following Units 3, 6, 9, and 12 reinforce key vocabulary and grammar points while teaching students valuable test-taking strategies to improve their performance on common standardized tests. Additional material includes a Starting Out section (providing a brief introduction to the course), a pronunciation table (referenced to the *Longman Advanced American Dictionary*), Vocabulary Expansion activities for each unit, and a comprehensive grammar reference section at the back of the book.

Workbook

The Workbook provides further practice and reinforcement of vocabulary and grammar, as well as additional interactive speaking activities and listening tasks. A self-review page (You're In Charge!) at the end of each unit allows students to assess their own progress.

Teacher's Guide

The Teacher's Guide contains complete teaching suggestions for the Student Book and references to corresponding Workbook practice exercises. Answers to all Student Book exercises are now highlighted in boxes on the Teacher's Guide pages. Audioscripts to all Student Book and Workbook exercises, along with the Workbook Answer Key, can be found in the back of the Teacher's Guide. Each Teacher's Guide unit ends with suggestions for evaluating language and communication skills. The Teacher's Guide also includes information on basic teaching techniques and Scope and Sequence charts. As an added feature, *In Charge 1* and *2* also provide reproducible Vocabulary Expansion Activities that provide additional vocabulary-enrichment work.

Audio Program

All material appearing on the audio program is indicated in the Student Book and Workbook pages with the symbol 🎧. The audio program is available in two formats, audiocassettes and audio CDs. Both contain conversation models as well as materials for the Warm Up, Listen, and Pronunciation sections in the Student Book and selected listening exercises in the Workbook.

Test Booklet

The new Test Booklet provides an additional option for evaluation. The Test Booklet contains midterm and final tests as well as an achievement test for each unit and an answer key.

A Student Book Unit

In response to teachers' feedback on the first edition, the unit organization of the new edition has been restructured for greater clarity and ease of use. Each unit is divided into four distinct sections, each identified by a different color, which highlight the pedagogic features and language skills.

GETTING STARTED

This unit opening section consists of three parts.

Warm Up

Warm Up activates students' prior knowledge of the unit theme. It introduces the theme by means of a short listening passage indicated by the symbol 🎧. Interactive activities get students talking about how the theme relates to their knowledge, feelings, and life experiences.

Figure It Out

Figure It Out presents the new language in a functional context in the form of a conversation, mini-reading, or questionnaire. Students begin to acquire the language before they analyze it in the Grammar section. A Vocabulary Check exercise helps students discover the meaning of the target vocabulary from context. This exercise is indicated in the Student Book with the symbol ☑.

Talk About It

Talk About It provides students with the opportunity to practice one or more aspects of the target language in a controlled context. This is an intermediary step between cue dependency and real production.

GRAMMAR

This section presents the target grammar of the unit. Grammar presentations and practice focus on structure, meaning, and usage, and are designed to encourage students to analyze the language by means of inductive and deductive reasoning. A variety of exercises give students the opportunity to practice language structures individually and in pairs or groups. Check Your Understanding exercises allow students to test their understanding of specific situations in which particular tenses and other grammar points are used. These exercises are indicated with the symbol ☑ . A culminating Express Yourself activity allows students to use the language communicatively in personalized contexts. This activity is indicated with the symbol ⊠ .

LISTENING and SPEAKING

This third section integrates listening and speaking strategies, skills, and activities.

Before You Listen

These activities focus on anticipating meaning and applying prior knowledge to the listening task. These pre-listening activities are followed by strategies such as listening for gist, listening for details, and listening critically. These strategies are indicated with the symbol ➡ and are followed by a listening activity from the audio program which is indicated by the symbol ⌒ .

Speak Out

Speak Out activities develop fluency as the students share information, opinions, and experiences. In addition, each unit focuses on at least one discussion strategy, which is indicated with the symbol ➡ .

Pronunciation

This section provides practice in perceiving, predicting, and producing the phonology of English (sounds, intonation, stress, reduction, etc.).

READING and WRITING

This final section integrates reading and writing strategies, skills, and activities.

Read About It

Read About It contains high-interest readings that reflect and extend the unit themes. Pre-reading exercises (Before You Read) focus on applying students' prior knowledge of the topic. Reading strategies such as understanding sequence, making inferences, and evaluating supporting details are presented and then checked in comprehension exercises. These strategies are indicated with the symbol ➡ .

Think About It

Think About It presents activities that offer students further opportunities to apply strategies and share personal knowledge and experience related to the readings in open-ended, creative ways.

Write

This section focuses on specific writing tasks—such as writing a topic sentence, narrowing a topic, using supporting details—that prepare students to write with confidence in English. Writing strategies such as writing a persuasive essay and choosing and narrowing a topic are presented. These strategies are indicated with the symbol ➡ .

Write About It

Write About It tasks are purposeful and communicative because students are writing for a real audience of their peers. A new, culminating Check Your Writing exercise applies the important writing process steps of peer feedback and revision. These exercises are indicated with the symbol ☑ .

A Teacher's Guide Unit

Each unit in the Teacher's Guide starts with a list of unit objectives. These objectives are followed by complete teaching information for each section of the Student Book unit. The teaching information contains suggestions for previewing and presenting material, language and cultural notes, and a rich variety of optional extension activities, including ideas for discussion topics, games and competitions, and research projects. These optional activities add flexibility to the course length, depending on how few or how many of the optional activities are used.

- The **Preview** section gives suggestions for introducing content and for developing the target language. During the Preview, you will want to encourage students to say as much as they can about the content or theme. Model correct usage, but remember that the objective here is to get students involved and to give them the language they need to express their ideas.
- The **Presentation** section provides effective, step-by-step suggestions for presenting the lesson, using clear, practical teaching methods.
- A variety of **Options** provides flexibility so that you can adapt the lesson to the needs of your class and offer additional activities for reinforcement and enrichment.
- The **Evaluation** section at the end of each unit contains suggestions for four different ways to evaluate your students' progress. See pages Txi–Txii for more information.
- **Workbook** links suggest points at which the corresponding material in the Workbook may be assigned, indicated with the symbol [Link] .
- **Language Notes** explain colloquial English, foreign words, and idiomatic expressions, and provide additional information about usage.
- **Culture Notes** give information on cultural contexts and historical backgrounds relevant to the unit themes.

Presenting a Unit

GETTING STARTED

Warm Up

Each unit of *In Charge* opens with a Warm Up section that both introduces students to the theme of the unit and involves them in the theme. It typically consists of a listening passage to which students must respond and one or more interactive exercises in which they talk about the unit theme.

Preview suggestions include the introduction of the target language through the use of pictures, realia, and mime. Depending on students' abilities, you may wish to skip this section and have the students learn the language directly from the recording and the Student Book pages.

In general, all the target language appears in the Warm Up and Figure It Out sections. These sections have been carefully designed so that students can discover the meaning of the new language through the pictures and context. Because of this, you should begin the presentation of each unit by reading the unit title and the Warm Up section with the class.

Encourage students to say as much as they can about the pictures and text. Model any language they need. Use the Preview suggestions to clarify or for reinforcement or review.

Play the recording and have students complete the corresponding exercises. Use the procedures outlined in Listen on page Tix.

Figure It Out

This section demonstrates the use of the new language in functional situations.

There are several ways to present this section to students. You will want to choose the method that best suits your classroom and your method of teaching.

Whatever method you use, first have students comment on any pictures and predict what the section is about. Using prior knowledge and anticipating meaning are valuable comprehension tools.

Many of the units contain conversations. In presenting them, you can emphasize listening and aural comprehension by reading the conversations aloud as students listen with their books closed. You might wish to set up a comprehension task. For some classes, ask a simple factual question and tell students to listen for the answer. For more advanced students, you should set more difficult tasks, such as inferring where the speakers are, what their relationship is, etc. You may find it valuable to have students read the comprehension questions before they listen.

Next, have students work in pairs or groups to read the conversations aloud. They might also answer the comprehension questions and do the meaning-from-context exercise at this time.

Finally, ask for volunteers to perform the conversations for the class. Encourage students to adapt or add to the conversations by introducing new topics or adding additional speakers as their level of proficiency permits. Simple props will make performing the conversations fun and meaningful.

For units that contain mini-readings or questionnaires, see Read About It on page Tx for ideas and suggestions.

Presenting Vocabulary

Active and Receptive Vocabulary

In Charge includes both active and receptive vocabulary. The active vocabulary has been selected for its usefulness and frequency of occurrence in real communication. In addition, receptive vocabulary appears throughout the unit. Students are not expected to learn these non-target words. Instead, they should learn to develop a tolerance for uncertainty with respect to unknown vocabulary. As long as they can complete the activities, understanding every word is not necessary. Students should be encouraged to try to make intelligent guesses about meaning based on the use of context, cognates, word families, and other strategies.

Introducing Vocabulary

Every opportunity should be taken to involve students in the learning process. Encourage students to provide synonyms, antonyms, examples, or simple definitions. Many English words are similar in form and meaning to words in other languages. Students should be trained to recognize these cognates (and cautioned on the dangers of false cognates).

Help students understand and use the techniques of paraphrasing and circumlocution to elicit and communicate new, unfamiliar vocabulary—for example, to say "the thing you cut bread with" for *knife*, or "go behind (someone)" for *follow*. As often as possible, help them understand meaning through the use of word associations. For example, the meaning of many verbs can be demonstrated through the use of different complements—e.g., *run out of gas* on the highway, *run out of money* at the store, *run out of eggs* while making a cake.

Finally, encourage students to use monolingual dictionaries. Bilingual dictionaries force students to see English in terms of their own language instead of as a distinct tool for communication. Translation should be used only as a last resort. The *Longman Advanced American Dictionary* is an ideal companion for *In Charge*.

Vocabulary Notebooks

Encourage students to keep notebooks of new vocabulary and to include both the words they learn in the Student Book and words they want to know in order to express their own ideas. Have students make up sentences to illustrate the meaning of the new words. This can be done individually or in pairs or groups. Write the best examples on the board for students to copy into their notebooks. If students group the words by meaning and function, at the end of the year they will have their own personal dictionaries. (You may want to collect and check the notebooks periodically to make sure that students' example sentences are correct.)

You might also wish to have a class vocabulary list. Students can alternate being responsible for writing down new vocabulary and presenting it to the class at the end of each week.

Talk About It

This mini-dialogue presents a series of connected conversational cues (a discourse chain) that trains students to relate roles, functions, and language. Have students work in pairs to read the situation and identify the roles; for example, in Unit 1 the situation is a health study, and the roles are a medical researcher and a subject being interviewed about his or her use of food-based "home remedies." Check that students understand the organization of the chart. Explain that while the model conversation contains *examples* of the language functions that appear in the right-hand column, it is possible to use other language. Go over the functions, and elicit other example language for the functions. Then have one pair read the model conversation aloud for the class. Assign or let students choose roles. Have them read the functions and the mini-dialogue aloud. Answer any questions about vocabulary or grammar. Then have the pairs work together to create their own conversations. Encourage them to come up with their own examples and to expand on the conversations. Circulate and offer help. Make notes of any student errors and review them with the class after the activity is finished. Ask selected pairs to present their conversations to the class.

Refer to your notes and write errors on the board without identifying who made them. Then focus attention on the exercise cues; in Unit 1, these cues are the list of "remedies" (see Student Book, page 5). Do one example with a student or ask a pair to do one example as a model. Then have the pairs work together to complete the exercise. Encourage students to cover the model conversations, looking only at the functions, and use their own examples as their proficiency develops.

GRAMMAR

In this section, students are given a brief grammatical description of the target language and are asked to apply those rules (deductive reasoning), or they are given a number of examples and are asked to use the examples to formulate rules (inductive reasoning).

This presentation is followed by exercises designed to accomplish two purposes: to train students to use the language accurately and to encourage them to use it fluently. The exercises designed for accuracy can be done by the students independently, in class or as homework; however, you will probably find it preferable to have students complete them in pairs or small groups. In this way, students can help each other form the correct answers. Check Your Understanding exercises follow to allow students to test their understanding of the specific situations in which the particular points are used. These exercises are done individually and then students are encouraged to check their answers with a partner. The Express Yourself exercises should be done in pairs to promote fluency and proper use of new vocabulary. Cooperative learning and peer correction are invaluable in developing both accuracy and fluency.

LISTENING and SPEAKING

Listen

The listening selections on the audio program provide practice in understanding ordinary English discourse. Listening selections include casual conversations, radio interviews, panel discussions, and lectures. These listening selections are *representative* rather than authentic. The language in these passages has been chosen for its frequency, its illustration of the grammar and theme, and the likelihood that students will encounter it. Each listening section begins with Before You Listen pre-listening questions, which establish the context and help students activate and share prior knowledge. The pre-listening questions are followed by a specific listening strategy, highlighted with ➡. You will want students to answer the pre-listening questions, to comment on any pictures, charts, etc., and to discuss the strategy before you play the recording or read the selection aloud. Always remind students that they don't have to understand every word of the selection in order to do the exercise.

The first time you play the recording or read the selection aloud, you may wish to have students listen with their books closed. Set a purpose for listening by asking a simple, factual question and having students listen for the answer. When they answer the question, have them tell you anything else they can remember about what they heard.

Have students open their books and reread the directions. Play the recording or read the selection again and tell them to listen for the specific information the exercise asks for. According to students' ability, you can have them mark the exercise at this time or during a third listening.

After students have written their answers, play the recording or read the selection again for students to check their work.

Pronunciation

To communicate understandably, a speaker must use the patterns of word stress, intonation contours, and rhythms that are characteristic of a language. The listener, too, must participate actively, using his or her knowledge of those elements to derive meaning. Good pronunciation evolves gradually. However, students should be encouraged from the start to listen carefully to the way English sounds are produced and to attempt the pronunciation of all of them.

A book alone cannot teach pronunciation; it can only serve as a guide. It is your voice and the voices on the recordings that must provide the models for the class. Speakers on radio and TV, recordings, and class visitors who are native speakers can provide additional models. Good models, consistent patterns, and ample opportunity to listen and speak are essential for developing good pronunciation.

In Charge focuses on enabling students to perceive and produce such aspects of English phonology as plural and past tense endings, word and sentence stress, intonation, reduction, and elision. Most students will not be able to produce such things as intonation and stress with perfect accuracy. Concentrate instead on their understanding of these aspects of English.

Have students read the explanation and make predictions about the target sound. Play the recording or read the examples several times while students listen. Remember that they must be able to perceive a sound before they can produce it. Next, play the recording or say each word or sentence, to be repeated first by the class, then by groups, and finally by individual students. Then have students complete the exercises and formulate the rule, if required.

You will find it valuable to have students work in pairs or groups to read the examples to each other. This gives additional, needed practice in forming the target sounds correctly.

Speak Out

Begin by setting up a situation familiar to the students in which the target discussion strategy would be used. For example, if the strategy focuses on persuading, you might ask students, if you have young students, how late they are allowed to stay out on weekday evenings and how they would try to get permission from their parents to stay out later. If students are parents, ask how late they allow their children to stay out and how their children try to get permission to stay out later. Elicit examples from the class and/or refer them to the strategy presentation box in the

Student Book. Have one or more pairs of students use the expressions in a conversation based on your example.

Divide students into pairs or groups according to the activity, and have them read the directions. Answer any questions they have. For some units, you may wish to model a conversation for the class or have students do so. Then have students complete the activity. Monitor the groups, but do not interrupt for correction. Instead, take note of repeated errors for later reteaching or review.

Encourage students to use the language in the strategy boxes as much as possible, inside and out of class. The purpose of this activity is to help students gain confidence in their oral performance. The constant reinforcement of this language will result in greater fluency.

READING and WRITING

Read About It

The reading selection in Read About It extends the theme of the unit and provides the opportunity for improving reading strategies and critical thinking skills. The section opens with Before You Read pre-reading questions, which introduce the content and help students recall prior knowledge of the subject. Additional previewing is done by drawing attention to illustrations and/or using strategies such as skimming and scanning. Pre-reading questions are followed by specific reading strategies (highlighted with ➡) aimed at helping students focus their attention on reading for specific information, examples, or main ideas or on such strategies as guessing meaning from context and making inferences.

Most reading done for information or pleasure is silent reading, so students should read the selections silently. Encourage them to read without dictionaries. Stopping to look up unknown words interrupts the flow of reading and makes it more likely that students read word for word rather than for general meaning. In addition, the selections have all been carefully written to enable students to use cognates and to understand meaning from context.

The reading may be assigned as homework, but you may find it more beneficial to have students read in class. Set a time limit to encourage them to keep reading without stopping at each unknown word. Watch to make sure they are not relying too much on dictionaries but are using context clues to help them comprehend new words.

Think About It

A final Think About It section presents challenging, creative activities related to the reading. These open-ended activities offer students further opportunities to develop critical thinking skills and share personal knowledge and experience.

Write

In the Write sections, specific elements of paragraph writing are presented—such as identifying what makes a good introduction, components of an essay, narrowing a topic, writing a thesis statement, adding supporting details, and writing a conclusion—along with other important academic writing skills and forms such as summarizing and using text citations. The presentations are immediately followed by one or more exercises that allow students to apply and practice the target elements or skills.

Write About It

Write About It tasks are purposeful and communicative. Students write for a real purpose related to the unit theme and for a real audience of their peers.

In Charge also incorporates key elements of the writing process to help students brainstorm and organize ideas, write their first drafts, and then edit and revise their paragraphs and essays. The new Check Your Writing exercises at the end of each unit focus students' attention on key points from the unit and help them edit and revise their drafts, applying the important writing process steps of peer feedback and revision. The following steps highlight and summarize key aspects of the writing process. Depending on your teaching objectives and classroom situation, you may follow these steps as guidelines for using the writing process more extensively and comprehensively.

1. Prewriting
Prewriting includes the important strategies of brainstorming, focusing, and organizing information. These strategies help students to generate, select, and organize ideas so that they can write a first draft of a paragraph or essay on a specific topic.

In **brainstorming**, students make a list of as many ideas about a particular topic as they can. The purpose of brainstorming is to generate and explore lots of possible ideas. Students should not worry at this point whether or not their ideas are good or bad but should just write them down.

Once students have a list of possible ideas, they can then focus on choosing the best, most useful ideas for inclusion in a paragraph or essay. In **focusing**, students should keep the ideas that relate to the topic they will write about and eliminate ideas that do not.

After students choose the ideas they want to write about, they are ready to organize them in a paragraph or essay. Each Write section focuses on a specific element—such as writing topic sentences, narrowing a topic, or writing supporting sentences—for **organizing** ideas in a paragraph or essay. These sections have been expanded and improved in the new edition to include more examples and models of the target elements.

Most students find it beneficial to do some or all prewriting with a partner because this enables them to invent and generate more new ideas from each other's ideas.

2. First Draft

Many students do not realize that good writing is usually the result of many revisions or drafts. Knowing that they will write more than one draft allows students to focus on different aspects of their writing in each draft. As students write their first drafts, they should concentrate on composition, not mechanics (such as grammar, spelling, and punctuation). Have them work with partners to write good topic sentences. Remind them that every supporting sentence should amplify the topic sentence and that the sentences should be in a logical order. Assure them that good writers revise several times.

3. Revision

Revision includes making such changes as adding new information, deleting nonessential information, and arranging the information in the best order. Editing for mechanics—to check grammar and proofread for correct spelling and punctuation—is a final step of revision. Students should understand that you expect correct grammar, spelling, and punctuation in the final copy, but that revision of these comes last in the writing process.

Peer editing is an effective tool for second-language writers. Have students exchange papers with a partner and read the partner's paper for interest and accuracy of content. Do they understand what the other person is trying to say? Do they have any questions they would like answered to make the passage clearer? Do they see anything that is out of place or irrelevant? The new, culminating Check Your Writing exercises can help students focus their attention on these and other questions. After peer editing, have students work independently to improve their drafts. Partners can then get back together to discuss

the improvements and to work on mechanics. You may wish to have partners sign each other's final drafts. This gives each person a stake in the other's success.

4. Correction

When correcting students' writing, concentrate on structure and ideas over grammar, punctuation, and spelling. You might use one color to comment on content and another color to mark errors in mechanics.

Student compositions will probably contain many mechanical errors. For this reason, you may wish to concentrate on only one aspect in a particular composition. For example, if a student is having difficulty with punctuation, you might mark only the punctuation errors. Or you may wish to mark only the errors in the target language of the unit.

However you do it, be sure to let students know that you and the rest of the class are interested in what they have to say by providing some means of presenting their work.

5. Presenting

All writing should be done with an audience in mind. Public acceptance of the writer's product validates both the writer and the writing process. Therefore, you should arrange to have students present their writing to the class—if they so wish.

Some suggestions for presenting:

- Have students read their paragraphs or essays aloud to a group or to the class.
- Display the papers on a bulletin board.
- Place a number of samples from an assignment in a notebook to be shared by interested members of the class.

A process-oriented approach based on these five stages makes students confident writers, providing them with both a blueprint and the necessary skills for crafting and polishing their paragraphs and essays.

Remember that good readers often become good writers. By providing a variety of English language materials for students to read (magazines and newspapers as well as books, fiction as well as nonfiction), you will be increasing their understanding of writing in English.

Evaluation

The second edition of *In Charge* offers a new supplementary test booklet containing midterm and final tests, as well as an individual achievement test for each unit. These new achievement tests complement and expand on the other ways of evaluating students' progress provided in the first edition: a self-test of vocabulary and grammar, an interactive dictation for aural comprehension and writing, and a check of oral proficiency.

Achievement Tests

There are new achievement tests for each of the twelve units. Each unit test measures students' progress in grammar, vocabulary, listening and speaking, reading, and writing. There are separate scales for different parts of the test, so you can test all or selective skills, depending on your teaching objectives.

Self-Check

Each unit in the Workbook ends with a review called You're In Charge!, allowing students to assess their own progress. Encourage students to complete these sections without looking back at their student books. You may want to have students complete them in class, however, so that you can record their results. Students are interested in their own progress and will take responsibility for review.

Portfolios

A portfolio approach to evaluation provides a means of assessing competence over the long-term rather than gauging a student's progress solely on the basis of "make-or-break" spot testing. Additionally, it helps students to overcome test anxiety and enables them to balance their strengths against the weaknesses that will inevitably be pointed out in Achievement Tests and Progress Checks. *In Charge* provides a suggested list of portfolio samples in the Evaluation section at the end of every unit. These include the main writing assignment for that unit as well as two oral communication activities for recording. The decision on what to include in student portfolios is left to the teacher, or even to the student, if the teacher sees fit to do it that way. You will no doubt wish to make your own scoring rubric (rating scale) in order to reflect your teaching situation. However, scoring rubrics for both writing and oral communication as well as a photocopiable portfolio assessment can be found on pages Txvi–Txix for your convenience.

Interactive Dictation

Dictation can be a valuable diagnostic tool. By careful correction, you can discover which areas need reteaching or review. For example, if students consistently drop the third-person singular, simple present tense ending, you will want to do additional practice on hearing, saying, and spelling that ending. Additionally, interactive components help you to assess student ability with the target grammar and structures, as well as eliciting additional vocabulary. Information on giving and correcting dictations can be found on page Txv.

Evaluating Oral Communication Skills

Oral communication has one primary goal— to get the message across as clearly as possible. The ability to communicate orally in a second or foreign language involves a complex set of competencies or abilities, each of which may develop at its own pace. We define oral communication skills in terms of five competencies. See the Oral Communication Rubric on page Txix.

Oral assessment can make students anxious, so use strategies that help students feel safe. Engaging in small talk before the beginning of an oral exam—for example, asking students how they are or talking about the weather and other simple topics—can help students feel more relaxed and at ease. You can also make students feel more comfortable by using clear directions and procedures so that they know what to expect.

You may choose to assess students individually or to have them work in pairs or small groups, depending on your objectives. (For example, if you want to assess students' ability to manage a discussion, you need to have students interacting in small groups.) Audio- or videotaping students during oral exams is an effective tool for learning and assessment. This allows you to listen several times and score what you observe. Audio- or videotaping also gives you the option of involving students in self- or peer assessment— that is, students can listen/observe and evaluate themselves or each other.

However you conduct oral assessment, introduce students gradually to the criteria of correctness so that they understand the objectives and know how to improve. In the beginning, you might want to assess only one category (for example, fluency), and then gradually add more. You can use the scale provided in the Oral Communication Rubric or modify it to suit your needs.

An oral assessment based on a single day's performance has obvious drawbacks. For that reason, you may wish to conduct assessment over an extended period of time by having students make audio or video recordings for inclusion in their portfolios. Two oral communication options are included in the evaluation section at the end of each unit.

Vocabulary Expansion Activities

The twelve reproducible, supplementary activities (one for each unit in the Student Book) provide students with additional tools for becoming independent learners by increasing their active and receptive vocabularies. They present vocabulary-building skills such as recognizing prefixes and suffixes, understanding noun compounds, and inferring extended meanings. Topics of other activities include idioms, empty verbs (*take, have, break,* etc.), phrasal verbs, and other specific difficulties of English vocabulary.

A good time to present the expansion activities is after students have completed the unit. As students complete each activity, encourage them to think of as many additional examples of the specific topic as possible. Answers to the vocabulary expansion activities appear at the end of the teaching notes for each unit.

Teaching Techniques

Using Realia

The use of realia in the classroom will motivate students and make them realize the relevance of their language study. Realia includes anything from the real world: guest speakers, radio and TV programs, films, records and tapes, printed materials such as brochures, tickets, schedules, ads, maps, menus, food, clothing, toy vehicles and furniture, photos and other pictures. *In Charge* makes extensive use of realia throughout the units, in authentic readings, listenings, and graphics.

Working in Pairs and Groups

Most of the language practice and skill development activities in *In Charge* can be done in pairs or in groups of three or four. There are many advantages to having students work in pairs or groups.

Student involvement and participation are maximized. Each student gets the opportunity to speak many times during each class. In addition, each student practices all the examples in an exercise instead of eight or ten students each practicing one example.

Students are able to collaborate on answers and rehearse them before speaking in front of the whole class. The pair or group is responsible for each member's participation. Students can confirm their knowledge or learn from their partners or groups. Anxiety is reduced, which increases success.

Face-to-face interaction simulates real-life social contact, encouraging the use of eye contact, proper intonation, emotional tone, rejoinders, exclamations, etc., which are difficult when reciting in front of the class.

Forming Groups

You will want to give each student in the class the opportunity to work with as many different partners or groups as possible during the term or year. You might assign partners and/or groups at the beginning of each week or even at the beginning of each class. You can do this in a variety of ways. The simplest is just to have students sitting next to or in front of and behind each other work together. You can put two to four slips of paper numbered 1, two to four slips numbered 2, etc., in a bag for the students to draw from. (The 1s work together, the 2s work together, etc.) Or you can put the names of half the students in the bag for the other half to draw from. Sometimes you may want to have students choose their own partners or groups.

No matter how you assign the groups, you will want one member of each group to act as leader. It is the group leader's task to keep the group working smoothly and talking in English. The leader should take any necessary notes and report any conclusions to the class. At first you may want to choose those students who have greater English fluency for this position, but it is important that every student be given the opportunity to act as a group leader.

Procedures

Always make sure everyone understands what to do. Have students read the instructions and any examples or models. They can do this silently or by reading aloud to each other. To encourage effective reading of the directions, set a time limit. Then have students close their books and tell each other what they are supposed to do. Answer any questions the pairs or groups have.

Always read the example, or model one of the items with a student. If you like, you can then ask for volunteers to do the next item as an additional model for the class. Establish a time limit. This will help keep students on task. Most activities in *In Charge* can be completed in no more than five minutes. Longer activities can have a longer time limit, but don't let students continue beyond their ability to speak English.

As students are talking, walk around the class and monitor as many groups as possible. Encourage students to speak only in English. Answer questions and provide any language they need. Students will make mistakes, but don't interrupt for error correction. Students should feel free to express themselves however they can. Repeated errors should be noted for later reteaching and review.

Remind students that error correction is the learner's responsibility as well as the teacher's. Encourage them to recognize their own mistakes. Peer- and self-correction are valuable tools in learning because students feel less pressure than they do from teacher correction. Train students to help each other give the correct answers before you step in to help. You might give them copies of the Oral Communication Rubric to help them evaluate themselves and each other. Keeping a record of their performance in each unit will help them assess their progress.

Conclude the activity by having a few pairs do parts of the activity for the class or by having group leaders report the group's conclusions.

Remember that this kind of practice gives all students the chance to use their new language often. This extended listening and speaking time will greatly improve their confidence and ability.

Pair or group work can result in a noisy classroom, but remember—it's the sound of students communicating in English!

Games and Activities

Chain Drills

For some classes, a chain drill is an excellent intermediary step for practicing language after modeling by the teacher and before working in pairs. It can be done in small groups or as a class. In a typical chain drill, each student holds an object or picture or focuses on a picture in the Student Book. You begin the chain by showing an object or picture to the first student and asking a question. After answering, that student turns to the next student and asks the question. Continue until everyone has had a chance both to ask and to answer.

Teacher: (*Shows eraser*) What's this?

Student A: It's an eraser. (*Shows pen to Student B*) What's this?

Student B: It's a pen. (*Shows book to Student C*) What's this?

Spelling Bees

Spelling bee techniques can be adapted for many kinds of language practice. To begin a typical spelling bee, ask students to stand. Give the first student a word to spell. If that person spells the word incorrectly, he or she must sit down and the second student gets a chance to spell the same word. If that student spells it correctly, the next student is given a different word to spell. The game continues until only one student is left standing.

The game can be played in teams or in small groups, with the group leader giving the words.

Surveys

Having students survey each other provides real language practice. Students enjoy surveys because they find out new information about their classmates and because they can compare their own lives and attitudes with those of their peers.

Begin a survey by having students tell you the questions they want answered about a topic. Write the questions on the board. You need one question for each student to ask. Have each student ask every other student his or her question and record the answers. (If your class is large, have students do the survey in groups with one member of each group asking the same question.)

Next, have each student summarize his or her results and write them on the board. You may wish to have students make a graph of the class's responses.

Finally, talk about the answers. Were any of them surprising? Which questions was the class evenly divided about? Were there any that everyone answered the same?

Interactive Dictations

Dictations are an excellent means for students to gain proficiency in aural comprehension and writing. Dictations can also be valuable diagnostic tools. By careful correction, you can discover which language skills need reteaching or review. For example, if a student consistently drops past tense endings, you will want to give that student extra practice in hearing and saying those sounds. By adding interactive components, in which students are asked to respond creatively to the material being dictated, the dictation can also be used to assess productive ability.

There are many kinds of dictations—single words, sentences, short dialogues, or paragraphs. Here are a few simple rules and ideas.

- At first, dictate passages that are familiar to the students. For example, after students have listened to a dialogue, read it silently, and answered comprehension questions, you can use it as a dictation. You may wish to have students prepare by reading the passage again as homework.

- Mark the passage for pauses before you read it to the students. The pauses should be after logical phrase groups and at the ends of sentences. (You may want to practice reading the passage aloud.)

- For the first few dictations, name the punctuation marks as you read. First, write the marks on the board and present the English names. Then, as you read the passage, name the marks as they occur. As students become more familiar with English, you can begin to omit the names of the punctuation marks from your reading.

- Write proper names, unknown vocabulary, and words with unusual spellings on the board. If you are dictating a dialogue, write the speakers' names so that the passage is easier to follow.

- Read the selection three times. First, read it at a normal pace while students listen for gist. Next, read it with pauses so that they can write. Allow a few minutes for them to check their work. Then read it again, this time at a pace slightly slower than normal but without long pauses. (In some classes, you may want to vary the speed of the last reading and/or read the passage a fourth time.) In all readings, try to use normal stress and intonation.

There are many ways to correct dictations. You might simply mark all the errors. Another method is to mark only those mistakes in vocabulary and structure that are covered in the unit you are working on. Or you might correct those errors in red and other errors in a different color. However you decide to do it, be sure to praise students for what they do get right.

PORTFOLIO ASSESSMENT: WRITING REPORT

Name: _____   Class: _____

Date: _____   Activity: _____

DELIVERY	RATING	COMMENTS
Content	1 2 3 4 5	_____
Style	1 2 3 4 5	_____
Organization	1 2 3 4 5	_____
Grammar	1 2 3 4 5	_____
Mechanics	1 2 3 4 5	_____

ADDITIONAL COMMENTS

_____

_____

_____

RATING KEY

1 = EXCELLENT   2 = GOOD   3 = SATISFACTORY   4 = NEEDS SOME IMPROVEMENT   5 = NEEDS IMPROVEMENT

PORTFOLIO ASSESSMENT: ORAL COMMUNICATION REPORT

Name: _____   Class: _____

Date: _____   Activity: _____

DELIVERY	RATING	COMMENTS
Fluency	1 2 3 4 5	_____
Accuracy	1 2 3 4 5	_____
Pronunciation	1 2 3 4 5	_____

ADDITIONAL COMMENTS

_____

_____

_____

RATING KEY

1 = EXCELLENT   2 = GOOD   3 = SATISFACTORY   4 = NEEDS SOME IMPROVEMENT   5 = NEEDS IMPROVEMENT

PORTFOLIO ASSESSMENT: Sample Scoring Rubric for Writing

Scores	Descriptors
CONTENT **1: Excellent**	Topic is relevant, engaging, and appropriate in scope; purpose and audience are clear; ideas are well-expressed; arguments are logical and persuasive.
2: Good	Topic is relevant, but not very engaging; scope is somewhat inappropriate; there is some sense of purpose and audience, but it is not consistent; some of the ideas are clearly expressed; some of the examples aren't logical and/or persuasive.
3: Satisfactory	Topic is somewhat relevant but scope is inappropriate; there is not much sense of purpose and audience; some of the ideas aren't clearly expressed; some of the arguments aren't logical and/or persuasive.
4: Needs Some Improvement	Topic is consistent with the assignment, but the scope is inappropriate; purpose and/or audience are unclear; ideas aren't clearly presented; arguments are illogical and/or inconclusive.
5: Needs Improvement	Topic is not consistent with the assignment, and the scope is inappropriate; purpose and audience are unclear; ideas aren't clearly presented; arguments are illogical and/or inconclusive.
STYLE **1: Excellent**	There is an identifiable tone or attitude; the level of formality is appropriate; sentence structures are varied; vocabulary is accurate and appropriate.
2: Good	There is tone or attitude, but it needs to be clearer; level of formality is not consistent; sentence structures are mainly or exclusively compound/complex; vocabulary is occasionally inappropriate.
3: Satisfactory	There is some sense of tone or attitude, but it needs to be clearer; level of formality is either slightly too high, or slightly too low; sentence structures are mainly compound/complex; vocabulary is sometimes inaccurate or inappropriate.
4: Needs Some Improvement	Tone or attitude is unclear; level of formality is not consistent; sentence structures are predominantly simple; vocabulary is basic.
5: Needs Improvement	Tone or attitude is unclear; level of formality is too low; style is inconsistent; sentence structures are simple; vocabulary is basic and often inaccurate.
ORGANIZATION **1: Excellent**	There is an introductory paragraph, with a clear thesis statement; the body of the essay develops and supports the thesis; there is a concluding paragraph that restates the thesis and concludes the argument; essay follows a clear organizational pattern; essay is unified by its main idea. Essay includes a title and bibliography, where needed.
2: Good	There is an introductory paragraph, but the thesis statement could be clearer; the conclusion lacks either a restatement of the thesis or a conclusion of the argument; essay includes a title and bibliography, but the formats are incorrect.
3: Satisfactory	There is an introductory paragraph, but the thesis statement is not clear; there is a concluding paragraph, but it lacks either a restatement of the thesis or a conclusion of the argument; the essay has an organizational pattern but occasionally departs from it; the essay occasionally digresses from its main idea; essay includes a title and bibliography, but the formats are incorrect.

4: Needs Some Improvement	The first paragraph doesn't introduce the topic, or there is no thesis statement; the body of the essay doesn't support the thesis; the final paragraph either doesn't restate the thesis or conclude the argument; there is a clear organizational pattern, but the essay frequently digresses from the main idea; essay includes a partial or inaccurate title.
5: Needs Improvement	There is no introduction and no thesis statement; the body of the essay doesn't develop and support an argument; there is no conclusion; there is no clear organizational pattern; the essay frequently digresses from the main idea.
GRAMMAR **1: Excellent**	Subjects and verbs agree throughout; tenses are used accurately and appropriately; word order is correct; there are no fragments or run-on sentences.
2: Good	There are occasional errors with subject and verb agreement, or tenses are occasionally used inaccurately; there are occasional errors in word order; there are one or two sentence fragments or run-on sentences.
3: Satisfactory	There are occasional errors with subject and verb agreement; tenses are occasionally used inaccurately or inappropriately; there are occasional errors in word order; there are a few sentence fragments or run-on sentences.
4: Needs Some Improvement	There are some errors with subject and verb agreement; tenses are often used inaccurately or inappropriately; there are errors in word order; there are sentence fragments and/or run-on sentences.
5: Needs Improvement	There are frequent errors with subject and verb agreement; tenses are often used inaccurately or inappropriately; there are frequent errors in word order; there are numerous fragments and run-on sentences.
MECHANICS **1: Excellent**	There are no spelling errors; appropriate punctuation and capitalization has been used throughout.
2: Good	There are a few spelling and/or punctuation errors; there are a few errors in capitalization.
3: Satisfactory	There are some recurring spelling errors; there are a few errors in punctuation and in capitalization.
4: Needs Some Improvement	There are spelling and punctuation errors; there are numerous errors in capitalization.
5: Needs Improvement	There are numerous spelling and punctuation errors; there are numerous errors in capitalization and in paragraph formatting.

PORTFOLIO ASSESSMENT:
SAMPLE SCORING RUBRIC FOR ORAL COMMUNICATION

SCORES	DESCRIPTORS
FLUENCY	
1: Excellent	Conveys ideas accurately and naturally; speaks without excessive pauses; keeps communication going smoothly; effectively requests and offers clarification.
2: Good	Has some trouble conveying ideas accurately; speaks with some pauses; uses limited strategies to keep communication going; uses some strategies to request and offer clarification.
3: Satisfactory	Ideas are occasionally unclear; pauses are somewhat frequent and/or occasionally too long; allows lapses in the conversations; somewhat haltingly requests and offers clarification.
4: Needs Some Improvement	Ideas are often unclear; speech has fairly numerous long pauses; has few strategies to keep communication going; has few or limited strategies to request and offer clarification.
5: Needs Improvement	Ideas are unclear; speech has numerous long pauses; has very few strategies to keep communication going; has difficulty requesting and offering clarification.
ACCURACY	
1: Excellent	A variety of grammatical structures are used correctly; vocabulary is used accurately; level of politeness and formality is always appropriate in context.
2: Good	There are occasional errors in grammar or vocabulary; level of politeness and formality is usually appropriate.
3: Satisfactory	There are some errors in grammar; avoids complex structures; vocabulary is occasionally inaccurate; level of politeness and formality is slightly or occasionally inappropriate.
4: Needs Some Improvement	There are errors in grammar; uses simple structures exclusively; vocabulary is often inaccurate; level of politeness and formality is often and/or substantially inappropriate.
5: Needs Improvement	There are numerous errors in simple grammatical structures and vocabulary; level of politeness and formality is often and/or substantially inappropriate.
PRONUNCIATION	
1: Excellent	Stress is used appropriately to convey meaning in context; intonation is used appropriately to convey meaning in context; vowel and consonant sounds are accurately pronounced.
2: Good	Stress is occasionally lacking; intonation is occasionally lacking or inappropriate; there are occasional errors with vowel and consonant sounds.
3: Satisfactory	Stress is sometimes lacking or inappropriate; intonation is occasionally lacking or inappropriate; there are occasional errors with vowel and consonant sounds.
4: Needs Some Improvement	Sentence stress is generally lacking; syllable stress is sometimes inappropriate; intonation is generally lacking or often inappropriate; recurring errors of certain vowel or consonant sounds.
5: Needs Improvement	Sentence stress is generally lacking or often inappropriate; syllable stress intonation is generally inappropriate; errors with vowel or consonant sounds cause comprehension problems.

SCOPE AND SEQUENCE

UNIT	Functions	Grammar	Listen	Pronunciation
▪1▪ **Food for Thought** Page 3	• Giving personal information • Stating preferences • Describing habits • Suggesting remedies	**Review of present tenses:** • simple present • present progressive • present perfect • present perfect progressive • stative verbs	A pizza maker gives a talk on the origins of pizza ➡ Listening for gist and details	−s endings in present tense verbs and plural nouns
▪2▪ **Memorable Moments** Page 15	• Giving information about past events • Asking for more information • Describing experiences	**Review of past tenses:** • simple past • past progressive • past perfect	A conversation about personal firsts ➡ Listening for sequence	Verbs and adjectives
▪3▪ **The Future of Film** Page 27	• Asking for and making predictions • Giving opinions • Offering evidence for opinions • Reaching a compromise	**Review of future:** • *will* • *going to* • simple present • present progressive	A panel discussion on digital technology's effects on films ➡ Evaluating arguments	Differing stress patterns for noun/verb homophones

PROGRESS CHECK (Units 1–3) ▪ Page 39

UNIT	Functions	Grammar	Listen	Pronunciation
▪4▪ **I Beg to Differ** Page 43	• Describing a conflict • Empathizing • Asking for and giving advice • Disagreeing politely	**Gerunds and infinitives:** • subject position • object position • changes in meaning • *It's* adjective + infinitive	A lecture on conflict resolution ➡ Applying background knowledge	Using contrastive stress
▪5▪ **Odd Jobs** Page 55	• Describing jobs • Stating abilities • Conveying likes and dislikes • Expressing surprise	**Passive voice:** • simple present • present progressive • simple past • past progressive • past perfect	A radio interview with a storm chaser ➡ Recognizing categories	Using stress and rhythm patterns in compound nouns and adjectives
▪6▪ **Beholding Beauty** Page 67	• Describing traits • Specifying details • Talking about regrets • Speculating about the future	**Conditionals:** • first • second • third	A lecture on the role of symmetry in beauty ➡ Identifying cause and effect relationships	Using intonation for stress

PROGRESS CHECK (Units 4–6) ▪ Page 79

Txx

Speak Out	Read About It	Write About It	Discussion Topics
Stages of discussions ➡ Opening a meeting or discussion	"The World's Most Popular Beverage" ➡ Using contextual clues	Reviewing audience and purpose ➡ Linking paragraphs to essays	• The social role of food • Influences behind food preferences • Traditional remedies
Defining social issues ➡ Defining an issue	"Paul MacCready's Flying Circus" ➡ Perceiving time organization	Responding to an essay question ➡ Analyzing essay questions	• Significant personal events • Important moments in history • Risk-taking
Debating the ethics of producing violent films ➡ Speaking persuasively	"Virtual Actors Cause High Anxiety in Hollywood" ➡ Reading critically	Writing a persuasive essay ➡ Analyzing a persuasive essay	• New technologies and the film industry • Virtual reality • Virtual actors

Speak Out	Read About It	Write About It	Discussion Topics
Resolving a conflict ➡ Managing conflict	"Say What You Mean" ➡ Evaluating point of view	Writing a composition on conflict ➡ Choosing and narrowing a topic	• Personal conflicts • Conflict management styles • Communication styles • Intercultural communication styles
Explaining and paraphrasing ➡ Maintaining understanding	"A Sweet Job" ➡ Using graphic organizers	Writing an introductory paragraph of an essay ➡ Analyzing introductions	• Unusual jobs • Dream jobs • Advantages and disadvantages of different careers
Giving opinions on fashion fads ➡ Keeping a discussion on track	"Our Obsession with Beauty" ➡ Evaluating supporting examples	Writing good supporting paragraphs ➡ Analyzing supporting paragraphs	• Differing standards of beauty • Yearly budget spent on appearance • The social advantages of attractiveness

SCOPE AND SEQUENCE

UNIT	Functions	Grammar	Listen	Pronunciation
▪ 7 ▪ **Feeling Left Out** Page 83	• Describing problems • Describing objects • Offering solutions • Giving additional information	**Relative clauses:** • identifying • non-identifying	A lecture on the brain ➡ Listening to summarize	Linking and assimilation
▪ 8 ▪ **You're Not My Type** Page 95	• Describing personality traits • Explaining preferences • Requesting specifics	**Phrasal verbs:** • separable • non-separable	A conversation about birth order ➡ Personalizing information	Stressed syllables in phrasal verbs
▪ 9 ▪ **Tech Trends** Page 107	• Describing changes • Speculating about future trends • Evaluating behavior • Stating needs	**Definite and indefinite articles:** • reference • countability	A conversation about tech pets ➡ Identifying implications	Using stress to confirm information

PROGRESS CHECK (Units 7–9) ▪ Page 119

UNIT	Functions	Grammar	Listen	Pronunciation
▪ 10 ▪ **Space Exploration** Page 123	• Stating and defending opinions • Making predictions • Discussing probability	**Future forms:** • future progressive • future perfect	A class discussion about Planet X ➡ Interpreting relationships between ideas	Emphasizing new information
▪ 11 ▪ **Adventure Vacations** Page 135	• Comparing and contrasting • Describing experiences • Expressing regret • Making complaints	**Wishes and regrets:** • *I wish...* • *Had I known...* • *If only...*	Three radio commentaries ➡ Identifying tone	Forming thought groups
▪ 12 ▪ **A Way with Words** Page 147	• Reporting information • Giving interpretations • Paraphrasing • Agreeing and disagreeing	**Reported speech:** • reported statements • reported questions • reporting verbs	A panel discussion on Esperanto ➡ Drawing conclusions	Expressing emotion with intonation

PROGRESS CHECK (Units 10–12) ▪ Page 159

Speak Out	Read About It	Write About It	Discussion Topics
Planning an awareness campaign ➡ Keeping a discussion going	"Life in the Left Lane" ➡ Evaluating generalizations	Writing a conclusion ➡ Analyzing concluding paragraphs	• Difficulties faced by left-handers • Brain activity and handedness
Planning a class project ➡ Having the floor	"Personality's Part and Parcel" ➡ Making inferences	Analyzing compare and contrast essays ➡ Organizing information	• Blood type and personal traits • Birth order and character • Factors that influence personality
Discussing trends in technology ➡ Managing disruptive behavior	"Enhanced Intelligence: A Smart Idea?" ➡ Assessing purpose and function	Writing a point by point essay of comparison ➡ Using transition expressions for comparison	• Computer ethics • Computer fraud • Tech pets • Genetic engineering
Debating use of funds ➡ Citing sources for support	"A Hotel with a Million Stars" ➡ Applying concepts to new information	Block-style essay of comparison ➡ Analyzing block-style organization	• Probability of space tourism • Role of exploration in developing new technology • Exploring new frontiers
Planning an excursion ➡ Endorsing others' opinions	"Junko Tabei: Conqueror of Mountains" ➡ Recognizing comparisons and contrasts	Writing block style essay of contrast ➡ Using transition expressions for contrast	• Dream vacations • Risk and excitement • Situations we wish had gone differently
Concluding a discussion on translation ➡ Closing a discussion	Two translations of Rilke's "The Panther" ➡ Focusing on language choice and style	Self- and peer editing ➡ Using a checklist for self-assessment in writing	• Comic mistranslations • Favorite quotes • Role of translators • Pros and cons of a global language

SECOND EDITION

IN CHARGE
TEACHER'S GUIDE
1

An Integrated Skills Course for
High-Level Students

Starting Out

Getting Acquainted
(pages 1–2)

Preview

Ask students what they usually do when they are in a new situation and want to get to know the people around them. Elicit that it is necessary to ask people questions and share something about yourself in order to get acquainted with others. You might want to have a class discussion about what kinds of questions are appropriate to ask when you are just getting to know someone.

Presentation

Have students read the opening paragraph at the top of page 1. Have each student introduce himself or herself and give one reason why they're studying English.

Note: It is important to respect the feelings of a student who chooses not to answer specific questions.

❶ Have students read the directions. Make sure they understand all the cues and what they are to do. Then have students move around the room and ask their classmates questions using the cues. Remind students that they should look for a different classmate for each cue and talk to as many students as possible. Have students share their results with the class.

❷ Have students read the directions and find two classmates to talk to. Give the activity a time limit and tell students when to change to a new partner. Have students share their results with the class.

❸ Have students read the directions. Discuss the difference between strengths and weaknesses. If necessary, provide one example of how to fill in the chart. For example:

Grammar Strength: memorizing verb forms

Grammar Weakness: perfect tenses

Grammar Goal: use perfect tenses easily

Elicit examples from students of how they might use their strengths and weaknesses to achieve the best results in this course. Have students complete the task individually.

❹ Have students share their charts in small groups and discuss their goals. Remind them to talk about how to measure their goals and also to give feedback to each other on whether the goals are realistic. Encourage students to offer advice and ask follow-up questions to get clarification or additional information.

❺ Ask students to look at the illustration and explain what they see in it. Tell students that they are going to play a simple and fun game. Then have them read the directions and example sentences. Make sure that students understand the premise of the game. Divide the class into groups of three. Demonstrate with a few volunteers how to play the game. Students can add more sentences if they choose as long as they continue to use the pattern of words that begin with the same sound as the last sound of the previous sentence. Walk around the room to monitor whether the students are playing the game correctly. Encourage students to repeat the game and to have someone else in the group start the "trip."

FOOD FOR THOUGHT

OBJECTIVES

Students will be able to:

*   Talk about food and culture
*   Use the present tenses
*   Listen for gist and for details
*   Pronounce /s/, /z/, and /ɪz/ endings
*   Use context clues to improve reading
*   Review paragraph structure
*   Plan and draft an essay
*   Understand and use compound adjectives

GETTING STARTED

Warm Up (page 3)

Preview

*   Discuss the meaning of the title "Food for Thought" with the class. Ask students what they have heard recently that might be considered "food for thought."

Language Note: *Food for thought* is an expression used for something that is interesting or important to think about. In this expression, the subject of our thoughts is called "food" to show that it is a necessary nourishment, just as food is necessary for our bodies. However, in this unit, the "food for thought" is actually *food*.

*   Ask students to discuss the pictures with a partner. What cultures do the food items represent? On what kinds of occasions might these foods be eaten?

Presentation

❶ Have students read the question. Point out that they can include food that is traditional for a formal occasion (for example, a wedding cake), food that is commonly associated with everyday activities (for example, popcorn at the

movies or pizza with friends), or food that they eat at certain times out of personal preference (for example, ice cream at a shopping mall). Have students discuss their answers with their partners.

❷ Review the factors. Check that students understand all the terms, as well as the ranking system—1 is for the *most* important factor in their opinion. Have students do the exercise and compare answers with their partners.

🎧 ❸ Have students read the directions. Play the recording or read the script aloud one or more times. Remind students that they don't have to understand every word of the conversation, that they only have to note the snack foods mentioned. Go over answers to the first question with the class. If necessary, help students understand any unfamiliar snacks mentioned in the recording.

Audioscript: The audioscript for Exercise 3 appears on page T130.

> **Answers**
> pizza, doughnuts, popcorn, and fruit

Culture Note: *Pizza Margherita* is the name for a common type of pizza that is made with mozzarella cheese, tomato, and basil.

Language Note: *Comfort food* is food that we eat when we want to make ourselves feel better. It is usually food that we liked as children, such as sweets and snack foods, or foods we associate with specific occasions.

🏃 **Option:** Have students discuss with a partner what "comfort food" they eat when they want to feel better.

 Workbook: Practice 1

Figure It Out *(pages 4–5)*

Preview

Introduce the proverb in the introduction: "Eating is heaven." Have students discuss their reactions to this proverb with a partner.

Option: Ask students to think of proverbs about food or eating from their own culture and discuss them with a partner. For example, "Eat to live, not live to eat." "Eat to live" means that eating is a necessity to fuel our bodies; "live to eat" means that eating is a pleasure that gives purpose to our lives. Ask how many students in the class think they "eat to live" and how many think they "live to eat."

Presentation

4 Have students read the introductory paragraph. Ask them to predict some of the other factors involved in food choice. If necessary, check for understanding of the following words: *fermented* (allowed to age until it acquires a sharp taste); *fungus* (a type of plant growth that can live on the surface of food); *consuming* (eating); *associations* (mental and emotional connections or memories); *cultivate* (grow). Then ask students to read the article independently to check their predictions.

☑ **5 Vocabulary Check** Ask students to do the exercise alone. Be sure students are aware there is one extra meaning on the list to make the activity more challenging. Review the answers with the class.

Answers
1. c   2. f   3. a   4. b   5. d   6. g

Option: Have students scan the article and make a list of the foods that are mentioned. Ask them to check (✔) food items that they think they would like, and to place an **X** on items that they think they wouldn't like. Ask for volunteers to share their answers with the class.

Option: Display pictures of different kinds of food, such as octopus, hummus, tamales, hamburgers, and cheese. Ask the students to note the name of the food (provide vocabu-

lary where needed) and the first two words they think of when they see it. Place students in groups and have them discuss their associations.

 Workbook: Practice 2

6 Have students discuss the questions with partners. For the first question, you might suggest that they relate a particular food to a particular experience, such as "Whenever I eat ice cream, I think of the time when I was seven and I . . ."

Talk About It *(page 5)*

Option: If you feel that your students need extra help in using present tenses (simple, perfect, and progressive), you might want to postpone this activity until after the grammar presentation (pages 6–9).

Preview

Ask students to look at the picture and discuss with a partner: *What is the person doing, and why?* Explain that gargling with salt water is a traditional remedy (medicine) in North America for sore throats. Elicit some more traditional remedies from the class, and write them on the board.

Presentation

Note: This activity is designed to develop fluency. It is best not to interrupt students to correct errors. Make notes of student errors for review with the class after the activity has finished.

7 Have students read the instructions and the model conversation. Explain that a *subject* in this situation is a person who participates in a study. Check that students understand the organization of the chart. Explain that the model conversation contains *examples* of language used to complete the functions in the next column. It is possible to use other language. Go over the functions and elicit other examples for the functions. Then have one pair read the model conversation aloud for the class. Have students work in pairs, using the cues to create their own conversations. Encourage them to come up with their own examples and to expand on the conversations. Circulate and offer help. Note any persistent errors that you hear. Ask selected pairs to present their conversations to the class. Refer to your notes, and write errors on the board without identifying who made them.

 Option: Elicit alternatives to the remedies in the book. Then have students create new conversations using the new cues.

 Option: Have students cover the model conversation. Using only the function column on the right, improvise a conversation with a student to demonstrate variations on possible language. Students then improvise new examples as proficiency permits.

Workbook: Practice 3

GRAMMAR

The Simple Present and Present Progressive Tenses (page 6)

Preview

Write two sentences on the board:

a. *I make spaghetti.*

b. *I'm making spaghetti.*

Ask students what questions could be asked to elicit each answer (for example, **a.** *What do you usually have for comfort food?* **b.** *What are you making now?*). Point out that this example presents the contrast between two of the most common uses of the simple present and present progressive, but that there are others.

Presentation

Have students read the grammar examples in the boxes. Ask them to identify which of the examples in the boxes use the tenses in the same way as the example sentences in the preview above.

☑ ❶ **Check Your Understanding** Check that students understand they must write the numbers from the example sentences in both boxes next to the

tense rule, and that in some cases more than one answer is possible. Have students first work alone and then compare answers with a partner. Review the answers with the class. Review the usage rules, giving additional examples and responding to any questions and problems students may have.

> **Answers**
> *Possible answers:*
> **a.** 9   **b.** 5   **c.** 1, 2, 3, 4   **d.** 6   **e.** 10
> **f.** 7, 8   **g.** 7,8

 Option: Have students work in pairs. One partner selects a usage rule from the list in Exercise 1, and the other partner must create a sentence that follows it.

Workbook: Practice 4

Stative Verbs (pages 6–7)

Note: For a list of common stative verbs, see page 165 in the Grammar Reference tables of the Student Book.

Preview

Ask students to look at the picture of the chefs on page 7. Elicit sentences referring to their appearance and activities: "He's tall." "He has black hair." "He's holding a plate with a lobster." Discuss the difference between present activity (*holding a plate*) and physical attributes (*has black hair*): one is an action and is subject to stopping and starting, and the other is a state and is either unchanging or requires positive action in order to change (e.g., the chef will always be tall, but he could change the color of his hair).

Presentation

• Have the students read the first grammar explanation and the examples in the first box. Point out the relatively unchanging nature of the verbs used.

• Remind students that there are some special cases in which stative verbs can be used in the progressive. Have them read the second grammar explanation and the examples in the second box.

Give additional examples if necessary, such as *I'm not hearing you very well right now* for a telephone connection that has just gone bad.

Culture Note: The Food Network on cable television carries a popular Japanese cooking program, *Iron Chef*, in which the challengers compete to create—in a set amount of time and with no advance preparation—the tastiest dish that incorporates one specific ingredient. Dubbed versions (translated voices) of this program are becoming popular worldwide.

❷ Read the instructions aloud and read the first sentence of the exercise in the manner of a TV commentator. Have the students complete the exercise independently, and then check their answers with a partner. Review answers with the class.

Answers
1. am observing **2.** looks **3.** is building
4. prefers **5.** see *or* am seeing **6.** is attempting
7. is using **8.** brings **9.** think **10.** is doing
11. appears **12.** is pouring **13.** believe
14. is planning **15.** are grilling

☘ Option: After students have checked answers with a partner, ask for volunteers to read the sentences aloud in the manner of a TV commentator. You might want to have one student read the entire commentary, or go around the class sentence by sentence, with students competing for the best delivery.

 Workbook: Practice 5

The Present Perfect and the Present Perfect Progressive Tenses (*pages 8–9*)

Preview

Have students work in pairs to discuss "unusual food" experiences. One partner thinks of an unusual food that he or she has eaten and then asks the other *Have you ever eaten . . . ?*

Presentation

Have students read the explanations and the examples in the box. Draw a timeline on the board, with a clear indicator for the "time of speaking." Go over the example sentences, and indicate where each one would occur on the timeline. Note that for many uses of the present perfect, it is impossible to pinpoint the exact time: the event occurred at some unspecified time before the time of speaking. However, for others, the time of the event can be narrowed down or precisely pinpointed, for example, *I've just tasted the spaghetti sauce* and *I've been here since 7:30.*

❸ Point out that not all of the signal words have been used in the example sentences. Then, have students work alone and compare answers with a partner. Review the answers with the class.

Answers
Possible answers:
a. 2, 5 **b.** 1, 6 **c.** 3 **d.** 4 **e.** 7 **f.** 8

☘ Option: Have students quiz each other in pairs. One student chooses a rule, and the other finds the example sentence that matches it. Students continue until all matches have been made, and then compare answers with those of another pair.

Have students read the explanation at the bottom of page 8 and the examples in the box on page 9. Point out that although the present perfect and the present perfect progressive have similar uses, the present perfect progressive often indicates ongoing actions. Note especially that with verbs such as *live, study, teach,* and *work,* both the present perfect and the present progressive tenses have similar meanings.

4 Have students work alone and then compare answers with a partner. Review the answers with the class. Where multiple answers are possible, discuss nuances with the class, for example, *people have enjoyed chocolate* suggests that the article may discuss history, whereas *people have been enjoying chocolate* suggests that the article may concentrate on the present.

Answers

Possible answers:
1. have been enjoying *or* have enjoyed
2. has spread 3. provide 4. has focused *or* has been focusing 5. comes *or* has come
6. possesses 7. have competed *or* have been competing 8. is 9. have been consuming *or* have consumed

Option: For additional practice, write the following pairs of sentences on the board, and ask students if the sentences share the same meaning. If the meaning is different, have students work with a partner to rewrite either the first or the second sentence so that the meanings are the same. Share selected results with the class.

a. People have been using spices for thousands of years.

 People started using spices thousands of years ago and are still using them today.

b. Robin Howe has written a wonderful book on soups.

 Robin Howe is still working on that book.

c. Emeril Lagasse has been doing cooking shows on TV for several years.

 Emeril Lagasse has stopped doing cooking shows on TV.

Option Answers

Possible rewrites are in italics:
a. same b. different (first sentence: . . . *has been writing* . . .) c. different (second sentence: . . . *is still doing* . . .)

 Workbook: Practice 6

5 **Check Your Understanding** Have students work alone and then compare answers with a partner. Review the answers with the class.

Answers

Possible answers:
a. present progressive, simple present, present perfect b. simple present, present perfect c. present perfect

6 **Express Yourself** Have students read the instructions and create their own dialogues using the situations in the chart in Exercise 5. Encourage them to use different present tenses. Monitor the dialogues, and select pairs to present their dialogues to the class.

Note: This activity is designed to develop fluency. It is best not to interrupt students to correct errors. Make notes of student errors for review with the class after the activity has finished.

Option: Students work in pairs to write an original situation requiring use of the present tenses. They exchange situations with another pair and create a dialogue. Pairs then get together to perform their dialogues for each other.

 Workbook: Practice 7

LISTENING and SPEAKING

Listen: Pizza Passion *(page 10)*

Presentation

❶ **Before You Listen** Have students work in pairs to answer the questions.

⊛ **Option:** Poll the class for their results, announcing such results as *the most popular topping, the most unusual topping,* and so on.

➡ **Listening for Gist and Details** Read through the strategy with students, reviewing the meaning of *gist* if necessary. Explain that listening for gist involves following the speaker's overall argument and summarizing it, whereas listening for details involves listening for specific information. Ask for situations where listening for gist might be important (for example, summarizing a story or a class lecture). Ask for examples of situations in which students need to listen for details (for example, listening to instructions, announcements, or messages).

🎧 ❷ Have students read the directions. Play the recording or read the audioscript aloud. Then have students answer the question and compare answers with a partner. Review answers with the class.

Audioscript: The audioscript for Exercise 2 appears on pages T130–T131.

Answer
c

Language Note: In American English slang, the word *dough* also means *money.* The expression *I'm rolling in dough* means *I have a lot of money.*

❸ Read through the directions with the students. Ask them to go through the questions before they listen, making brief notes of what kinds of words, such as *dates, places, names of people,* and *names of foods,* they will need to listen for to answer the questions. Play the recording, or read the audioscript again. Have students first work alone and then

compare answers with a partner. Review the answers with the class.

Answers
a. the Greeks **b.** Naples **c.** a baker named Raffaele Esposito of Naples; to honor King Umberto the first and Queen Margherita when they came to visit Naples in 1889 **d.** true buffalo mozzarella, tomatoes, and fresh basil **e.** flour, yeast, salt, water **f.** the second half of the 19ᵗʰ century

⊛ **Option:** For mixed ability classes, do Exercise 3 as a jigsaw exercise. One partner answers **a, c,** and **e** and the other partner answers **b, d,** and **f.** Play the recording or read the audioscript only once, and then have partners ask each other for the missing information. Then if necessary, play the recording or read the audioscript one or more times, so that both partners can listen for answers that either of them may have missed.

 Workbook: Practice 8

Pronunciation *(pages 10–11)*

Preview

Write the following sentence on the board (with each final *s* underlined): *He gives her chocolates and roses on Valentine's Day.* Read the sentence aloud several times. Ask students how many *different* final *s* sounds there are in this sentence. Have them discuss their answers with a partner. Review answers with the class. The answer should be *three:* /z/ (first and last words), /s/ (second word), and /ɪz/ (third word).

Presentation

Explain that final *s* is used with most *plural* nouns and some *singular present tense* verbs. Read through the explanation with the students, and read the examples in the box aloud, having students repeat them after you. Review the pronunciation symbols for the various sounds. Refer students to the pronunciation symbols on page 163 of their Student Book.

❹ Draw a chart with one column for each sound—/s/, /z/, and /ɪz/—on the board and have students copy the chart. Tell students to read the directions, then work with a partner and write the underlined words in the appropriate column of the chart.

❺ Play the recording or read the audioscript once. Have students compare answers with a partner. Then play the recording or read the audioscript a second time, and have students work with their partners to resolve any differences.

Audioscript: The audioscript for Exercise 5 appears on Student Book page 11.

Answers

mixes: /ɪz/   elements: /s/   Spices: /ɪz/
peppers: /z/   seeds: /z/   dishes: /ɪz/
foods: /z/   peas: /z/   lentils: /z/
carrots: /s/   cucumbers: /z/   drinks: /s/

---

❻ Read the directions with the students. Monitor pairs and make corrections as they are practicing. Have selected students read the sentences to the class.

Option: Dictate the following exercise to the students, or write the sentences on the board or on an overhead transparency, or make copies. Have students work with partners to determine the final *s* sounds in the sentences. Go over the answers with the class, and then have students practice reading the sentences with their partners.

a. Shitake <u>mushrooms</u> may help prevent tooth decay.

b. Eating <u>peanuts</u> may reduce the risk of heart disease.

c. <u>Eels</u> are a traditional Christmas dish in Italy.

d. *Churrasco* is a traditional way of grilling <u>meats</u> in Brazil.

e. Jamaican jerk is a spice mixture for grilled <u>foods</u>.

f. Fish <u>sauces</u> are typical of the Filipino diet.

g. Taro root and <u>coconuts</u> formed the basic Samoan diet.

Option Answers

a. /z/ **b.** /s/ **c.** /z/ **d.** /s/ **e.** /z/ **f.** /ɪz/ **g.** /s/

 *Workbook: Practice 9*

Speak Out (*page 11*)

Preview

Ask students to work with a partner and discuss the differences between casual conversation and formal meetings. Allow some time for discussion, and have selected students share their conclusions with the class. If it hasn't already come up, point out that not only is the language different in formal situations, but that formal meetings follow a much more clearly-defined format.

Presentation

➡ **Opening a Meeting or Discussion**

Have students read the strategy and the expressions in the box.

Note: This activity is designed to develop fluency. It is best not to interrupt students to correct errors. Make notes of student errors for review with the class after the activity has finished.

❼ Have students work in small groups. Ask them to read the instructions and then choose a topic for discussion. Limit groups to three students, and be sure that the groups generate one topic of their own so that each speaker will have a topic to introduce. Monitor the groups, and review persistent errors at the end of the activity.

Option: Extend the activity in Exercise 7 by pointing out that there is more sample language possible for each stage in the chart. Elicit a few other possibilities for each function, and put them on the board. Have groups generate their own topics, and use the expanded range of language possibilities to open their discussion.

 Workbook: Practice 10

READING and WRITING

Read About It (pages 12–13)

Presentation

❶ **Before You Read** Have students read the instructions and take the quiz. Review answers with the class.

Answers
1. False 2. False 3. False 4. False 5. True

➡ **Using Contextual Clues** Have students read the strategy. Put the following sentence on the board: *This coffee is so* **unclambrious** *that I can't drink it.* Ask students what they can tell you about the word **unclambrious**. Elicit the fact that it is an adjective (the *–ious* suffix and the intensifier *so*), that it is grammatically negative (the *un-* prefix indicating *not clambrious*) and that, since the coffee is not fit to drink, we can probably assume that *clambrious* is a good quality and *unclambrious* is bad. Then tell them, if they didn't already know, that it is a nonexistent word.

❷ Have students read the instructions and the article. Ask them to take notes of unfamiliar words, either by circling them in the text or making a list on paper. Have students review their lists when they have finished reading and, without using a dictionary, try to narrow down the meanings of unfamiliar words as much as possible.

⊕ **Option:** Have students work in pairs after they have finished reading. Have them compare lists and help each other with unfamiliar words. For words that are on both lists (words that neither partner knows), have students discuss context clues and try to come up with a meaning.

⊕ **Option:** Have students work in pairs and go back through the article, rewriting words that they identified in Exercise 2. They should concentrate on giving enough information to make the point without using the same vocabulary.

Example:

…they had to contend with **smugglers**, who secretly took coffee plants and seeds to sell…
… they had to contend with people who secretly took coffee plants and seeds to sell…

☑ ❸ **Vocabulary Check** Have students work alone, and then compare answers with a partner. Be sure students are aware that there is one extra meaning on the list to make the activity more challenging. Review the answers with the class.

Answers
1. c 2. f 3. a 4. b 5. g 6. h 7. d

❹ Have students work alone, and then compare answers with a partner. Review the answers with the class.

Answers

a. Coffee can be served with ice; steaming hot; black; with milk; with lemon peel; with whipped cream; with spices such as cinnamon, ginger, and cardamom; with chocolate; with brandy or whiskey; and even with a pinch of salt or pepper.

b. Around the year 1100, Arabs roasted coffee berries to make qahwa.

c. The two types of coffee are Arabica and Robusta. Arabica is highly prized because of its rich flavor and aroma. It takes a great amount of care to cultivate. Arabica coffee accounts for 75 percent of the coffee grown around the world. Robusta coffee requires less care, and grows more successfully in West Africa and South East Asia. It can tolerate different climates better than Arabica can, and contains twice the caffeine, but the flavor and aroma can't compare to Arabica. Robusta coffee accounts for 25 percent of the coffee grown around the world.

d. Physical effects are: stimulates the central nervous and cardiovascular systems; increases blood pressure; increases secretion of gastric acid, thus aiding digestion; makes people more alert and less tired; fights migraine headaches.

Think About It (page 14)

Presentation

5 Have students read the questions independently. Then have them discuss the questions in pairs, small groups, or as a class. Share selected responses with the class.

Write: Review of Paragraph Structure (page 14)

Preview

Review the terms *topic*, *audience*, and *purpose*. Diagram an essay on the board, using boxes for paragraphs. Label the paragraphs *intro-duction*, *body*, *conclusion*, and draw arrows between them labeled *transitional* expressions.

Presentation

➡ Have students read the strategy. Go over it with the class, checking that they under-stand the following:

- distinction between *topic* (the broader subject) and *main idea* (the writer's own point of view)

- distinction between *topic sentence* (a sentence that identifies the main idea of each paragraph) and *thesis statement* (a statement of the main idea of the entire essay)

Write About It (page 14)

Presentation

6 Have students read the directions and choose a topic. Then have students list their main idea, audience, and purpose. Review these with the students individually, if possible, before they begin writing.

☑ **7** **Check Your Writing** Go through the instructions with the students. Have students make notes on their partner's work to facilitate feedback.

 Workbook: Practice 11

Vocabulary Expansion: Compound adjectives See page T118.

> ### Answers
> **A.** **1.** honey-glazed ham **2.** honey-mustard dressing **3.** full-figured women **4.** mind-boggling assortment **5.** oven-roasted chicken **6.** lip-smacking desserts
> **B.** *Possible answers:*
> half-eaten pie/half-eaten apple/dishwashing liquid/strawberry-rhubarb pie/pie-eating contest

EVALUATION

See pages Txi–Txii.

Unit 1 Achievement Test

Self-Check See **You're In Charge!**, page 8 of the Workbook.

PORTFOLIO

Writing Revised essay from **Write About It**, Exercises 6 and 7, page 14.

Oral Communication

1. Record a monologue describing a typical meal in your family: the foods served, the roles of different family members during the course of the meal, the sequence of events, etc. (If you live alone, describe meals on holidays or whenever your rela-tives or friends gather.)

2. Record a dialogue with another student in which you describe an unusual dish or meal that you have eaten. For your tape, describe the food, and answer your partner's questions. Then change roles for your partner's tape.

Interactive Dictation

Dictate the following sentences to your students. Have them complete the sentences, replacing the blanks with information about themselves. For more information on dictation, see page Txv.

1. Food that we eat to make ourselves feel better emotionally is called "comfort food." We often choose foods that were served to us as children, such as _____.

2. My friend eats _____ when he's feeling down. He has been eating _____ for as long as I've known him.

3. I have eaten it once or twice myself, but I don't like it very much. For comfort, I prefer _____. I'm thinking about _____ right now, and my mouth is watering.

4. Maybe I'll have a piece of _____ with that. Maybe two pieces!

MEMORABLE MOMENTS

OBJECTIVES

Students will be able to:
- Discuss milestones
- Use the past tenses
- Listen for time expressions and a sequence of events
- Listen for and identify emotions
- Perceive and pronounce different –ed endings for verbs and adjectives
- Define an issue for discussion
- Read for dates and times and a sequence of events
- Analyze an essay question
- Understand and use idioms for expressing emotions

GETTING STARTED

Warm Up (page 15)

Preview

- Have students look at the photos at the top of page 15, and ask them what is being shown. Elicit *the first automobile* and *the first man on the moon*. Ask them what the significance of each event was: What impact did it have when it happened? How did it shape the world we live in today?

- Have students read the title, "Memorable Moments." Ask them what other words they can think of related to *memorable*. Elicit as many as possible: *memory, memorial, memorize, memento, memoir, remember, remembrance*. Point out that *memorable* has a very positive connotation: something that is "worth remembering."

Presentation

Have students read the introduction. Ask if they know the year of the Apollo XI mission (1969). Ask them what events from their own childhood could be classified as equally memorable.

T12

Language Note: *Moment* as it is used here refers not only to a time period, but to a significant event that happens during that time period; *defining moments* are events that are so significant that they give meaning to an era, a generation, or an individual life.

❶ Have students read the instructions and work independently to create their lists. Then have them discuss their answers in small groups.

❷ Have students work alone. Then have them discuss their answers with their groups. Ask selected groups to summarize this discussion and the previous discussion for the class.

Language Note: *Firsts* are first-time events: in this case, an adjective form is used as a noun, in much the same way that the word *premiere* has come to mean the first performance or opening event.

🎧 ❸ Check that everyone knows what to do. Play the recording or read the audioscript. Have students discuss their answers in small groups.

Language Notes:

- *Deal?* The woman's question is short for *Is it a deal?* or *Do we have a deal?* meaning *Do you agree to the arrangement or proposition?* The man replies *You're on*, meaning that he accepts the offer.

- *No way* means that something is impossible. It is a shortened form of *There is no way that . . .*

Audioscript: The audioscript for Exercise 3 appears on page T131.

Answers
Event 1: Elvis teaching teens how to rock 'n' roll
Event 2: the first landing on the moon
Event 3: Gandhi's civil disobedience in 1915

Option: Extend the discussion by having students choose the events that they think were more significant than those in the dialogue and report their results to the class.

 *Workbook: Practice 1*

Figure It Out *(pages 16–17)*

Preview

With books closed, write *Edmund Hillary and Tenzing Norgay*, *Akio Morita*, and *Toni Morrison* on the board. Ask students if they know who these people are and what their achievements were. Write some of the guesses on the board, whether correct or incorrect. Explain that the students will each read a short text about these people.

Presentation

Tell students they are going to read about the lives and achievements of some pioneers in various fields. Point out that this type of biography usually goes into the background of the person and describes how that background led to the achievement that the person is noted for.

Option: With the class, brainstorm one or two other notable people and make lists on the board of their achievements, significant dates, biographical information, and other relevant information.

❹ Have students read the directions. Make sure they are aware that they should read only **one** of the readings. Have students count off one, two, three. Then have them read the section that corresponds to their number and fill in the chart information relating to it. Remind them that brief answers are sufficient. When students have finished with their portion of the chart, have them get into groups and fill in the information on the other readings.

Option: As an alternative, have one group work on each biography. Answers could then be shared in the manner of a press conference: group members face the class and respond to questions from the members of the other groups, who fill out their charts as they ask the questions.

Answers

A. Edmund Hillary and Tenzing Norgay
Personal or World "First"
First human beings to ascend Mount Everest.
Important Dates
May 29, 1953: ascended Mount Everest.
Biographical Information
Norgay: professional mountaineer from the Sherpa community in the Everest foothills.
Hillary: beekeeper from New Zealand.
Other Important Information
Answers may include: Mt. Everest is the highest mountain in the world, at 29,028 feet (8,848 meters). Both became the most celebrated citizens of their countries. Both devoted much of their lives to ensuring the happiness of the Sherpas.

B. Akio Morita
Personal or World "First"
Started his own company, Sony. Invented Walkman. Sony's other products included miniature transistor radio, 8-inch TV, videotape recorder.
Important Dates
1955: miniature transistor radio.
Biographical Information
From Nagoya, Japan. Left family sake-brewing business to start his own electronics company.
Other Important Information
Answers may include: Name *Sony* came from *sonus*, meaning *sound*, and the American word *sonny*. Morita developed Walkman after he saw people listening to music in cars and outdoors. Walkman is a worldwide hit.

C. Toni Morrison
Personal or World "First"
First African-American to receive the Nobel Prize for Literature.
Important Dates
1931: born in Lorain, Ohio. 1993: won the Nobel Prize for Literature.
Biographical Information
Large family with sense of heritage and tradition of storytelling. Spent childhood absorbing language and stories from people around her. Later relocated to NYC.
Other Important Information
Answers may include: While working as an editor, noticed the lack of books by and about black women and decided to change that. First African-American to win the Nobel Prize, eighth woman to do so.

☑ ❺ **Vocabulary Check** Have students read the instructions and do the exercise independently. Review the answers as a class. Be sure students are aware there is one extra meaning.

Answers
1. d 2. f 3. a 4. h 5. b 6. c 7. e

 Workbook: Practice 2

Talk About It *(page 18)*

 Option: If you feel that your students need extra help in using the simple past, past progressive, and past perfect, you might want to postpone this activity until after the grammar presentation (pages 18–21).

Presentation

Note: This activity is designed to develop fluency. It is best not to interrupt students to correct errors. Make notes of student errors for review with the class after the activity has finished.

❻ Have students model the conversation for the class. Then have students work in pairs to improvise conversations using the language in the model. Circulate and offer assistance. Make

notes of student errors. Select pairs to present their conversations to the class. Refer to your notes, and write the grammar errors on the board without identifying who made them. Then correct the errors as a class.

 Option: Extend the activity by having the class interview one student, in press-conference style, on his/her most memorable moment.

 Workbook: Practice 3

GRAMMAR

The Simple Past and Past Progressive Tenses *(pages 18–19)*

Note: The grammar points here will be review. Although your students probably understand the difference between simple past and past progressive, students will undoubtedly benefit from looking at them again. The contrast is an important one.

Preview

Ask the class: *What were you doing when you heard about . . . ?* Use a fairly recent event that is likely to be familiar to all students, such as the death of Princess Diana or the World Trade Center attack. Write the question on the board, and select a few students to share their answers with the class. Write several responses on the board. Draw a line on the board to illustrate the continuing action in the past and an *X* on the line to show that the action in the simple past interrupted it.

Example: *I was listening to the radio in my car when I heard about the World Trade Center attack.*

Choose one of the responses and ask a question about it:

Example: *What did you do when you heard about the attack?*

Elicit the response:

When I heard about the attack, I pulled the car over and called my mother on my cell phone.

✪ **Option:** Extend this activity by continuing to ask questions based on one of the student responses; for instance, continuing the previous dialogue:

> **Teacher:** What was your mother doing when you called her?
>
> **Student:** She was reading the newspaper.
>
> **Teacher:** What did she do then?
>
> **Student:** When I told her the news, she dropped the paper and turned on the television.

Presentation

Have students work alone and read the exercise. Check understanding of the distinction between simple past for a single completed action (*I ran in the Marathon in 1992.*) and simple past for a completed series of actions (*I ran in the Marathon every year in high school.*).

Review the use of *while* and *when*. Then ask students to look at the examples in the second box. Point out that each example contains two clauses, and that in some instances the same tense is used in both clauses, while in others a different tense is used in each clause.

✪ **Option:** Have students create timelines for each of the examples in the box. Have them represent ongoing actions or habitual actions with brackets along sections of the line and completed actions with an **X** at a point on the line.

❶ Have students read the instructions and do the exercise independently, and then compare answers with a partner. Review the answers with the class.

Answers
a. 2   b. 1   c. 3

---

❷ Have students read the directions and example. Check that students understand they have to revise the second sentence so that it accurately reflects the information given in the first. Also, remind them they should avoid simply restating the first sentence. Have students work alone, and then compare answers with a partner. Review the answers with the class.

Answers
Some possible answers:
a. He participated in politics when he was a law student.
b. Pulitzer worked in sweatshops before he went west.
c. He had already established himself as a journalist when he began to build his newspaper publishing empire.
d. He didn't know his place in history before he thought up the prize.

✪ **Option:** Have students work independently to write two more alternatives for each answer in the previous exercise. Then have them compare answers with a partner and discuss. Monitor discussions and suggest corrections.

❸ Read through the instructions with the class. Point out that one partner can prompt the other with questions, as in the preview activity. As students work, monitor them, and note persistent errors for future reteaching and review.

✪ **Option:** Have students work in small groups to create a fictional "chain story." One student begins with a sentence such as "When the dam broke, I was at home sleeping." The next student must make another sentence beginning with *while* or *when*, such as "When the water came through my window, I woke up." Students continue the story, using *while* and *when*, simple past and past progessive, until they reach a logical ending or can't go any further.

 Workbook: Practice 4

The Past Perfect Tense (*pages 20–21*)

Preview

Begin by asking a student to list several actions done earlier in the day and write these and the times they were done on the board. Then make sentences about these actions using the past perfect and the phrase *by the time . . .*

Option: On the board, write: *I wasn't nervous when I took my final exams.* Elicit the question: *Why not?* Answer the question: *I wasn't nervous when I took my final exams because I had studied a lot.* Write the new sentence on the board. Point out that the action of studying was finished by the time of the exam. Contrast this with the sentence: *Before I took the test, I studied a lot,* which focuses on the time before the test, not on the speaker's condition at the time of taking the test.

Presentation

Have students read the introduction. Go over the introduction and the examples in the box with the class. You might want to point out that the last two examples in the box could start with *When* instead of *After*: the sense is that one action immediately follows the other.

❹ Have students read the instructions and do the exercise independently. Then have them compare answers with a partner. Review the answers with the class.

Point out that the information on the time-line itself is given in the present tense. This is generally the case with picture captions and headlines as well. The sense is that the information is a label for what you see on the page and refers to a present condition, not to the historical event portrayed or described. The headline *Canadian skaters get gold medal* means *Here is a story about Canadian skaters getting a gold medal.* The story itself will use past tenses to accurately present the time frame.

Culture Note: *That's Incredible* was a popular American television program that ran from 1980 to 1984. It was known for presenting bizarre stunts and unbelievable facts.

Answers
a. was watching; began **b.** became **c.** was studying; won **d.** had turned; had (already) won **e.** became **f.** had (already) earned

---

❺ Have students read the instructions. Put a sample timeline on the board: a line with dates indicating when significant events occurred. Label the first date *born* but don't label any of the other dates. Have

students guess the events using statements rather than questions, as follows:

Student A: In June of 1995, you graduated from high school.

Student B: No—by 1995, I had already finished high school.

Student A: So you had finished high school by the time you were 16.

Student B: Yes, that's right.

 Workbook: Practice 5

☑ ❻ **Check Your Understanding** Have students read the instructions and do the exercise independently. Then have them compare answers with a partner and discuss. Monitor the discussions and suggest corrections. Review selected responses with the class.

Option: Assign Exercise 6 as homework, asking students to choose **one** of the topics and write a paragraph.

❼ **Express Yourself** Have students read the instructions independently and then do the exercise with their partners. Monitor the discussions, and make notes for future reteaching and review.

Option: If Exercise 6 was done as homework, have students exchange paragraphs with a partner, read their partner's paragraph, and then ask and answer questions. Monitor the discussions, and make notes for future reteaching and review.

 Workbook: Practices 6, 7

LISTENING and SPEAKING

Listen: Bungee Jumping and Whitewater Rafting (pages 21–22)

Presentation

❶ **Before You Listen** Have students read the instructions independently and then discuss the question in small groups. Monitor the discussions, and share information with the whole class if it seems that some groups have more background information than others.

Option: Put the phrase *extreme sports* on the board. Have students work in groups to brainstorm the topic. What extreme sports do they know? Have they ever tried any?

Language Note: *Extreme sports* are sports that involve thrills and a high level of personal danger. They may be non-traditional sports, such as skateboarding and bungee jumping, or variations on traditional sports, such as extreme skiing (skiing off a high cliff) and big-wave surfing.

➡ **Listening for Sequence** With their books closed, elicit words the students listen for to determine the order of events. Then have students open their books and read the strategy and the time words listed there.

🎧 ❷ Direct students' attention to the steps for each extreme sport in the chart, and check that everyone knows to number the events *in the order they happened*, not the order they are mentioned. Play the recording or read the audioscript. Have students do the exercise independently and then compare answers with a partner. Review answers with the class.

Audioscript: The audioscript for Exercise 2 appears on pages T131–T132.

Answers	
Bungee Jumping	**Whitewater Rafting**
4	2
2	5
1	3
3	4
	1

❸ Have students read the instructions. Play the recording or read the audioscript again and have students focus on the emotions they hear. Point out that the speakers use certain expressions or idioms to convey their emotions and that students should pay attention to that.

Answers
fear and excitement

Language Notes: To *chicken out* is to be too afraid to do something; *chills down one's spine* refers to the physical feeling of fear; *butterflies in one's stomach* refers to the physical feeling of nervousness or mild fear; to *be a goner* means to be about to die; *on top of the world* describes a feeling of extreme happiness; *the thrill of one's life* means the most thrilling experience that one will have in one's entire lifetime.

❹ Have students read the instructions independently and then work in groups to complete the activity. Encourage listeners to question the speaker. Monitor the discussions, and take notes on points to review once the activity has finished.

 *Workbook: Practice 8*

Pronunciation (*page 22*)

Preview

Put the following sentence on the board: *At school we _learned_ about Aristotle, who was a very _learned_ man.* Read the entire sentence aloud. Point out the different pronunciations of the underlined words. Then ask the class what part of speech each word is: adjective, adverb, or verb?

Presentation

Have students open their books and read the rules and examples in the box. Read the examples out loud to the class. Point out that the /ɪd/ pronunciation for *-ed* adjectives is somewhat rare, and that, in most cases, the adjective form has the same pronunciation as the past-tense verb form; for example, *a closed mind, loved ones, tossed salad.* Have students practice the examples in the box with partners.

❺ Have students work alone and then compare answers with a partner.

🎧 ❻ Play the recording or read the audioscript for students to check their predictions. Review answers with the class.

Audioscript: The audioscript for Exercise 6 appears on Student Book page 22.

Answers
a. /ɪD/   b. /ɪD/   c. /d/   d. /ɪD/

---

❼ Have students work with their partners. Circulate and note student errors. Refer to your notes, and go over errors on the board without identifying who made them. Then correct the errors as a class.

 Option: Have students write several sentences using adjectives and past-tense verbs with *–ed* endings. Then have them exchange sentences with a partner, and then read the sentences to each other, checking each other's pronunciation of the *–ed* endings.

Link *Workbook: Practice 9*

Speak Out (page 23)

Preview

Tell the students that you would like to discuss *crime*. Ask them if they know what you will talk about. Elicit words related to crime, such as, *robbery*, *burglary*, and *murder*, and write them on the board. Then tell them that you actually want to talk about *white-collar crime*, such as tax fraud and embezzlement. Introduce the concept of defining terms in the early stages of a discussion. Point out that, in this case, *defining* doesn't refer to determining the literal meaning of a word, but to narrowing down a broader meaning to the exact set of specifics that are relevant to the discussion.

Presentation

➡ **Defining an Issue** Have students read the strategy and the examples in the box. Encourage students to prompt each other with questions. Demonstrate by expanding on some of the examples with specifics, as follows:

T18

Student A: We have a crime problem in this company.

Student B: What do you mean by *crime*? Have there been muggings in the parking lot or something?

Student A: When I say *crime*, I mean *white-collar crime*. The accounting department has made some disturbing discoveries . . .

Note: This activity is designed to develop fluency. It is best not to interrupt students to correct errors. Make notes of student errors for review with the class after the activity has finished.

❽ Have students work in groups of three or four to define and discuss the issues. Be sure that students understand they need to come to a group consensus about what constitutes each category. Have them report their definitions to the class.

 Option: Extend the activity by having students write down two or three serious issues that they want to discuss. With students of different nationalities or age groups, this might prove an interesting cross-cultural awareness activity.

Link *Workbook: Practice 10*

READING and WRITING

Read About It (pages 23–25)

Presentation

❶ **Before You Read** Have students name some world firsts in engineering. Some examples might include suspension bridges; steel-frame construction (skyscrapers); synthetic materials (plastic, fiberglass); wireless transmission (radio, TV, satellite communications); silicon-chip circuitry (computers). Have them name firsts in aviation. Some examples might include lighter-than-air craft (balloons); powered flight; jet-powered flight; supersonic flight; space flight. Write some examples on the board in order to facilitate discussion. Then have students form groups of three or four, read the instructions and the questions, and then discuss them.

➡ **Reading for Time Organization** Have students read the strategy, and point out that this is the same strategy that was used in the Listening section. Elicit sequence words they will be looking for. Have them read the selection and make notes of the signal words as they read by circling them in the text.

✈ **Option:** Have students read the excerpt as homework and create a timeline of the major events in Paul MacCready's life.

Language Notes:

* The phrase *his enthusiasm gets the better of him* usually means *defeats*; in this situation, it means that he tries to control his enthusiasm, but fails, and gets excited.

* A *rush of endorphins* refers to the feeling of physical well-being following exercise. *Endorphins* are chemicals created by our bodies that cause feelings of pleasure; a *rush* is a slang word for a sudden feeling of excitement and pleasure.

* The *Gossamer Condor* is the name of MacCready's aircraft. *Gossamer* is an adjective for something light and delicate, like cobwebs; a *condor* is a large bird, native to the Andes of South America, that lives on the flesh of dead animals. The name contrasts images of lightness and beauty with images of heaviness and ugliness.

* The phrase *buy(s) engineers by the acre* refers to the practice of large companies hiring many engineers in hopes that some of them will produce valuable work. An *acre* is a measure of land, and *buying by the acre* refers to purchasing vast quantities rather than selecting carefully; it is an image of quantity, not quality.

Culture Notes:

* The Wright Brothers were the first to achieve a controlled, powered flight. After many experiments with gliders

and powered aircraft, they finally succeeded on December 17, 1903, when their aircraft *Flyer 1* made a flight of 852 feet at Kitty Hawk, North Carolina.

* Charles Lindbergh made the first non-stop solo flight across the Atlantic Ocean. In 1927, at the age of 25, he flew from New York to Paris in his plane, the *Spirit of St. Louis*. He instantly became an international celebrity.

❷ This can be done as homework or in class. Have students work alone and then compare answers with a partner. Review answers with the class.

Answers

* childhood: grew up in New Haven, Connecticut; spent his free time collecting moths and butterflies and collecting model airplanes; by his early teens, he had begun building flying machines
* age 16: became a licensed pilot
* age 20: introduced to the sport of soaring . . . glider flying
* 1957: married Judy Leonard and started an engineering career; started Meteorology Research, Inc.
* 1970: left Meteorology Research, Inc. and began AeroVironment in order to develop renewable energy sources like wind and solar power
* 1977: designed the first human-powered airplane

✈ **Option:** To review the answers to Exercise 2, draw a timeline of Paul MacCready's life on the board. Write in the dates, and elicit the events from students. Use points or *X*s to indicate completed actions, and brackets to indicate ongoing ones or recurring ones.

☑ ❸ **Vocabulary Check** Have students read the instructions and do the exercise independently. Point out there is one extra meaning. Encourage them to use context clues as much as possible. Then have them compare answers with a partner. Review the answers with the class.

Answers
1. d **2.** f **3.** h **4.** g **5.** b **6.** e **7.** a

Think About It (*page 25*)

Presentation

❹ Have students read the instructions independently and then discuss the questions with a partner. Monitor discussions, and have selected pairs report their conclusions to the class.

⚙ **Option:** Have students work in groups to discuss the three inventions that they think had the most impact on the world. They must reach a consensus and report their results to the class, giving reasons for their choices.

⚙ **Option:** Have students work in groups to brainstorm other solutions to the human-powered flight problem. Tell them that they don't need to worry about engineering principles but should be as creative as possible. Groups will discuss options and create a proposal to be presented to the class.

⚙ **Option:** Assign a homework activity in which each student chooses a flight pioneer and researches that person's achievement. Students will prepare a timeline and a brief chronological summary of the achievement and present it to the class. Some possible pioneers: the Montgolfier brothers, Otto Lilienthal, Leila Marie Cody, the Wright brothers, Louis Bleriot, Vickers Vimy, Charles Lindbergh, Amelia Earhart.

Write: Analyzing Essay Questions (*page 26*)

Preview

Ask students if they have ever taken an essay test and if they can remember some of the questions. Most students will probably not remember the actual questions but will remember the topic. Ask if any have taken essay tests in English. Explain that many well-known proficiency tests, such as the TOEFL®, the Michigan Test, and some of the Cambridge exams, require the students to answer essay questions. Elicit some sample questions/topics, and write them on the board. Discuss what students found most difficult about essay tests. Have students look at the topics/questions, and ask them if the topic requires *description* or

persuasion. If necessary, review the differences between these two functions.

Presentation

➡ Have students read the strategy. Ask them to think about what key words in a question would call for description and what key words would call for persuasion, and list some on the board. Some examples might include: *what were some, discuss, agree or disagree, which, why.*

Note: These skills will be particularly useful in test-taking, both in language skill assessment testing and in content-area testing, for those who wish to pursue higher education in an English-speaking environment. Emphasize this to the students.

❺ Have students work alone and then compare answers with a partner. Review the answers with the class. Elicit these key words for description: *what were some, discuss.* Elicit these key words for persuasion: *agree or disagree, which, why.*

Answers
1. D (What were some)
2. D (discuss)
3. P (agree or disagree)
4. P (Which, why)

Write About It (*page 26*)

Presentation

❻ Have students do the exercise as homework.

☑ ❼ **Check Your Writing** Have students work in groups of three or four to present their paragraphs and get feedback from group members. Review the questions in the box. Remind group members to take notes as each writer presents. They should then give oral feedback to the writer, and the writer should take notes of their comments to use for revision.

 Workbook: Practice 11

Vocabulary Expansion: Idioms of emotion
See page T119.

Answers

A.

Fear	Sadness
• one's heart is in one's throat	• to be down in the dumps
• to be petrified	• to be all choked up
• to have chills down one's spine	• to be blue

Anger	Happiness
• to go ballistic	• to be on cloud nine
• to hit the ceiling	• to be walking on air
• to blow a fuse	• to be on top of the world

B. *Answers will vary.*

EVALUATION

See pages Txi–Txii.

Unit 2 Achievement Test

Self-Check See You're In Charge!, page 16 of the Workbook.

PORTFOLIO

Writing Revised paragraphs from **Write About It**, Exercises 6 and 7, page 26.

Oral Communication

1. Record a dialogue with a partner describing a *rite of passage*: an event in your life that marked a transition from one stage to the next, like graduating from high school or college, getting your first job and/or first apartment, getting married, etc. For your tape, describe a rite of passage in your own life, and answer your partner's questions. Then reverse roles for your partner's tape.

2. Imagine it is twenty years from now and you are looking back at the last twenty years. Record a short speech describing significant achievements of the past twenty years in the sciences, medicine, the arts, and so on.

Interactive Dictation

Dictate the following sentences. For more information on dictation, see page Txv.

1. I attended my first wedding last week.

2. When I say *my first wedding*, I don't mean that I was getting married.

3. I mean that it was the first time I had attended anyone's wedding.

4. A wedding is one of those blessed events that makes everyone feel good.

5. The couple who were getting married looked like they were on top of the world.

Then have students compose five sentences of their own about a first-time event, using simple past, past progressive, and past perfect tenses.

THE FUTURE OF FILM

OBJECTIVES

Students will be able to:
- Talk about films and the film industry
- Make and discuss predictions about the future
- Use future tenses
- Listen for supporting details
- Produce shifts in stress to distinguish between homophones
- Speak persuasively in a discussion
- Critically analyze examples when reading
- Analyze a persuasive essay and identify its main parts
- Use high-tech idioms and coinages

GETTING STARTED

Warm Up (page 27)

Preview

- Have students brainstorm words associated with films and filmmaking, for example, *movie, cinema, director, producer, actor/actress, camera, lighting, special effects,* etc.

- Have students look at the picture at the top of page 27. Ask them when and where they think the picture was taken, and what clues tell them this.

Presentation

Have students read the introduction, and ask them to think of other ways that filmmaking has changed.

❶ Have students read the question and discuss answers with a partner. Have selected pairs share their answers with the class.

Option: Have students work with a partner or conduct a class survey to answer the following questions:

What are your three favorite movies?

Do you think they will be remembered fifty years from now? Why or why not?

🎧 **❷** Have students read the directions independently. Review the chart, and explain that the task is writing in the expressions used in the conversation to describe these elements. Remind them that they don't have to understand every word of the dialogue to complete the activity. Play the recording or read the audioscript one or more times. Have students work alone and then compare answers with a partner. Review answers with the class.

Language Note: *Awesome* in formal diction is very strong, and means *exceptional* or *extraordinary*; it is sometimes used informally in American English to simply mean *excellent*. This usage is most common among young people.

Audioscript: The audioscript for Exercise 2 appears on pages T132–T133.

Answers

Story: Complex storyline; events are like a puzzle with pieces that don't fit together until the final scene; full of suspense

Direction: Awesome, full of new ideas; images are brilliantly put together; characters are nicely blocked

Acting: Performers are believable; the actor who played Mr. Bernstein was fantastic

Photography: Incredible camerawork: long shots and tight close-ups, good use of light and shadow

 Workbook: Practice 1

Figure It Out *(pages 28–29)*

Preview

Tell students to look at the picture. Read the situation, and ask students to work with a partner to predict some questions an interviewer might ask a businessperson like Harjiv.

Presentation

❸ Have students read the conversation alone and then read the conversation aloud in pairs. Dictate or write the following questions on the board, and have the students answer them. Have them work in pairs to answer the following questions. Review answers with the class.

1. How will digital movies be transmitted to theaters? What are the advantages over the way movies are distributed now?

2. What has to be done to a movie before it can be transmitted in this way?

3. Besides ease of transmission, what are some other advantages of digital movies?

4. What does Harjiv invite Margo to do tomorrow?

5. What time does the screening start?

Presentation Answers

1. By satellite. No more shipping, no more spools, no more splicing; distribution and transmission will be much cheaper, easier, and faster.

2. It has to be scanned, digitized, and turned into a gigantic computer file. Then it has to be compressed and encrypted.

3. Digital movies will give audiences pristine images and sound at every screening; images will be stable, with no scratches, dirt, burns, or splices.

4. To join himself and several film industry CEOs for an experimental screening of a digital movie.

5. It starts at 11:00 a.m.

🌐 **Option:** Extend the activity by having students discuss the following questions in pairs or small groups. Have selected groups share answers with the class.

1. What are some potential disadvantages of satellite transmission of digital movies?

2. How do you think the movie theater of the future will be different from movie theaters today? Think of size and layout as well as technical equipment.

Language Note: *CEO* stands for Chief Executive Officer, which is generally the highest-ranking position in a company.

☑ ❹ **Vocabulary Check** Have students work alone and then compare answers with a partner. Review the answers with the class.

> **Answers**
> 1. g   2. a   3. e   4. f   5. c   6. b

 Workbook: Practice 2

Talk About It *(page 29)*

🌐 **Option:** If you feel that your students need extra help in using future forms, you might want to postpone this activity until after the grammar presentation (pages 29–32).

Presentation

Note: This activity is designed to develop fluency. It is best not to interrupt students to correct errors. Make notes of student errors for review with the class after the activity has finished.

❺ Have students model the conversation for the class. Then have students work in pairs to improvise conversations using the language in the model. Circulate and offer assistance. Make notes of student errors. Select pairs to present their conversations to the class. Refer to your notes, and write the grammar errors on the board without identifying who made them. Then correct the errors as a class.

Note: 35mm is the standard film format for movies. Most movie theaters today are equipped with 35mm projectors.

Language Note: *Technologies:* the word *technology* is usually a singular, collective noun. However, it can be used in the plural, to refer to several distinct disciplines. For example, *sound technology, camera technology, lighting technology, and special effects technology are just some of the* **technologies** *that are involved in making a movie.*

✺ **Option:** Extend the previous activity by having students work in groups of four to six. Each student is assigned one of the topics and prepares to be interviewed. The other group members then conduct the interview, asking for explanations, clarification, examples, etc.

✺ **Option:** Each student prepares one of the topics by doing research at home. In addition to researching their own topics, students prepare lists of questions on the other topics. Each student is then interviewed by the class and asked for explanations, clarification, examples, etc.

 *Workbook: Practice 3*

GRAMMAR

Going to, Will, Present Progressive, and Simple Present *(pages 29–32)*

Preview

Put cues on the board such as:

new Russell Crowe movie / opens tomorrow / Garden City Cineplex / first show at 7:30 / guest appearance by Russell Crowe

Ask for different sentences using this information. If necessary, use sentence prompts such as: *The new Russell Crowe movie . . . / Russell Crowe . . . / I . . . The movie . . .* Elicit sentences such as:

1. *The new Russell Crowe movie <u>is opening</u> tomorrow night at the Garden City Cineplex.*

2. *Russell Crowe <u>will be</u> there in person.*

3. *I'm definitely <u>going to go</u>. The movie <u>starts</u> at 7:30.*

Underline the future forms used in these sentences, and ask students to explain the different uses of each.

Presentation

Have students read the introduction and the examples in the first box. Explain that *will* expresses a definite belief but can also be used to announce intentions that were just decided on at the time of speaking, as in *I have to go now—I'll see you later*; to make promises, as in *I promise I'll take you next week*; and to make offers, as in *You paid for the last movie. I'll get this one.* Also point out that the *going to* future form in a statement is not generally used when there is any uncertainty, such as when preceded by an *if* or *when* clause. Then have them read the second part of the introduction and the examples in the second box. It is possible to use different forms to describe the same action with little or no change in meaning, for example, *I'm going to the movies tomorrow*, or *I'm going to go to the movies tomorrow*.

❶ Have students read the instructions and the article and do the exercise independently. Then have them compare answers with a partner. Review answers with the class.

> **Answers**
> 'm playing, starts, 'll tell, going to be, is going to become, will revolutionize, will be able to do, will be able to (fly, jump, climb up), will be, will provide, will (not only spend, live)

❷ Have students work alone and then compare answers and discuss with a partner. Circulate and offer assistance, and review answers with the class.

Culture Notes:

- The *Cannes International Film Festival* is held in May every year in Cannes on the French Riviera and is known for focusing on cinema artistry rather than commercial success and for encouraging new directors.

- The *Oscars* are the annual awards given by the Academy of Motion Picture Arts and Sciences. The award, a statuette of a male figure, is called the *Oscar*. One story is that an early director of the Academy thought that the statuette resembled her Uncle Oscar.

Answers

Possible answers:
1. will be *or* is going to be
2. am going to watch; will visit
3. going to be; is . . . starting; *or* is . . . going to start

Option: Have students choose one example from the text for each future form and write sentences of their own using the same forms. Then have them discuss their sentences with a partner. Monitor the discussions. Review the sentences in class while monitoring, or collect them for correction and comment.

❸ Have students work alone and then compare answers with a partner and discuss. Review the answers with the class.

Culture Note: *Ratings codes* are voluntary designations used by film distributors in the United States to determine the suitability of films for different age groups. There are five classifications, ranging from G (general audiences) to NC-17 (no one 17 years of age or younger admitted).

Answers

Possible answers:
1. will give *or* is giving   2. is going to talk
3. is going to present   4. will argue
5. will probably influence   6. starts
7. takes   8. begins   9. is going to be *or* will be   10. will be *or* am going to be

☑ ❹ **Check Your Understanding** Have students read the directions independently. Point out that more than one tense may be *possible* in these situations but that they should think about which tense would be used *most*. Students should work alone, and then compare answers with a partner and discuss the reasons for their choices. Review the answers with the class.

Answers

a. *going to* **b.** *will* **c.** present progressive
d. simple present

❺ **Express Yourself** Go over the instructions with students. Monitor their dialogues as they are practicing and performing them. Have selected pairs present their dialogues to the class.

Option: Have students work at home to prepare an individual presentation on one of the topics, to be presented to the class in the manner of a television newscaster.

 Workbook: Practices 4, 5, 6

LISTENING and SPEAKING

Listen: The Future of Movies (*pages 32–33*)

Presentation

❶ **Before You Listen** Ask students how many own a digital camera. Ask how many own a video recorder. Have students read the instructions independently and then discuss in small groups. Have selected groups summarize their conclusions for the class.

➡ **Listening Critically** Have students read the strategy. Ask them how they evaluate an argument. What kind of support is convincing? Elicit examples, such as *logic*, *clear examples*. What kind of support is not convincing? Elicit examples, such as *emotional appeals*, *strong language*, etc.

🎧 ❷ Have students read the instructions and the list of predictions independently. Make sure they understand that they will hear only *some* of these predictions in the dialogue. Play the recording, or read the audioscript once for students to select answers. Review answers with the class.

Audioscript: The audioscript for Exercise 2 appears on pages T133–T134.

Answers
a, d, f

❸ Direct students to the picture on page 33. Ask them who made each prediction they checked. Have each student work with a partner. Each pair should choose one of the predictions. Play the recording or read the audioscript one or more times, and have students work alone to list the supporting arguments, then compare answers with their partners. Then have students form small groups and discuss whether or not they agree with the predictions and why. They must support their arguments with evidence.

🌐 **Option:** Students work in groups of three. Each student focuses on one of the predictions and the arguments.

 *Workbook: Practice 7*

Pronunciation (pages 33–34)

Preview

Write the phrase *Rebel Without a Cause* on the board. Ask students if they recognize it. (It is the title of James Dean's best-known film, released in 1955 and starring Dean, Sal Mineo, and Natalie Wood.) Ask for a volunteer to say the title out loud. Elicit the pronunciation *RE•bel Without a Cause.* Model the pronunciation *Re•BEL Without a Cause,* and ask if it would change the meaning. (It would make it an imperative sentence rather then a noun phrase, but it should be sufficient to point out the noun/verb distinction.)

Presentation

Have students read the rules and examples in the box. You may wish to point out that this stress shift does not occur with all verb/noun pairs (e.g., *LI•mit/LI•mit, AN•swer/AN•swer*).

❹ Have students read the instructions and do the exercise independently. Review answers with the class.

Answers
Rebel is a noun in the first sentence. It is a verb in the second.

❺ Have students read the instructions and do the exercise independently.

Language Note: *A druglord* is the head of a criminal gang that sells drugs.

Culture Note: Orpheus and his bride Eurydice are figures from Greek mythology. Orpheus and Eurydice were deeply in love. Eurydice died, and Orpheus was so filled with grief that he followed her to Hades (the world of the dead). Eurydice was allowed to follow Orpheus and return to the world of the living on the condition that Orpheus did not look back to see if she was there. He did look back, and Orpheus had to return alone to the world of the living.

🎧 ❻ Have students read the instructions independently. Then have them work with a partner to compare predictions from the previous exercise. Play the recording, or read the audioscript for students to check their predictions. Review the answers with the class.

Audioscript: The audioscript for Exercise 6 appears on Student Book page 33.

Answers
re-, -mits, con-, -trasts, in-, -gress

❼ Have students read the sentences with their partners, checking each other's pronunciation of the stressed syllables. Monitor their performances, and make corrections and suggestions as needed.

 Workbook: Practice 8

Speak Out (pages 34–35)

Preview

Make a strong statement expressing an opinion, such as: "Movies and all other forms of electronic entertainment will disappear in the near future and people will go back to reading books and attending live performances." Elicit questions for supporting reasons, and respond that you just think so. Ask them if they are convinced. Ask them why or why not.

Presentation

→ **Speaking Persuasively** Have students read the strategy independently. Point out that making concessions not only is less confrontational, but is also a means to persuade others. A stance often starts out with generally accepted ideas but eventually reaches a point where aspects of these ideas can be refuted. A counterargument is more effective if it begins by expressing agreement with ideas that are generally accepted.

Go over the examples in the box with the class. Provide complete sentences based on the prompts.

☼ **Option:** Have students work with partners to create and practice model sentences based on the prompts.

Note: This activity is designed to develop fluency. It is best not to interrupt students to correct errors. Make notes of student errors for review with the class after the activity has finished.

❽ Have students read the instructions independently. Review the instructions to make sure students understand that there are to be three unique roles in the discussion: the "for," the "against," and the judge. Have them read the situation and roles independently, and then do the activity in groups of three. Monitor the activity, and have selected students present their viewpoints to the class.

☼ **Option:** Select a pair of one "for" and one "against" from each group, and have them present their viewpoints to the class. Then have an open question-and-answer session in which class members ask for clarification, explanation, etc. Finally, poll the class to decide on the most convincing presentation.

☼ **Option:** As an alternative to Exercise 8, create three "teams" within the class: one "for," one "against," and one "neutral." Allow teams time to discuss and prepare their presentations: the "neutral" team can discuss both sides of the issue while the other teams are preparing their presentations. Then, after both sides have presented to the class, the neutral team will briefly discuss and then vote to decide the winning viewpoint.

☼ **Option:** Expand the situation. Place controversial statements on the board, such as, *In the future, people will be bored with simulated violence on screen, so studios will resort to live violence . . . ;* or *Twenty years from now all films will be made in Hollywood.* Tell students to brainstorm lists of possible reasons to support and refute these claims. They can be creative. Then have a discussion following one of the procedures in the options above.

 *Workbook: Practice 9*

READING and WRITING

Read About It *(pages 35–37)*

Presentation

❶ **Before You Read** Have students read the instructions independently and discuss the question in small groups. Have selected groups share their answers with the class.

☼ **Option:** Lead the students in a discussion about who their favorite actors are and why they like them. Brainstorm a list of the qualities of a good actor. Ask the students to provide specific examples. Then have students work in groups to discuss these qualities and narrow down the list to those they think are most important. Then poll the groups and compare results.

→ **Reading Critically** Have students read the strategy independently. Point out that this is the same strategy that they practiced in the Listening and Speaking section in a different context: noticing and evaluating supporting reasons.

❷ Have students read the article independently. Ask them to take notes of supporting details by marking them in the text or noting them by line number on a separate piece of paper.

Language Note: *Abuzz* is a predicate adjective meaning "talking excitedly." In the entertainment industry, the noun form *buzz* is often used to describe excitement about a new product or person, as in "There is a lot of *buzz* about the new *Star Wars* movie."

Culture Note: The character of Jar Jar Binks in the film *Star Wars: Episode 1—The Phantom Menace* was widely criticized as a racial stereotype. Even though this character was not human, many felt that its language and behavior represented a demeaning characterization of West Indian people. Some *Star Wars* fans have used video editing equipment to create an alternate version of the film in which the Jar Jar Binks character does not appear. This unofficial version has been titled *Star Wars 1.1—The Phantom Edit.*

Option: If you feel your students need help with unfamiliar words before they do the task, you may wish to do the Vocabulary Check exercise on page 37 before the following exercises.

❸ Have students read the instructions and do the activity independently. Remind them that they can use the notes they made while reading the article to help them answer the questions. Also remind them to put the answers in their own words as much as possible. Then have them compare answers with a partner.

Answers

a. It was thought that computers couldn't portray the range of emotions that a human actor could. A new digital technology called photo-realistic animation may finally make it possible to do so.

b. Actors are troubled and afraid, because they think that directors will use digital animation to alter the actors' performances without their knowledge or permission. They are also concerned about the emergence of digital competition.

c. Digital actors will do anything filmmakers want them to do, without any complaints or demands. They can be used for promotions and endorsements, and any extra money they bring in for endorsements goes to the studio.

d. Many people feel that computer animation can't create believable human characters. However, actors still feel threatened, because they fear losing control over the final outcome of their performance.

e. Other applications of this technology include inserting actors into film clips with historical figures, using long-dead stars in commercials, and changing an actor's appearance or age when necessary.

❹ Have students read the instructions and do the activity independently. Then have them compare answers with a partner. Review answers with the class.

Answers

a. paragraph 3 **b.** paragraph 1
c. paragraph 5 **d.** paragraph 6

☑ ❺ **Vocabulary Check** Have students read the instructions and do the exercise independently and then compare answers with a partner. Review the answers with the class.

Answers

1. c **2.** h **3.** g **4.** e **5.** i **6.** b
7. f **8.** a

Think About It *(page 37)*

Presentation

❻ Have students read the question independently and discuss it with a partner or in a small group. Monitor discussions, and review conclusions with the class.

Option: Assign pairs either the "pro" (*actors' fear **is** justified*) or the "con" (*actors' fear **is not** justified*) position on the question in Exercise 6. Allow time for them to prepare their position, and then match up each "pro" pair with a "con" pair and have them present their viewpoints and discuss. Monitor discussions, and have selected groups summarize their discussions for the class.

❼ Have students read the question independently and discuss it with a partner or in a small group. Monitor discussions, and review conclusions with the class.

☀ Option: Lead a discussion with the class on the questions in Exercises 6 and 7.

Write: The Analytical Essay (pages 37–38)

Preview

Ask students what we do when we analyze something. Elicit ideas like *break it down, examine closely, try to understand,* etc.

Presentation

Have students read the introduction. Ask whether the analytical essay's purposes are primarily persuasive or descriptive. Explain that they may be either.

➡ **A Persuasive Essay** Have students read the strategy. Point out that this persuasive essay will analyze its topic as a way of making its point. Also point out that there is a certain amount of description going on, but that the main purpose of the essay is persuasion. If necessary, review the terms outlined in the introduction, such as *thesis statement,* etc.

❽ Have students read the instructions and do the exercise independently. Then have them compare answers with a partner. Review answers with the class.

Answers

a. paragraph 1   b. paragraph 1
c. paragraph 2   d. paragraph 3
e. paragraphs 2, 3   f. paragraph 4

Write About It (page 38)

Presentation

❾ Have students read the question independently and write the essay in class or as homework.

☑ **❿ Check Your Writing** Have students use the bulleted questions to give written feedback on their partner's paper. Have them use feedback from their partner to revise their own paper.

 Workbook: Practice 10

Vocabulary Expansion: High-tech idioms
See page T120.

Answers

```
      ¹W E B C A M
      E
    ²B U R ³N
      C     O
      A     V
      S     E
  ⁴V I ⁵R T ⁶U A L
  I     A   P
  ⁷D O W N L O A D
  E     O
  O   ⁸C A M C O R D E R
      D
```

Across

1. Needed for a webcast [WEBCAM]

2. Record a CD [BURN]

4. —— reality [VIRTUAL]

7. Get from the Net [DOWNLOAD]

8. Two machines in one [CAMCORDER]

Down

1. Like TV on the Net [WEBCAST]

3. Basis for many films [NOVEL]

4. Not audio [VIDEO]

5. Uncooked or unedited [RAW]

6. Put on the Net [UPLOAD]

EVALUATION

See pages Txi–Txii.

Unit 3 Achievement Test

Self-Check See **You're In Charge!**, page 24 of the Workbook.

PORTFOLIO

Writing Revised essay from **Write About It**, Exercises 9 and 10, page 38.

Oral Communication

1. Record a dialogue with a partner, discussing the difference between films of ten, fifteen, or twenty years ago and those of today. For your tape, choose one film to represent each era and compare them. Answer your partner's questions. Then reverse roles for your partner's tape.

2. Record a dialogue with a partner discussing creative uses of digital technology in filmmaking. Suggest a new use for the technology, such as interactive storylines, etc., and answer your partner's questions. Then reverse roles for your partner's tape.

Interactive Dictation

Dictate the following sentences to the students. Then have them go back and insert a sentence between each of the dictated sentences to create a paragraph with a coherent flow. For more information on dictation, see page Txv.

1. Filmmaking is yet another area where traditional concepts are in conflict with the capabilities of technology.
2. (student's sentence)
3. Will movies of the future be high-tech spectacles in which robots battle each other against fantastic, futuristic backgrounds?
4. (student's sentence)
5. Already, some young filmmakers are rebelling against what they see as technology for its own sake, without art or soul.
6. (student's sentence)
7. Whatever the outcome, one thing is clear: technology is not going to go away.
8. (student's sentence)
9. As the saying goes, "The future starts today."
10. (student's sentence)

PROGRESS CHECK
Units 1–3

Progress Checks may be done as homework or may be used in class. As a class exercise, they may be done in several ways:

- as a quiz—students work alone and hand their papers in to you to be corrected

- as pairwork—students work alone and then compare answers with a partner

- as a class exercise—students work alone, and answers are reviewed with the class

➡ **Answering Multiple Choice Questions**
Have students read the strategy. Make sure they understand the difference between the "correct" answer and the "best" answer.

GRAMMAR (*pages 39–41*)

A Have students read the instructions and do the exercise. For a review of the simple present tense, refer students to Unit 1, page 6. For a review of the simple past, past progressive, and past perfect tenses, refer students to Unit 2, pages 18–21.

> **Answers**
> 1. B   2. C   3. C   4. B   5. D   6. A
> 7. A (or B)   8. D

➡ **Answering Error Detection Questions**
Have students read the strategy. Point out that, in most cases, they will have to look for errors in grammar and structure rather than in vocabulary and word choice. Therefore, in cases where it seems that there are two things that could be changed to make the sentence correct, it is safer to choose the one that illustrates a grammar error.

B Have students read the instructions and do the exercise. For a comprehensive review of tenses, refer students to: Unit 1, pages 6–9; Unit 2, pages 18–21; Unit 3, pages 29–32.

> **Answers**
> Section One
> 1. B   2. C   3. C   4. B   5. D
> Section Two
> 1. C   2. A   3. B

VOCABULARY (*pages 41–42*)

➡ **Answering Multiple Choice Vocabulary Questions** Have students read the strategy, pointing out that the "best" answer is sometimes determined by tone or nuance.

Have students read the instructions and do the exercise.

> **Answers**
> Section 1
> 1. B   2. B   3. B   4. D   5. D   6. A
> Section 2
> 1. A   2. B   3. D   4. C

I BEG TO DIFFER

OBJECTIVES

Students will be able to:

- Talk about conflict resolution
- Express sympathy
- Ask for and give advice
- Use gerunds and infinitives
- Listen for and evaluate supporting reasons
- Produce contrastive word stress for emphasis
- Manage conflict in discussions
- Apply prior knowledge to reading
- Choose and narrow a writing topic
- Use idioms of confrontation

GETTING STARTED

Warm Up (page 43)

Preview

Have students look at the photograph at the top of the page. Ask them what is going on. Elicit some possible answers, such as *a discussion, an argument, a fight*, etc. Introduce the term *conflict* as a word that covers all those meanings.

Presentation

Put the word *conflict* on the board. Explain that its meaning ranges from a polite disagreement to an undeclared war, as in *the conflict in the Middle East*. Point out other situations where conflict can occur, such as *a conflict of interest*, and *conflicting loyalties*. Also point out that *conflict* is one of the words that has a different stress depending on whether it is used as a noun or a verb: *CON•flict* (noun) and *con•FLICT* (verb).

❶ Have students work in small groups to discuss the questions. Monitor the discussions, and have selected groups summarize their discussions for the class.

❷ Have students read the instructions and then relate their experience to a partner. Have selected students share their experiences with the class.

Language Note: To *beg to differ* means to *politely disagree*. You are essentially asking the person for permission to disagree with him or her.

🎧 ❸ Have students read the instructions independently. Review the instructions, pointing out that on the first listening they only have to identify the subject of the conflict. Play the recording, or read the audioscript one or more times. Have them compare answers with a partner and then work with their partner to discuss possible resolutions to the conflict.

Language Notes:

- *Dispute* is a word that has essentially the same meaning as *conflict*.

- *In my book* is an idiom that means *according to my way of thinking*.

- *Showed up* is an idiom that means *arrived*.

- *Out of the blue* is an idiom that means *without warning, suddenly, unexpectedly*. The image is of something that fell from the sky.

- *You snooze, you lose* is an idiom that means *If you are asleep or not paying attention, you will lose your opportunity*.

Audioscript: The audioscript for Exercise 3 appears on page T134.

Answers

a. A mother is arguing with her daughter about staying out late.

b. Two men are arguing over a parking space.

c. Two co-workers are arguing over the male co-worker's Web-surfing during work hours.

Answers to the last question (possible resolutions) will vary.

 Workbook: Practice 1

Figure It Out (pages 43–44)

Preview

Ask students to work with a partner and discuss the following questions.

- Who did they have conflicts with most frequently as children, and how did they respond? Who do they have conflicts with most often these days?

- What are these conflicts about?

- How do they usually respond?

- Has their response to conflict changed over the years?

Have selected students report their answers to the class.

Presentation

Have students read the instructions, do the activity alone, and tally the results. Be sure to do the questionnaire yourself while they are working. After they have tallied the results, have them read the explanation at the end of the questionnaire.

Culture Note: This type of questionnaire is often found in popular magazines. Magazines from *Cosmopolitan* to *Psychology Today* carry "personality profiles" and other such questionnaires, sometimes referred to as "pop psych (for *popular psychology*) quizzes."

Language Notes:

- To *empathize* (verb form of *empathy*) is to understand someone's feelings and to experience them yourself to some degree, even if you don't altogether agree with the other person's motivations or conclusions. It is closely related to the word *sympathize*.

- To *validate* (someone's) *feelings* is to show that you think it is acceptable and understandable to have such feelings, even if you don't have those feelings yourself.

❹ Set up the activity by asking students how they think you yourself answered the questions. Have selected students guess your answers to specific questions and volunteer reasons for their answers. Explain that students will work with a partner and try to guess each other's

answers. They can either go through all the statements first, mark those they think their partner checked, and then go back through and review the answers with their partners; or simply guess and review as they read the questionnaire.

🌐 **Option:** Poll the class to determine and compile results: What were the score ranges? What percentage of the class could be considered to be "good at conflict resolution"?

🌐 **Option:** Expand the activity by having groups discuss the validity of the questionnaire. The interpretation mentions "recommended conflict resolution strategies." Have students discuss why these strategies are recommended. Ask them to suggest alternatives and additions to the statements in the questionnaire.

🌐 **Option:** Have students discuss cultural differences in conflict resolution. Ask them to discuss which culture they think this questionnaire came from (North American) and to give examples of situations that reflect the cultural attitudes in which and for which it was created. Ask them what other questions might appear in another culture.

☑ ❺ **Vocabulary Check** Have students work alone and then compare answers with a partner. Review the answers with the class.

Answers
1. d   2. e   3. b   4. a   5. c

 Workbook: Practice 2

Talk About It (page 45)

🌐 **Option:** If you feel that your students need extra help in using gerunds and infinitives, you might want to postpone this activity until after the grammar presentation (pages 46–49).

Presentation

Note: This activity is designed to develop fluency. It is best not to interrupt students to correct errors. Make notes of student errors for review with the class after the activity has finished.

❻ Direct students to the picture and ask them to describe what is happening. Have students read the instructions and discuss the situation with the class. Ask students what they would do if they had a problem with their supervisor at work. Discuss different ways of responding such as *discussing the problem with a co-worker, talking directly with the supervisor, writing an anonymous letter to the supervisor, talking to their boss's supervisor, leaving the job*. Ask students which of these options they would choose and in what order. Explain that in North America, it is common to discuss a problem first with a co-worker or with the supervisor directly; written complaints are usually taken seriously. Speaking with your boss's boss is usually the solution of last resort. Have a pair of students read the conversation for the class. Then have students work in pairs to improvise conversations, using the cues and the language in the model as a guide. Select pairs to present their conversations to the class.

Language Notes:

- A *sympathetic* listener is one who shares your feelings. As mentioned earlier, *sympathy* is closely related to *empathy*, but with the sense that the listener not only understands your feelings but also shares them and supports you.

- *Swamped* means burdened with more than one can handle; the image is of being in a swamp; that is, being partially underwater.

- To *take some weight off (someone's) shoulders* is to help someone with a task that is too much for that person; the image is of helping someone to carry a heavy load.

- To *take a sick day* means to use one of the allotted number of days that one is allowed to stay home from work due to an illness, without losing any pay.

 *Workbook: Practice 3*

GRAMMAR

Gerunds *(page 46)*

Preview

Put the following sentences on the board:

Someone was <u>talking</u> during the test.

<u>Talking</u> is not allowed during tests.

Underline the word *talking* in each sentence, and then ask students if there is a difference in meaning between the two sentences. Ask them if there is a grammatical difference. Elicit *yes* or *no* answers, but stop short of describing what that difference is.

Presentation

Have students read the introduction and the examples in the box. Have them contrast the use of *taking* in the following two sentences:

*I enjoy **taking** classes on conflict resolution.*

*I am **taking** a class on conflict resolution this semester.*

Elicit the fact that *taking* in the first sentence is a gerund (noun form of the verb), while in the second sentence, *taking* is a present progressive verb. Point out that gerunds can function exactly like nouns in sentences.

❶ Review the directions with the students and explain the task. The first part (**a.**) asks them to find examples of gerunds in the questionnaire. The second, third, and fourth parts (**b., c.,** and **d.**) ask them to classify these gerunds according to function. Have students do the exercise independently and then compare answers with a partner. Review answers with the class.

Answers

Possible answers (with questionnaire numbers):

a. getting, leaving (1), convincing, thinking (3), saying (4), talking (5), empathizing (6), resolving (7), bringing (9), discussing (10), talking, doing (11), expressing (12), saying (13), Being (14)

b. Being (14), talking (5)

---

c. getting (1), bringing (9), doing (11), saying (13)

d. leaving (1), convincing, thinking (3), saying (4), empathizing (6), resolving (7), discussing (10), talking (11), expressing (12)

Verbs with Gerunds or Infinitives (pages 46–47)

Presentation

Have students read the introduction and the examples in the box. First focus on the verb + gerund structure. Put a few sample sentences on the board to illustrate the use of this structure, for example, *I **enjoy solving** my problems on my own, I can't **help getting** angry when he talks like that.*

Option: Have students write one or two sample sentences alone. Ask selected students to read their sentences for the class.

Then focus on the verb + noun phrase + gerund structure, and have students look at the examples in the box. Put sample sentences on the board, or ask students to provide their own sentences to illustrate the use of this structure; for instance, *He **accused me of taking** his bicycle, I **criticized her for talking** about family problems to outsiders.*

Then write this sentence on the board:

He agreed _____ to my teacher tomorrow. (talk)

Ask students to use the verb in parentheses to fill in the blank. Elicit the infinitive. Have students look at the list of phrases in the box. Put additional sample sentences on the board, or ask students to provide their own sentences to illustrate this structure. Then put this sentence on the board:

I asked _____ to her about my grade.

Ask the question, "Why did he agree to talk to my teacher?" Ask students to fill in the blank above to answer the question. Elicit *I asked <u>him to talk</u> to her about my grade.* Have students look at the phrases in the third

box. Put additional sample sentences on the board, or ask students to provide their own sentences to illustrate the use of this structure.

Gerunds or Infinitives and Their Meanings (pages 47–49)

Preview

Put the following sentence on the board:

Do you like _____ tests? (take)

Ask students to complete it using a form of the verb in parentheses. Elicit both *Do you like taking tests?* and *Do you like to take tests?* Point out that in many cases with verbs that can take both gerunds and infinitives, there is little difference in meaning. In the case above, for example, there is no real difference. In some cases, however, the gerund meaning is more "hypothetical," as in, *Would you like **doing** the dishes?* (Hypothetical—If you were to do the dishes, would you enjoy it?) The infinitive meaning is more "actual," as in, *Would you like **to do** the dishes?* (Actual—I am politely suggesting that you wash the dishes.)

Presentation

Have students read the introduction and the examples in the box. Put a few additional sample sentences on the board.

*I can't stand **doing** laundry./I can't stand **to do** laundry.* (little difference)

*I would love **going** with you!/I would love **to go** with you!* (little difference)

❷ Have students read the instructions and do the exercise independently. Then have them check answers with a partner. Review answers with the class.

> **Answers**
> 1. to do 2. wearing 3. going out
> 4. being 5. to help 6. to listen 7. going
> 8. taking 9. being 10. trying

Next, put this sentence on the board:

He forgot _____ the key. (leave)

Ask students to complete the sentence with a form of the verb in parentheses. Elicit both the gerund and infinitive forms, and their differences in meaning. For example:

He forgot <u>leaving</u> the key. (He left the key but didn't remember doing so.)

He forgot <u>to leave</u> the key. (He didn't leave the key because he forgot that he was supposed to.)

Have students read the introduction and the examples in the box at the top of page 48. Put a few additional sample sentences on the board, illustrating the use of this structure.

❸ Have students work alone and then compare answers with a partner. Review the answers with the class.

Answers
a. 1   b. 2   c. 3   d. 4   e. 5   f. 6

Option: Have students work in pairs. Put the words *forget, remember, stop* in one column on the board and the words *do, give, take, ask, smoke, send, tell* in another column. Point to one word from each column, and have students compete to come up with two sentences, one using the gerund form of the second verb and one using the infinitive form. Award points for the first pair to complete two acceptable sentences. Before awarding points, have the winning pair explain the difference in meaning.

❹ Have students read the instructions independently. Tell them that they should try to use a mixture of both gerund and infinitive forms in their conversation. Have them work with a partner to create and perform the short conversations. Monitor the conversations, and have selected pairs present their conversations to the class.

Using *It* + Infinitive Instead of a Gerund (*page 49*)

Presentation

Have students read the introduction and the examples in the box. Point out that this structure is usually used to make a general

observation with adjectives such as *essential, important, necessary, unusual, common,* etc.

Option: For additional practice, ask students to explain the grammatical differences between the second and third examples in the box. Explain that the third sentence adds the preposition *for* and its object *employees* to indicate who must do the resolving. The two sentences could be paraphrased as follows:

It's essential to *resolve problems in a collaborative manner.*

= *Problems should be resolved in a collaborative manner.*

It's essential for employees *to resolve problems in a collaborative manner.*

= *Employees should solve problems in a collaborative manner.*

Then have them create example sentences of their own, following the pattern of the examples in the box.

☑ ❺ **Check Your Understanding** Have students read the instructions and do the exercise independently. Then have students compare answers with a partner. Review the answers with the class.

Answers
1. making a distinction 2. Treating *or* To treat
3. not to be 4. doing 5. to interrupt
6. doing 7. to find out

Option: Expand Exercise 5 by asking students to rewrite the passage exchanging gerund/infinitive usages wherever possible; for example, using gerunds in place of infinitives and vice versa, rewriting sentences to use plain forms of verbs rather than gerund/infinitive forms, rewriting *it* + infinitive sentences as gerund-as-subject sentences, etc.

❻ **Express Yourself** Set up the task by having students brainstorm different situations where Mexicans and Americans might interact: as tourists, on business trips, meeting a new family member. Then describe a situation in which a Mexican businessman meets an American colleague for a business lunch at a charming restaurant in Mexico City.

The Mexican businessman is thirty minutes late. Improvise a model conversation with a student, or have students improvise their own conversation in pairs. Then have students work with a partner to create their own situation, write and practice dialogue, and then perform it for another pair. Have selected pairs perform their dialogues for the class.

 Workbook: Practices 4, 5, 6

LISTENING and SPEAKING

Listen: Resolving Conflict (*page 50*)

Presentation

❶ Before You Listen Have students read the instructions and the statements independently. Check understanding, and then have them do the task. Then have students form small groups to discuss their opinions. Monitor the discussions, and have selected groups report their conclusions to the class.

➡ **Applying Background Knowledge**
Before students read the strategy, ask them the advantages of knowing something about the topic before they listen to a lecture about it. Answers could include that students are familiar with the vocabulary, it's easy to pick out key information, etc. Elicit the advantages of relating a reading to their own lives. Possible responses could include that remembering information is easier, they can put information to immediate use, they can grasp nuances, and they can decide how reliable the information is.

Have students read the strategy. Review the concept of using past information and background knowledge to evaluate a speaker's viewpoint. Suggest that students use the question *How does this fit in with what I know about X?* when evaluating a viewpoint.

❷ Have students read the instructions and questions. Remind them of the

importance of taking notes. Suggest that they review the question to see what they are listening for and prepare a notebook page for this information. In this case, they will need to identify styles of conflict resolution and the characteristics of each, so they might prepare a two-column page with "style" on the left and "characteristics" on the right. Play the recording or read the audioscript, and have them do the exercise independently. Then have them compare answers with a partner. Review answers with the class.

Audioscript: The audioscript for Exercise 2 appears on pages T134–T136.

Answers

a. The five styles the speaker mentions for dealing with conflict are:
1. Withdrawing or avoiding the conflict
2. Accommodating
3. Competing (or win/lose approach)
4. Compromising
5. Collaborating (or win/win approach)

b. Characteristics of each style:
1. Refusing to discuss the problem when confronted.
2. Preferring to suppress the conflict, to smooth things over, or to refuse to acknowledge the fact that a conflict exists.
3. The win/lose approach. It's often a power struggle in which one person comes out on top. Generally, this is not a good solution to the problem because one person gains at another's expense. In rare situations, though, it can be useful.
4. Adopting a middle-of-the-road approach. Can be the fairest approach to take.
5. The win/win approach. Develops mutually satisfying solutions. Requires that one find out more about the situation first and explore options before one comes up with a final solution. New options can be designed.

❸ Have students read the instructions and the questions independently. Play the recording, or read the audioscript again, and have them answer the questions. Then have them compare answers and discuss with a partner. Have selected pairs report on their discussion to the class.

 *Workbook: Practice 7*

Pronunciation *(pages 50–51)*

Preview

Write this sentence on the board:
It's tomorrow night.

Ask for a volunteer to read it aloud. Don't comment on the stress pattern. Then ask the question:

When is the meeting?

Ask for another volunteer to read the first sentence as an answer to your question. Elicit the word stress pattern *It's tomorrow **night***. Then ask the question:

Is the meeting tonight or tomorrow night?

Ask for a volunteer to read the original sentence as an answer to your question. Elicit the word stress pattern *It's **tomorrow** night*.

Presentation

Have students read the rules and example dialogue in the box. Model the stress in the example dialogue, and have them practice reading it with a partner.

❹ Have students read the instructions and work with a partner.

❺ Play the recording or read the audioscript one or more times for students to check their predictions. Then have them compare answers with a partner.

Audioscript: The audioscript for Exercise 5 appears on Student Book page 51.

Answers
A: Tuesday, Thursday
B: Thursday
A: 204, 206
B: Not sure, schedule
A: tonight, tomorrow
B: thing, tomorrow, busy, date, Steve

❻ Have students read the instructions and work with their partners to read the dialogue from Exercise 4, focusing on contrastive stress. Monitor their performance, and have selected pairs present the dialogue to the class.

 Workbook: Practice 8

Speak Out *(page 51)*

Preview

Ask for a volunteer to give an opinion on a topic; for example, *What do you think of the idea of a government tax on e-mail messages?* When the volunteer has given his/her opinion, respond with *That's ridiculous!* After a brief pause, respond with *I'm sorry, but that's not how I see it.* Ask students which response they preferred.

Presentation

➡ **Managing Conflict** Have students read the strategy. Make the distinction between clarity and strong tone, and point out that it is possible to make one's point very clearly yet politely. Point out that this will not only make your viewpoint more acceptable to the person with whom you are disagreeing, but it will also make objective bystanders view your position more favorably.

❼ Have students read the instructions and do the exercise independently. Review the answers with the class.

Answers
1. P 2. I 3. P 4. P 5. I 6. P 7. I 8. P

Option: Discuss the concept of *register* (formal and informal) with the students. Give the class different situations, for example, a father talking to a child, two siblings arguing, a disagreement between two close friends, an assistant listening to his boss, the company president talking to a low-ranking worker. Ask students in which situations each response is *most likely* to be heard. Have their answers about politeness changed? Why or why not?

 Option: Have students read the written responses to one another, emphasizing emotion, and discuss the facial expressions and gestures that might accompany these statements.

❽ Have students read the instructions and the situation independently. Then have them work with a partner and brainstorm supporting points for the viewpoints. Then put pairs together into small groups. Divide each group into *students* and *administrators*, and have them discuss the issue. Remind them of the importance of using *softeners*. Monitor the discussions, and have selected students present examples of the use of softeners to the class.

Note: This activity is designed to develop fluency. It is best not to interrupt students to correct errors. Make notes of student errors for review with the class after the activity has finished.

Workbook: Practices 9, 10

READING and WRITING

Read About It (pages 52–53)

Presentation

❶ Before You Read Check that students understand the situations. Have students read the instructions and the situations independently, and then discuss them with a partner. Have selected pairs share the results of their discussion with the class.

Language Note: *In front of the class*, in this case, simply means *while other students are present*. It does not necessarily mean the student is physically at the front of the classroom.

➡ **Evaluating Points of View** Have students read the strategy. Point out that this is essentially the same as the strategy used in the Listening section.

❷ Have students read the instructions and do the exercise independently. Suggest that they use two columns to take notes as they read: one column will be the author's points, and the other the students' own experiences and/or prior knowledge. They can then examine their notes in order to answer the questions.

Language Notes:

- A person who is *self-conscious* is timid and easily embarrassed.

- To *summon the courage to do something* means to overcome one's fear in order to do what needs to be done.

- *Mortified* means extremely embarrassed (literally, *embarrassed to death*).

 Option: If you feel your students need help with unfamiliar words before they do the task, you may wish to do the Vocabulary Check exercise on page 53 before the following exercise.

❸ Have students read the instructions and the questions independently and then discuss them in small groups. Have selected groups share their responses with the class.

Answers

a. The two most common causes of miscommunication are listeners not paying careful attention or listeners taking for granted that they understand what a speaker means, when in fact the speaker had intended a completely different meaning. Cross-cultural differences and different communication styles are other causes.

b. The teacher suggested that Susanna took her professor's comment the wrong way and that Susanna should meet with her psychology professor after class and ask him what he really meant. *For the last two parts of this question, answers will vary.*

c. *Answers will vary.*

✪ **Option:** Alternatively, after students have read the instructions and the questions independently, divide the class into three groups, and have each group discuss one of the questions. After a brief discussion period, have groups share their responses with the class.

✪ **Option:** Expand the activity by having students discuss these questions with a partner:

> Can you think of some examples of each communication style? What are some possible advantages and disadvantages of each style? Which style more closely resembles your own? What can you do to improve it if need be?

Have selected pairs share the results of their discussion with the class.

☑ ❹ **Vocabulary Check** Have students read the instructions and do the exercise independently, and then compare answers with a partner. Review the answers with the class.

Answers
1. f 2. h 3. g 4. a 5. d 6. c 7. b

Think About It (page 54)

Preview

Have students look at the cartoon, and ask them what the difference is between the waiter's idea of the food and the customer's. This is an example of "miscommunication." Ask if something similar has ever happened to them (it helps to have some personal experience to relate to). You could expand this by relating a "miscommunication" story of your own in a foreign language. Ask students to discuss similar experiences with their partners.

Presentation

❺ Have students read the questions and answer them independently. Then have them discuss their answers with a partner. Have selected students share their answers with the class.

Write: Choosing and Narrowing a Topic (page 54)

Preview

Draw an inverted triangle on the board. Across the top line, write *money;* somewhere in the middle of the triangle, write *the Euro;* at the bottom point, write a question mark. Elicit narrowed topics for the bottom point of the inverted triangle, for example, *problems in adapting to the Euro.*

Presentation

Have students read the introduction. Review it with them, pointing out that it is essential to narrow a topic in order to arrive at a clear thesis.

➡ Have students read the strategy. Point out that the length of the paper often determines the narrowness of the topic. Review the given example (*conflict resolution*), and point out that the broad topic could easily generate an entire book and would still need to be narrowed somewhat.

✪ **Option:** Have students decide which of the topics below are appropriate for a short paper and discuss their choices with a partner.

- Conflict Resolution in Brazil
- Conflict Resolution in the Tourist Industry
- Conflict Resolution in Retail Sales
- Resolving Arguments about Teenagers' TV Viewing Habits

Write About It (page 54)

Presentation

❻ Have students read the question independently and write the essay in class or as homework.

☑ ❼ **Check Your Writing** Have students use the bulleted questions to give written feedback on their partner's paper. Have them use feedback from their partner to revise their own paper.

 Workbook: Practice 11

Vocabulary Expansion: Idioms of confrontation See page T121.

Answers

A.

1. e (conflict) **2.** h (resolution)

3. f (conflict) **4.** b (conflict)

5. d (resolution) **6.** a (conflict)

7. c (conflict) **8.** g (conflict)

B. *Answers will vary.*

EVALUATION

See pages Txi–Txii.

Unit 4 Achievement Test

Self-Check See **You're In Charge!**, page 32 of the Workbook.

PORTFOLIO

Writing Revised essay from **Write About It**, Exercises 6 and 7, page 54.

Oral Communication

1. Record a monologue about your own approach to dealing with conflict. Describe your overall approach, relate it to experiences that you've had, and make generalizations based on these experiences.

2. With a partner, record a role-play of one of the situations below. For your own tape, play one of the **(a)** roles.

   Situation 1: (a) *a person who has to be up for work at 4:00 A.M., and* **(b)** *a neighbor who is having a loud party.*

   Situation 2: (a) *a person giving his/her choice for Person of the Year, and* **(b)** *someone who strongly disagrees.*

   Situation 3: (a) *an employee who thinks the company's dress code is too strict, and* **(b)** *a supervisor.*

Interactive Dictation

Dictate the following sentences to the students. After each sentence, have students write a sentence of their own, using either a gerund or an infinitive form of the verb in parentheses, or that verb plus another gerund or infinitive. Altogether, the sentences should have a coherent flow. For more information on dictation, see page Txv.

1. People often treat conflict as something to be won.

2. (*resolve*)

3. Conflict-resolution experts often talk about "win-win scenarios."

4. (*attempt*)

5. Empathy is important.

6. (*validate*)

7. An awareness of varied communication styles is also vital.

8. (*interpret*)

9. Impartial mediation is another valuable tool.

10. (*advise*)

ODD JOBS

OBJECTIVES

Students will be able to:
- Talk about unusual jobs
- Express surprise and ask for clarification
- Use the passive voice
- Listen for sequence of events
- Make inferences while listening
- Produce rhythm patterns in compound nouns and adjectives
- Clarify in a discussion
- Use graphic organizers to analyze reading
- Write effective introductory paragraphs
- Understand and use job names and titles

GETTING STARTED

Warm Up *(page 55)*

Preview

Tell students to look at the picture at the top of page 55. Ask them to name the job. Ask them if they know anyone who does this job or one like it for a living. If there are any students who do, ask them to elaborate on who it is and how they know this person. Ask them if they've ever heard the expression "odd jobs," the title of this unit. Ask if anyone knows what it means. Elicit or point out the fact that it is a pun; this common expression refers to having assorted part-time jobs rather then a steady (or *usual* job), but the adjective *odd* also means *unusual* in the sense of *strange*.

Presentation

Have students read the introduction alone. Point out that some of the jobs that we consider unusual are high-profile (circus performer, advice columnist), while others such as chocolate taster or dog groomer are not so. Also point out that jobs that are statistically rare, such as movie actor or head of state, are not really considered "unusual" because they have such a high status.

❶ Ask students to read the instructions independently and then discuss with a partner. Remind them to choose jobs that are truly unusual, for example, statistically rare and not very high profile. Then have pairs share their lists with the class. Ask the class to judge which of the jobs listed could be classified as "glamorous" and tell why they think so.

🎧 ❷ Have students read the instructions independently. Then play the recording or read the audioscript. Have students write their answers on a separate piece of paper and compare their answers with a partner. Then, if necessary, play the recording or read the audioscript again for them to confirm their answers. Review answers with the class.

Audioscript: The audioscript for Exercise 2 appears on page T136.

> **Answers**
> The male from the first conversation is a videogame reviewer. The female in the second conversation is an ice sculptor. The male in the final conversation is a subway pusher.

 Workbook: Practice 1

Figure It Out *(pages 55–56)*

Preview

Begin by eliciting jobs that are combinations of two jobs, for example, *underwater welder* or *singing waiter*. Have students work in small groups to brainstorm jobs that are variations on common jobs or combinations of two jobs, and are therefore unusual. Monitor the discussions, and compile a list on the board. Poll the class to see which job they think is the most unusual.

Presentation

- Read the situation with the class, and ask students what job is being described. Have students skim the conversation quickly on their own to answer the question.

- Have students read the dialogue independently. Then dictate the following questions to the students, or write them on the board and have students work with a partner to answer the questions.

1. How do people feel about their skydiving experiences? (*They cherish them.*)

2. How does Terry carry his video cameras when he makes his jumps? (*His cameras are attached to his helmet.*)

3. How does the automatic function on one of Terry's cameras work? (*A switch has to be pressed for it to start filming.*)

4. What happens to the video after it is shot? (*It is edited and dubbed, and music is added.*)

Then have selected pairs share their answers with the class.

Option: Extend the activity by having students practice reading the dialogue aloud in pairs after they have answered the questions. Have selected pairs present sections of the dialogue to the class.

Culture Note: Skydiving is an increasingly popular sport in the U.S. and Canada. United States Parachute Association statistics show that 311,500 people made 3.4 million jumps in 1999 and that those numbers are increasing by two to three percent per year. [Source: www.nationalgeographic.com]

Language Note: *A tad* means *a little bit.*

☑ ❸ **Vocabulary Check** Have students work alone and then compare answers with a partner. Be sure they're aware that one item in the right column has no match in the left column. Review the answers with the class.

Answers
1. e   2. a   3. b   4. f   5. c   6. g

 Workbook: Practice 2

Talk About It (*page 57*)

 Option: If you feel that your students need extra help in using the passive voice, you might want to postpone this activity until after the grammar presentation (pages 57–60).

Presentation

Note: This activity is designed to develop fluency. It is best not to interrupt students to correct errors. Make notes of student errors for review with the class after the activity has finished.

❹ Refer the students to the picture. Ask what the people in the picture are doing and what kinds of people take "night classes" in areas such as ceramics, jewelry design, weaving, cooking, or wine-tasting. Explain that adults in North America often take these classes at night after work to relax and to meet new people. Then read the instructions, and have a pair of students read the conversation for the class. Have students work in pairs to improvise conversations using the cues and the language in the model. Select pairs to present their conversations to the class.

Language Notes:

- *A keen sense of smell*: the adjective *keen* as used here means *sharp.*

- *Sharp* can be applied to senses, especially eyesight, as meaning *specific* and *accurate.*

Workbook: Practice 3

GRAMMAR

The Passive Voice: Past and Present (*pages 57–58*)

Preview

Write on the board the name of a famous work of art such as the *Mona Lisa*, or show the class a photograph of it or another famous work of art. Ask them for as much information as they can provide about it. After the initial recognition, prompt students with passive-voice questions to elicit additional information, such as:

It's called La Gioconda *in Italian.*

It was painted in 1506.

It was painted by Leonardo da Vinci.

Go on to give the students additional information, such as:

It was stolen in 1911 and recovered in 1913.

People who search for lost and stolen works of art are called art detectives.

Presentation

Have students read the introduction. Point out that the standard subject-verb-object word order is changed to make passive sentences; the object becomes the subject, because we are focusing on the action and not on the *agent* or "doer." In many cases where the passive is used, the agent is unimportant or unknown, or the speaker does not wish to name the agent, as in *I was given bad advice.* Elicit situations where the emphasis might be on the action, such as *scientific writing* or *describing a process.* Refer back to the examples in the preview, and point out that the focus in most cases is on the painting and what happened to it.

Alternatively, ask students to close their books. Then copy the sentences below on the board, and have the students convert them from the active voice to the passive voice. Do the first one as an example, and ask them to complete the chart with a partner. When they have finished, have them check their passive voice sentences with the sentences

in the example box on page 58 of the Student Book.

1. People consider George Zambelli the King of Fireworks.

2. The Zambelli family is still producing fireworks.

3. Descendants of Italian immigrants have produced more than 25 percent of fireworks used in the U.S.A.

4. Zambelli family members wrote down the Zambelli fireworks recipes in a little black book and carried them across the Atlantic at the beginning of the 20th century.

5. When I visited the Zambelli Fireworks factory, one of the workers was packing the firework explosive chemicals into a small tube.

6. By the end of the 20th century, the Zambelli Fireworks company had already produced thousands of tons of fireworks.

Go through the examples in the box with the class, pointing out how the passive voice is formed in the various tenses. Draw their attention to the position of *still* in progressive forms and the position of *already* in perfect forms. Go through the examples in the box with the class.

Option: Have students rewrite the example sentences in the active voice. Have selected students share their answers with the class.

Point out that, in some cases, the active and passive work equally well:

Da Vinci **created** *his most famous work, the* Mona Lisa, *in 1506.* (active)

Da Vinci's most famous painting, the Mona Lisa, **was created** *in 1506.* (passive)

However, if the agent is more important, the active voice is preferable:

In his lifetime, Leonardo da Vinci **painted** *several masterpieces.* (active)

Several masterpieces **were painted** *by Leonardo da Vinci in his lifetime.* (passive)

❶ Have students read the instructions and the passage and answer the questions independently. Then have them check answers with a partner and discuss the reasons for their answers. Review the answers with the class. You might want to point out that *get paid* in the advertisement is an example of a passive that uses the auxiliary *get* instead of *be*. This usage is becoming more common.

> **Answers**
> 1. give, has asked, begins, hasn't washed, enters, noticing, rushes, took
> 2. come, going, looks,
> 3. a, c

Language Note: *Going undercover* means to have one's real identity or work hidden in order to catch criminals or find out information; people's *covers* are their alternate identities.

Option: Extend Exercise 1 by having students rewrite sentences containing the underlined verbs in the passive voice wherever possible. Have them work independently and then check answers with a partner. Review answers with the class.

Option Answers

Answers will vary. Some sample answers:
. . . the quality of service that **is given** to the customers of a certain store, . . .
. . . she **has been asked** to do a general review . . .
. . . they **haven't been washed** in at least a week . . .

Option: Have students go back to the dialogue about skydiving on pages 55–56 and circle all the examples of the passive voice. Then have them work with a partner and discuss why the passive voice was used. Have them refer to specific information in the text, rather than just saying "The passive voice was used to emphasize the action," etc.

Option: Expand on the use of passive *get*. Explain that this is more common in conversation than in written English. Dictate the following questions to your students, and have them discuss their answers with a partner.

Where do you get your hair cut?
Where do you get your pictures developed?
Where do you get your teeth fixed?

The Passive Voice: Modal Verbs *(pages 59–60)*

Preview

Set the situation: A student is going to have a pair of shoes custom-made for him or her. Tell students that there are several steps involved.

*First, someone **will measure** your feet.*

Ask if it is possible to put this sentence in the passive voice, and elicit the following:

*First, your feet **will** be measured.*

Underline the word *will* in the new sentence, and ask them what part of speech it is. Elicit the fact that it is a modal auxiliary.

Presentation

Have students read the introduction and the example sentences in the box. Point out that when using modals in the passive voice, the verb *be* is in its base form. In other words, there is no subject-verb agreement when using passive modals.

❷ Direct the students to the photo. Ask them if they have seen masks such as these before and where they saw them. Explain that these masks are from Venice and are worn during the festival of *Carnival*, the Roman Catholic holiday preceding Lent. Ask students if masks are ever worn in their countries and, if so, on what occasions. Then have students read the directions, do the activity alone, and then compare answers with a partner. You may want to pre-teach the following words: *enterprise* (activity), *prescribed rituals* (necessary ceremonies), *conventions* (customary ways of doing things), *adhere* (keep to). Circulate and offer assistance. Have selected students share their answers with the class.

Answers
1. are made
2. play
3. is presumed
4. is felt
5. should be followed *or* ought to be followed *or* must be followed *or* have to be followed *or* are followed
6. is believed
7. should be handled *or* ought to be handled *or* must be handled *or* have to be handled *or* are handled
8. are adhered *or* have been adhered
9. is considered
10. is worn
11. believe
12. is absorbed

Language Notes:

- *Apprenticeship* refers to the situation in which a young person serves as an assistant (or *apprentice*) to a master craftsman for several years in order to learn the craft.

- *Conventions* in this context refers to the customary way of doing things.

☑ ❸ **Check Your Understanding** Have students read the instructions and do the exercise independently. Then have them compare answers and discuss their reasoning with a partner. Review the answers with the class.

Answers
a, d

 ❹ **Express Yourself** Have students read the instructions and do the exercise with a partner. Monitor discussions, and have selected pairs share their answers with the class.

Workbook: Practices 4, 5, 6

LISTENING and SPEAKING

Listen: Storm Chasers (*page 60*)

Presentation

❶ **Before You Listen** Direct students to the picture. Ask them how they would react if they were driving in that sort of weather. Point out that people react differently to extreme weather conditions. Remind them that the unit theme is unusual jobs and elicit from them what kind of job they expect to hear about. Then have students read the instructions and discuss the questions with a partner. Monitor the discussions, and have selected pairs share their answers with the class. Ask students what type of person they think would become a *storm chaser* and whether they themselves would like doing this job.

➡ **Recognizing Categories** Have students read the strategy independently and review to make sure they understand the separate concepts of categorizing information and inferring information. You might also want to teach them the phrase *making inferences*, as it is a common way to refer to this strategy. Give one or two examples, for instance, *The whole class passed last week's quiz, but half the class failed this week's quiz. What can you infer?* Elicit responses such as *This week's quiz was more difficult* or *Fewer people studied this week.*

🎧 ❷ Place the following chart on the board, and ask students to copy it on a sheet of paper:

Categories of Storm Chasers	Characteristics
1.	
2.	
3.	
4.	

Have students read the instructions. Check to make sure that everyone understands that this exercise is related to categories only, and that they are to describe as well as name the categories. Play the recording or read the audioscript, and have students first write the names of the different categories. If necessary, play the recording or read the audioscript again several times to allow students to write down the characteristics of each type of storm chaser. Then have them check answers with a partner and discuss any differences. Review answers with the class.

Language Notes:

- *Yahoos* are uncontrolled, unsophisticated people. The expression may derive from the Yahoos, a race of crude humans in Jonathan Swift's *Gulliver's Travels*, or it may be related to a shout of excitement traditionally associated with cowboys: *Yahooo!*

- To *mess up* is to make errors or fail in a task.

- To *miss the shot* is to fail to get the desired photograph, usually by being too late.

- *Big-time* in this context means *serious* or *severe*.

Audioscript: The audioscript for Exercise 2 appears on pages T136–T137.

Answers
(Categories in bold: Descriptions follow.)
Scientists: Chase storms as part of their research.
Recreational: Photograph or videotape severe weather for their archives.
Spotters: Observe and report threatening weather. Often risk their life.
"Yahoos" or thrill seekers: Chase storms for the thrill of it. Often do so in an irresponsible manner. Often just compete with each other to see who can get the most extreme video but, in the process, place themselves and others in danger.

---

❸ Have students read the instructions and the statements. Tell them that that the

information they need is not directly stated and that they are going to have to make inferences. Then play the recording or read the audioscript one or more times, and have students complete the exercise independently. Have them compare answers in groups and discuss the information on which they based their inferences. Then review the answers with the class. You might wish to photocopy the audioscript, distribute copies to students, and point out specific portions of the dialogue that provided the bases for the inferences.

Answers
a. T   b. F   c. T   d. F   e. F

 *Workbook: Practice 7*

Pronunciation (*page 61*)

Preview

On the board, draw a stick figure bent under the weight of a huge boulder. Write the following sentences:

My back is breaking.

It's a back-breaking job.

Say both sentences out loud, with appropriate stress. Put accent marks over *back* and *break-* in the first sentence. Put accent marks over *back* and *job* in the second. Then underline *break-* in the second sentence. Say them both out loud again, clapping along with the stresses to demonstrate that the stress-timing of *back is breaking* is the same as that of *back-breaking job*. (It isn't necessary to introduce the term *stress-timing*; only demonstrate.)

Presentation

Have students read the introduction and example phrases in the box. Read the phrases out loud to demonstrate. Give the students a few more example phrases, such as *out-of-work actor, egg salad sandwich, box cutter, golf pro*. Have students read the phrases aloud with a partner. You can suggest that they clap along with the stress, unless class size makes clapping disruptive.

❹ Have students read the instructions. Remind them that syllables that would be stressed when a word occurs alone become secondary stresses when that word is the second part of a compound. Have them do the exercise independently and then compare predictions with a partner, discussing any differences.

🎧 ❺ Play the recording or read the audioscript once, and have students check their predictions. Give them time to confer with their partners and update their answers, and then play the recording or read the audioscript again for them to confirm any changes.

Audioscript: The audioscript for Exercise 5 appears on Student Book page 61.

Answers

móuthwatering, chocólate taster, chocólate tasters, América, master status, wéll-earned Ph.D., dessért classification system, high-grade, poór-quality, cocoa powder, vegetable oil, chocólate-tasting competition, blíndfolded competitors, chocólate bean, tóp five

---

❻ Students take turns reading the entire selection or alternate line by line. Monitor the practice, and have selected students read sentences to the class.

☣ **Option:** Extend the practice by having students make lists of their own examples, exchange lists with a partner, and practice saying the phrases with the appropriate stress while their partners check their pronunciation of the stresses. Monitor the activity, make corrections, and have selected students read their phrases to the class.

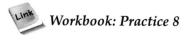 *Workbook: Practice 8*

Speak Out *(pages 61–62)*

Preview

Relate an experience of your own in which incomplete or misinterpreted information led to negative results. Discuss what could have been done to solve these problems.

If appropriate, elicit similar experiences from the students.

☣ **Option:** Alternatively, you might begin by making an unusual announcement to the class, such as that starting today you will give people extra credit for being absent and that people who have perfect attendance will be marked down; or, from now on you will be giving a 30-minute test during every class period, and grades will depend totally on students' performances on these tests. Ask if there are any questions. Elicit paraphrases of your information and requests for confirmation. Then discuss the importance of getting clarification.

Presentation

➡ **Maintaining Understanding in a Discussion** Have students read the strategy. Explain that clarifying information is vital in discussion and decision-making, since incomplete or misinterpreted information will lead to mistaken conclusions and ineffective action. Point out that it is especially important, and must be done often, when people are speaking a foreign language. Point out that paraphrasing is a valuable skill, both to be sure others understand you as well as to help others interpret the speech of a third person.

❼ Have students read the instructions and do the activity independently. Then have them compare answers with a partner. Point out that there are polite ways to ask for clarification, but that a high degree of politeness is not always necessary in informal discussion. Then review answers, and open the discussion to the class.

Answers

a. A   b. P   c. C   d. A   e. A   f. P
g. C   h. P   i. C   j. P

☣ **Option:** Have students work with their partners to discuss the *register* of the expressions in Exercise 7. Ask them which expressions, if any, are appropriate to use with a teacher, with a parent, or with a boss, and why. Have selected pairs share their answers with the class.

❽ Read the instructions independently, and then discuss the cartoons on page 62. You may choose to have all students in each group offer their interpretations and discuss among themselves (which would involve mostly third-party paraphrasing), or to have one student offer an interpretation and then have other students question that student (which would involve mostly asking for and giving clarification). Monitor the discussions, and have selected groups give their interpretations to the class.

Note: This activity is designed to develop fluency. Therefore, it is best not to interrupt students to correct errors. Monitor their speech, and make notes of student errors for review with the class after the activity has finished.

Option: Have students work in groups of three. Explain that two of the group members are going to look at and describe different cartoons. The student whose book is closed must ask questions for clarification until he or she understands both cartoons. Have one student in the group close his or her book, and the other two will take turns describing each cartoon, paraphrasing, and clarifying their descriptions. Then have all the students look at the cartoons and discuss which one is funnier and why they think so.

 *Workbook: Practice 9*

READING and WRITING

Read About It *(pages 63–65)*

Preview

Ask students to briefly brainstorm jobs involving food. Elicit some common jobs, for example chef, waiter, grocer, counterperson, etc. Then ask them to start thinking about unusual jobs involving food.

Presentation

❶ Before You Read Have students work with partners to discuss unusual jobs involving food. You might give them an example to get them started, such as

snail farmer (to supply French restaurants with *escargots*), etc. Have selected pairs share their results with the class.

➡ **Using Graphic Organizers** Have students read the strategy independently. Discuss the example of a cluster in the textbook. Point out that it starts with the broad topic and then identifies various sub-topics and possible supporting details for each sub-topic. Explain that this is just one way to take notes.

❷ Have students read the instructions independently. Tell them to make notes of the main topics as they read by either circling them in the text or writing them on a separate sheet of paper. Have them read the excerpt independently and then get together with a partner to compare and discuss answers.

Language Notes:

• A *sweet job* is a slang expression for one that is not hard and pays well; as used in the title, it is a pun on the fact that ice cream is a sweet-tasting food.

• *In his genes*: Our *genes* are where our bodies store information for physical characteristics that we inherit from our parents. If something is *in one's genes*, it means that it is a physically inherited characteristic, like height or hair color. In this case, it is simply an expression; the ability to distinguish variations in the taste of ice cream is probably something that is learned rather than inherited.

• *Caught on* means *became popular*.

• To *pass on (something)*, as it is used here, means to refuse an offer of something; if you are offered something that you don't really want, you can say, "No thanks—I'll pass." It is not related to the idiom to *pass (something) on* which means to transmit or relay something.

• To *taint* something is to spoil it by adding something else to it.

Option: If you feel your students need help with unfamiliar words before they do the task, you may wish to do the Vocabulary Check exercise on page 65 before the following exercise.

❸ Ask students if they have any questions on the reading. Then have them work with their partners to complete the cluster. Remind them to fill in supporting details for each sub-topic.

☑ ❹ **Vocabulary Check** Have students work alone and then compare answers with a partner. Review the answers with the class.

> **Answers**
> 1. c 2. b 3. i 4. j 5. f 6. a 7. h 8. g 9. d

Think About It (*page 65*)

Presentation

❺ Have students read the instructions independently and work in small groups to discuss the quotation. Monitor discussions, and have selected groups share their conclusions with the class.

> **Answers**
> *Answers will vary. Possible answer:*
> If you like your job, it will never feel like "work," but more like enjoyment.

🌐 **Option:** Extend Exercise 5 by asking students if there is another way to interpret the saying. Have them discuss this in small groups, and see if anyone comes up with the following: *If you only do things you like doing, you'll never be able to get a job.*

Write: Writing Introductions for Analytical Essays (*pages 65–66*)

Preview

Write the phrase *first impressions* on the board. Ask students if they have heard it and if they know what it means. Elicit the fact that it refers to people's image of you when they first meet you, and that it is considered very important to make a good first impression since people rarely change their opinions once they have formed them. Then point out that this is equally important in writing: The introductory paragraph

is often the basis by which a reader will decide to either continue reading a piece or put it down.

Presentation

➡ Have students read the strategy. Review the elements of the introductory paragraph. Emphasize the importance of an attention-getting first sentence.

❻ Have students read the instructions. Remind students of the difference between a broad topic and the writer's viewpoint on that topic (the main idea). Point out that some introductory paragraphs clearly spell out what will be discussed in the essay, while others are less explicit—in which case students will have to use their imaginations a bit more to determine how the writer will develop the main idea. Have them do the exercise independently and then compare answers with a partner and discuss.

> **Answers**
> a. **Topic:** Working as a costumed movie character
>   **Main Point:** Working as a costumed movie character is hard work.
>   **Development:** *Answers will vary.*
> b. **Topic:** Working on a cruise ship
>   **Main Point:** If you like to travel, live well, and meet new people, you might want to explore the possibilities of working on a cruise ship.
>   **Development:** *Answers will vary.*

🌐 **Option:** Extend Exercise 6 by asking students to judge the first sentence of each of the paragraphs: Is it interesting and attention-getting? Have them rate the sentences on a scale of 5 (*very interesting*) to 0 (*not interesting at all*) and rewrite the sentences to make them more interesting. Then have them compare results with a partner and discuss. Put selected rewrites on the board, and discuss them with the class.

Write About It (*page 66*)

Presentation

❼ Have students read the instructions independently and write the essay in class or as homework. Remind them that the term *odd jobs* here is used in the sense of *strange or unusual jobs*, not in the sense of *various part-time jobs*.

☑ ❽ Check Your Writing Have students use the bulleted questions to give written feedback on their partner's paper. Have them use feedback from their partner to revise their own paper.

 Workbook: Practice 10

Vocabulary Expansion: Job names and titles
See page T122.

Answers

Possible answers:

- A network administrator organizes information systems.
- A network administrator works with information systems.
- A home health aide works with people with disabilities.
- A home health aide works with people with health problems.
- A software engineer creates computer applications.
- A software engineer designs computer applications.
- A public relations manager explains a company's actions to the public.
- A human resources assistant works with the employees of a company.
- A human resources assistant advises the employees of a company.
- A restaurant critic reviews the food at restaurants.
- A loan underwriter reviews applications from people who want to borrow money.
- A wedding planner organizes celebrations.
- A residential counselor works with people with disabilities.
- A residential counselor works with people with health problems.

- A residential counselor advises people with disabilities.
- A residential counselor advises people with health problems.
- A comptroller supervises accounting procedures.
- A comptroller reviews accounting procedures.

EVALUATION

See pages Txi–Txii.

Unit 5 Achievement Test

Self-Check See **You're In Charge!**, page 40 of the Workbook.

PORTFOLIO

Writing Revised introductory paragraph from **Write About It**, Exercises 7 and 8, page 66.

Oral Communication

1. Record a dialogue with a partner, discussing "jobs of the future." For your tape, think of a new job that will be created within the next twenty years and give it a name. Discuss how it will be done, its advantages and disadvantages, and so on. Answer your partner's questions. Then reverse roles for your partner's tape.

2. Work with three other students to present a television game show, either live in the classroom or on videotape. The game is called "What's My Job?" In this game, a person with an unusual job answers yes/no questions from a panel of three. Students on the panel take turns asking questions. After each round of questions, they discuss the answers and see if they can guess the job. Rotate roles and play four complete games.

Interactive Dictation

Dictate the following paragraphs to the students. Then have them go back and select appropriate sentences to rewrite using the passive voice. For more information on dictation, see page Txv.

My uncle works for an office-machine company. He is a dust-accumulation engineer. Dust affects all kinds of machines. Someone has to measure the dust. He has to answer several important questions: Where does the dust settle? How quickly does it build up? How does the dust affect the machines?

The engineers measure the dust with high-tech electronic instruments. Then they write careful reports and send them to the design department. After that, it is up to the design engineers. They must design office machines that are as dust-proof as possible.

BEHOLDING BEAUTY

OBJECTIVES

Students will be able to:

- Talk about different standards of beauty
- Speculate about the past and present
- Ask about regrets and propose options
- Use first, second, and third conditionals
- Listen for clues to cause-and-effect relationships
- Pronounce intonation shifts that affect meaning
- Keep a discussion on track
- Evaluate supporting examples to improve reading
- Write effective supporting paragraphs
- Understand and use expressions for describing physical characteristics

GETTING STARTED

Warm Up (page 67)

Preview

Ask students to look at the photographs at the top of page 67 and brainstorm adjectives that apply to each one. Have them make a list of up to five adjectives for each photo. Then ask for students to call out their adjectives for each photo, and compile two lists on the board. Look over the lists, and ask students to think about why we react the way we do to these photographs.

Have students read the title of the unit. Review the verb "behold," meaning, "to look at something consciously and meaningfully." Elicit the fact that the title expression refers to the tastes and opinions of the person who is looking at something. You might also point out that this is an example of *subjectivity*, or the concept that there are no absolute standards of beauty.

Presentation

Have students read the introduction independently. Ask them to think about which factor is more influential in setting a standard of beauty: personal preference or cultural preference?

❶ Have students read the instructions and compile their lists independently. Then have them work with a partner to compare lists and discuss the reasons for their choices. Have selected pairs share their lists with the class.

❷ Have students read the instructions, answer the questions independently, and then compare results with a partner. Have selected pairs share their conclusions with the class.

🎧 **❸** Have students read the directions. Then play the recording or read the audioscript twice, and have students write down a brief answer to the question. Then have them work in pairs to discuss their answers. Have selected students share their answers with the class.

Language Note: To *have meat on one's bones* refers to weight and means to be not overly thin.

Audioscript: The audioscript for Exercise 3 appears on pages T137–T138.

Answers

The grandfather and grandson are discussing different views of beauty based on culture and generation. They first discuss how the ideal body type for women of today is far skinnier than the ideal woman of forty years ago, like Marilyn Monroe. Next, they discuss that in some countries, people prefer to have bodies that would be considered overweight in Western cultures. They then discuss how women in Japan used to dye their teeth black because they didn't like white teeth then. Finally, they discuss how the male members of some tribes in West Africa put on makeup, dance, and make faces to get women to notice them.

 *Workbook: Practice 1*

Figure It Out *(pages 67–68)*

Preview

Write *the ideal man* and *the ideal woman* on the board. Ask students to think for a minute about their *culture's* ideal man and ideal woman.

Presentation

Point out that *ideal* means *the best that one can imagine* and that, while we might think this is an individual concept, it is strongly affected by culture.

🌐 **Option:** If you feel your students need help with unfamiliar words before they do the task, you may wish to do the Vocabulary Check exercise on page 68 before the following exercise.

❹ Have students read the instructions independently. (You might want to point out that *ideal* in the directions is the noun form of the adjective *ideal* used in the preview.) Be sure they are aware that the exercise is not asking for their personal ideal but the ideal that is valued by their culture. Then have them complete the questionnaire. If there are questions about the vocabulary used for the descriptions, tell students to try to use context to determine the meaning. Have them compare answers with a partner. Ask them to discuss their choices with their partners, thinking about whether the choices were based mainly on personal or cultural standards.

🌐 **Option:** This exercise can be done as a gender-neutral exercise in which both men and women choose the traits of an ideal man and an ideal woman. Optionally, it could be done as an opposite-sex exercise, in which women describe the ideal man and men describe the ideal woman.

☑ ❺ **Vocabulary Check** Have students work alone and then compare answers with a partner. Review the answers with the class.

> **Answers**
> 1. e   2. h   3. c   4. g   5. b   6. d   7. a

 Workbook: Practice 2

Talk About It *(page 69)*

🌐 **Option:** If you feel that your students need extra help in using conditionals, you might want to postpone this activity until after the grammar presentation (pages 69–73).

Presentation

Put the word *regrets* on the board, and ask for volunteers to give a meaning. Elicit that *regrets* are bad feelings about the past. When we have regrets, we wish we could change the past; we can't change the past, but we sometimes think about doing so.

Note: This activity is designed to develop fluency. It is best not to interrupt students to correct errors. Make notes of student errors for review with the class after the activity has finished.

❻ Have students read the instructions and the model conversation independently. Have a pair of students read the conversation for the class. Elicit other sample language that has the same functions. Then have students work in pairs to improvise conversations using the cues and the functions. Select pairs to present their conversations to the class.

 Workbook: Practice 3

GRAMMAR

First Conditional and Second Conditional (*page 69*)

Tell the students that they are going to practice using conditionals, which are used to express cause-and-effect relationships. Write the following sentence on the board:

If you exercise regularly, you will be in good physical condition.

Ask students to identify the condition clause (*If you exercise regularly*) and the result clause (*you will be in good physical condition*).

Presentation

Have students read the explanation of the conditionals and the examples in the boxes in class or for homework. Then review the explanations with the class. For the second conditional, ask what time frame the past tense refers to in the "if" clause: past or present (present)? Ask students to supply additional sentences in the first and second conditionals.

Note: Point out that a comma separates both clauses when the "if" clause appears first.

Option: Alternatively, if your students prefer charts, you could draw the following grid on the board and ask where each type of conditional would be placed in the chart.

	Past	Now or Always	Future
Likely		✓	✓
Unlikely	✓		

Third Conditional: Speculating About the Past (*pages 70–72*)

Presentation

❶ Have students read the instructions and do the exercise independently.

Then have them compare answers with a partner. Review answers with the class, and then have students practice reading the dialogue out loud with their partners.

Note: *Were* is used with all persons in unreal "if" clauses.

> **Answers**
> 1. were 2. would have probably gotten
> 3. will tell 4. would still have guessed
> 5. weren't 6. didn't have
> 7. would have paid

Option: Alternatively, have the students complete the exercise independently and then practice reading it aloud with their partners. Partners can check each other's answers as they perform the dialogue. Then review the answers with the class, or select a pair of students to read the dialogue out loud to the class.

Language Notes:

- To *stick out* means to be obvious and noticeable.

- To *be into* something is to be interested in it. Saying that someone is *into* his/her looks is another way of saying that the person is somewhat vain.

❷ Have students read the instructions and the newspaper clipping. With mixed-ability classes, you might want to point out that conditionals can use modals other than *will/would*, such as *can/could*. You might also point out that they may have to use some negative constructions in order to achieve the desired meaning. Have them do the exercise independently and compare answers with a partner. Then review answers with the class.

Answers

1. are 2. is 3. were 4. had 5. would have
6. had worked out 7. wouldn't have gained
8. had 9. could get 10. would be
11. became 12. would get
13. wouldn't keep 14. could afford
15. were 16. would get away 17. changed

Language Notes:

- A *tummy tuck* is a surgical procedure in which fat and skin are removed from one's stomach and the muscles are tightened. The medical name for this operation is *abdominoplasty*.

- A *hunk* is a good-looking, physically fit man.

❸ Tell students to look at the picture of Peter and ask them what they think he is doing. Elicit the term *daydreaming*. Then tell them that he is going to discuss his daydreams with a friend. Have them read the instructions. Model the conversation and first cue with a selected student. Take the *Friend* role yourself, and prompt the student in the *Peter* role with further questions. Then have students continue the conversation in pairs, using the cues and the model conversation for reference, and alternating roles. Encourage the person in the Friend role to respond to Peter and prompt him with further questions; encourage the person in the Peter role to vary the structure of his answers, using *if* clauses occasionally in his answers. Monitor the conversations and make notes of student errors for review with the class after the activity has finished.

❹ Have students read the instructions. Review the situation, making sure that students understand that all of Peter's daydreams really came true, but that his mother is worried about his future. You might want to introduce the word *pessimist*. Ask the students if they know anyone like this. Then have students work with their partners and continue the conversation, using the cues and the model conversation for reference,

and alternating roles. Monitor the conversations, and make notes of student errors for review with the class after the activity has finished.

☯ Option: Extend the activity to the third conditional by telling students that everything went wrong for Peter. All his mother's fears came true. Now he is thinking about what happened, and having regrets. Put this sentence on the board:

If I <u>hadn't spent</u> all my money on that face lift and tummy tuck, I <u>could have gotten</u> an education.

Have students work independently to create sentences like the example, using the cues from Exercise 3. Then have them compare answers with a partner and discuss. Have selected students share their sentences with the class.

 Workbook: Practices 4, 5, 6

Other Expressions with the Conditional (*pages 72–73*)

Presentation

Have students read the explanation of *just in case* and *in the event that*, and the examples in the box. Then ask the students, "Is it going to rain tomorrow?" Get a few responses, and then tell them, "If it rains tomorrow, I'll wear my new raincoat." Write that sentence on the board, and below it write <u>In the event that</u> it *rains tomorrow, I'll wear my new raincoat*. Point out that the meaning is the same, but the second one is more formal. Tell students you are leaving your home now, and ask them, "Is it going to rain today?" Get a few responses, and then write on the board, "*I'll wear my new raincoat, <u>just in case</u> it rains.*" Point out that this meaning is slightly different, in that the speaker has already decided on what action to do; the speaker doesn't know if the event (rain) will happen or not but wants to *be safe*. Then write *In case it rains, I'll wear my new raincoat*, and point out that this sentence can go either way: *in case* in initial position, without *just*, is often used interchangeably with *in the event that*.

Review the examples, pointing out the difference in meaning.

❺ Have students read the instructions independently. Then have them do the exercise independently and compare answers with a partner. Review answers with the class, and discuss alternatives and nuances, for example, the difference between:

In the event that you decide to come with me, I'll buy an extra ticket. (You should tell me if you're coming or not; if you're not coming, I won't buy a ticket.)

I'll buy an extra ticket, just in case you decide to come with me. (I'm going to buy the ticket anyway, regardless of your decision.)

Answers

a. I'll give you the name of a tattoo place that's safe, (just) in case you want to get a tattoo.
b. In the event that the wounds after your surgery aren't healed in ten to fourteen days, you will have to go to the hospital.
c. In the event that my friend has this CD, can I exchange it?
d. I can recommend a good hairdresser, (just) in case you want to cut your hair.

Have students read the explanation of *only if* and *as long as*, and the examples in the box. Point out that these structures are used when the cause is **absolutely necessary** in order for the effect to take place. Go over the examples in the box, drawing attention to the inversion of the subject and auxiliary verb in sentences, such as in the example:

Only if I see dramatic results will I stay on this horrible diet.

✪ Option: Practice the *only if* and *as long as* structures by having students write sentences based on the following list of cues. The example gives all three possibilities; students only need to make one sentence for each cue but should vary the types of sentences they write. When they have finished, have them compare answers with a partner and discuss. Put selected sentences on the board.

get a makeover
I'll get a makeover only if it isn't too expensive.
Only if it isn't too expensive will I get a makeover.
I'll get a makeover, as long as it isn't too expensive.

get a new wardrobe
apply for a job as a model
color my hair green
grow a beard
join a gym
(your own idea)

 Workbook: Practices 7, 8

☑ ❻ Check Your Understanding Have students read the instructions and do the exercise independently. Then have them compare answers with a partner. Review answers with the class.

Answers

a. Second and third conditional.
b. First and second conditional (the third conditional is possible *if you've already won the lottery and experienced the consequences*).
c. First conditional.
d. First, second, and third conditional.

---

❼ Express Yourself Have students read the instructions independently and then do the activity with a partner. As students are working, monitor them, and note persistent errors for review with the class after the activity has finished. Have pairs perform their dialogues for another pair, or have selected pairs present their dialogues to the class.

LISTENING and SPEAKING

Listen: The Beauty of Symmetry *(page 73)*

Preview

Ask students to look at the picture of the rose window. Ask if they find it beautiful. If so, ask them why. Put the word *symmetry* on the board, and ask students if they know what it means. Elicit the concept of two sides being in balance.

Presentation

❶ **Before You Listen** Have students read the introduction and circle the elements that they consider essential for something to be beautiful, and then compare answers and discuss with a partner. Ask them to give reasons for their choices and use specific examples to illustrate their points.

➡ **Recognizing Cause and Effect** Have the students list situations in which they might hear a cause-and-effect relationship. Ask students what words they would listen for that might indicate a cause-and-effect relationship. Elicit *in case, in the event that, as if, provided that, only if*. Have students read the strategy. Review the list of expressions with them, and point out that they are going to be listening for definitions and examples, which is a form of cause-and-effect in the sense that a definition states, "If something meets these conditions (the *cause*), then it is a _____ (the *effect*)."

🎧 ❷ Have students read the instructions. Remind them they are only listening for the main ideas. Play the recording, or read the audioscript one or more times. Have them write down their summaries and then compare answers with a partner and discuss. Have selected pairs share their results with the class.

Audioscript: The audioscript for Exercise 2 appears on pages T138–T139.

❸ Have students look at the chart. Explain that this time they are to listen for definitions and examples. Play the recording or read the audioscript one or more times, and have them fill in the chart as they listen. Then have them compare answers with a partner. Review answers with the class.

> **Answers**
> **General definition of symmetry:**
> Symmetry is the property of being the same, or almost the same, on both sides of an imaginary central dividing line.
> **Example of bilateral symmetry:** Folding paper to cut out a paper heart.
> **Example of radial symmetry:** Snowflakes, a round pie, sunflowers, starfish, structure of crystals, humans.

✷ **Option:** Extend the activity by putting the following question on the board.

A round apple pie, on the condition that one cut divides it in half, is an example of _____.

Elicit the answer *radial symmetry*. Then put the following questions on the board, or distribute copies to the class:

1. In the event that babies have a choice of faces to look at, they prefer _____.

2. In the case of scorpion flies, females prefer _____.

3. Bees prefer symmetrical flowers, provided that _____.

4. Assuming that attraction equals desirability, symmetry equals _____.

Have students read through the questions. Then play the recording or read the audioscript again, and have students work with a partner to answer the questions. Review answers with the class.

Option Answers

1. symmetrical faces
2. mates with symmetrical, same-sized wings
3. the flowers have nectar
4. beauty

 Workbook: Practice 9

Pronunciation *(page 74)*

Preview

Put the word *Great!* on the board. Ask for a volunteer to read it out loud. If the reading is flat, ask them to read it "with feeling." Chances are that the person will read it excitedly. Then read it yourself, sarcastically. Change the exclamation point to a question mark, and repeat the procedure. Chances are that the volunteer will read it as a "checking-information" question, as meaning "Did you say 'great'?" Then read it yourself, with exaggerated surprise, as meaning "Could you possibly have said 'great'?"

Presentation

Have students read the explanation. Read the example dialogues aloud, and have students briefly practice them. Monitor the practice and model the dialogues once more.

Language Note: According to some experts, only about 20 percent of human communication is conveyed by the words themselves.

 **Option:** Read the conversations below to the students, and ask them the following questions:

1. Is the second speaker's intonation rising or falling?

2. How does the second speaker feel about the information?

Conversation 1

A: I just heard that there's a new rule: no makeup is allowed in school.

B: Fantastic! [*said with falling intonation, disgustedly*] And I just spent all my money on new lipstick!

Conversation 2

A: Did you hear that we're getting an extra day off next week?

B: Fantastic! [*said with initial rising intonation, excitedly*] I was hoping to have some time to go shopping.

4 Have students read the instructions and do the exercise independently. Then have them compare predictions with a partner.

5 Play the recording or read the audioscript once for students to check their predictions. Have them discuss their answers briefly with a partner and revise if necessary. Then play the recording or read the audioscript again for them to confirm their corrections.

Language Note: The phrase *she could put on a few (pounds/ kilos)* means that the speaker thinks the woman looks unhealthily thin and needs to gain some weight.

Audioscript: The audioscript for Exercise 5 appears on Student Book page 74.

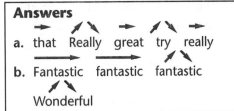

Answers
a. that Really great try really
b. Fantastic fantastic fantastic
   Wonderful

6 Have students read the conversations aloud with their partners, paying attention to the use of intonation to convey tone. Monitor their practice, and model correct pronunciation as necessary.

Option: Extend the practice by having students work in pairs. One pair writes a one-word expression (either an exclamation or a question) on a piece of paper, shows it to the other, and then gives a series of situations, to which the other student must respond with appropriate intonation, using the word on the paper. For example:

The expression is *Thanks!*

A: "Your haircut looks great!"
B: "Thanks!" (enthusiastically)

A: "I don't really like those shoes."
B: "Thanks!" (sarcastically)

Workbook: Practice 10

Speak Out (*page 75*)

Preview

Select a student, and ask him or her some questions related to the unit topic of appearances, such as current fashion in hair, shoes, or jewelry. After a few exchanges, begin wandering off the topic. Elicit the fact from the class that you are not *on track*. If this is expressed in some other words, teach the idiom *keeping/staying on track* (continuing to discuss the same subject; staying on the subject).

Presentation

➡ **Keeping on Track** Have students read the strategy. Point out the use of the word *digress* as a more formal way of saying *get off track*. Point out that cases of getting off track are rarely as extreme as the one you demonstrated; often digressions are related to the topic but are not appropriate in the context. For example, someone may have an interesting story related to the topic, but the story isn't relevant to the purpose of the discussion.

Model the examples in the box, and have students practice them with a partner. Stress politeness and the importance of acknowledging what the person has said before bringing the group back on track.

❼ Have students read the instructions independently. Then put them in groups of three and review the roles. Allow students to improvise the order of speaking and to choose roles on the spur of the moment, for example, the first speaker is whoever comes up with something to say first, the second speaker is the first person who can react to the statement, and so on. The only rule is that the person who digresses can't be the same person who brings the discussion back on track.

Note: This activity is designed to develop fluency. It is best not to interrupt students to correct errors. Make notes of student errors for review with the class after the activity has finished.

Option: For a mixed-ability class, follow a set procedure for the exercise: the first student makes a statement, the second student elaborates, the third student digresses, and the first student brings the conversation back on track. Then they shift roles and topics, and begin again.

 Workbook: Practice 11

READING and WRITING

Read About It *(pages 75–77)*

Presentation

❶ Before You Read Have students read the questions and jot down some short answers. Then have them compare answers with a partner and discuss.

If appropriate, have selected pairs share their answers with the class.

➡ Evaluating Supporting Examples

Have students read the strategy. Suggest to the students that they ask themselves questions as they read, in order to assess the strength of arguments or test the validity of the assertions. You might want to put some examples on the board, such as:

How do I know this is true?

Is this an isolated example, or part of a pattern?

Is it logical to assume this from the evidence?

❷ Have students read the instructions independently. Remind them to choose one general statement and two examples *that support the statement.* Then have them read the article, find the statement and examples, and then work with a partner to share and discuss their findings. Remind them that while reading, they should use context clues as much as possible to figure out the meanings of unfamiliar words.

Culture Notes:

Johann Wolfgang von Goethe was a German poet and philosopher of the late 18th and early 19th century, well known for his reflections on nature, morality, truth, love, and beauty. *Paul Klee,* a Swiss painter of the early 20th century, mixed elements of realism and abstaction in his work. *Robert Browning* was an English poet of the Victorian era. He is best known for his dramatic verse monologues and for the love poetry that he wrote to his wife, the poet Elizabeth Barrett Browning. *Montesquieu,* a French nobleman of the 18th century, was a political philosopher whose liberal ideas influenced the founders of the American government. *Aristotle,* the Greek philosopher and naturalist of the 4th century B.C., wrote extensively on beauty in his *Poetics,* his *Metaphysics,* and elsewhere. *Victorian times* refers to the reign of Queen Victoria, who ruled England from 1837 until her death in 1901. The term is generally associated with British culture of the middle and late 19th century.

Language Note: *To what end* means *for what purpose* or *toward what goal.*

☻ **Option:** If you feel your students need help with unfamiliar words before they do the task, you may wish to do the Vocabulary Check exercise on page 77 before the following exercises.

❸ Have students read the instructions and answer the questions independently. Then have them compare answers with a partner and discuss. Review answers with the class.

Answers

a. The time periods and countries or ethnic groups listed are: modern Western, Tuareg of the Sahara, African societies, East Asia, United States, European aristocracy, Victorian women, Victorian times, 17th century, Egyptians and ancient Egypt, ancient Greeks and Romans, Mayans, and Aztecs.

b. The aristocratic French male held a self-absorbed attitude when it came to beautification. He wore wigs of cascading curls, stockings, and high heels to show off his legs, and wore scented gloves and rouge. He was devoted to his appearance.

c. The author reaches the conclusion that we seek out beauty because of our natural instincts. A youthful, symmetrical appearance free of blemishes is what our prehistoric ancestors looked for in a mate, as those features were thought to mean that there was no obvious disease or disability that would result in premature death.

---

❹ Have students read the instructions and answer the questions on a separate sheet of paper. Then have them compare answers with a partner and discuss. Review answers with the class.

☑ ❺ **Vocabulary Check** Have students work alone, and then compare answers with a partner. Review the answers with the class.

Answers
1. f **2.** d **3.** a **4.** h **5.** i **6.** b **7.** c **8.** g

---

Think About It *(page 77)*

Presentation

❻ Have students discuss the italicized quotations from the text in groups. Have selected groups share summaries of their discussion with the class.

☻ **Option:** For mixed-ability classes, you might have them discuss the sayings below instead of the ones in the text. Ask them to deal with *all* the sayings and to discuss how they support or contradict each other.

- You can't judge a book by its cover.
- Everything has beauty, but not everyone sees it.
- Beauty is truth, and truth is beauty.
- Beauty is only skin-deep.
- There's no cosmetic that guarantees beauty like happiness.

☻ **Option:** Extend the activity by asking students to work in groups to create a new saying that they feel embodies an important truth about beauty. Have groups present their sayings to the class.

Write: Writing Supporting Paragraphs *(page 78)*

Presentation

➡ Have students read the strategy independently. Review the distinction between the main point of the essay, as expressed in the thesis statement, and the main idea of each supporting paragraph, as expressed in the topic sentence of that paragraph.

❼ Have students read the article and answer the questions independently, either in class or as homework. Then have them compare answers with a partner and discuss any differences. Review answers with the class.

Answers

a. **Thesis statement:** *(As a result,) your investment in skin-care problems may be hurting not only your bank account but also your complexion.*

b. *There are two supporting paragraphs.*

c. **Paragraph 2:** *When people buy expensive skin products, often what they're paying for are fancy containers.* **Paragraph 3:** *People also need to be aware of the ingredients in the skin products they buy.*

Write About It *(page 78)*

Presentation

❽ Have students read the instructions independently and write their paragraphs in class or as homework. Remind them to use topic sentences in their supporting paragraphs.

☑ ❾ Check Your Writing Have students use the bulleted questions to give written feedback on their partner's paper. Have them use feedback from their partner to revise their own paper.

 Workbook: Practice 12

Vocabulary Expansion: Describing physical characteristics See page T123.

Answers

A. *Possible answers:*

That person is . . .
stocky / slender / short

That person has . . .
almond eyes / smooth skin / bushy eyebrows / sturdy legs / broad shoulders / an oval face / high cheekbones / a slender figure/ pointy ears / short hair / short legs

B. *Answers will vary.*

EVALUATION

See pages Txi–Txii.

Unit 6 Achievement Test

Self-Check See **You're In Charge!**, page 48 of the Workbook.

Writing Revised introductory paragraph and supporting paragraphs from **Write About It**, Exercises 8 and 9, page 78.

Oral Communication

1. Work with a partner to record a dialogue on *makeovers*. Bring in a picture of a person who you think needs some fashion and grooming advice. Exchange pictures with your partner. Comment on what you think that person could or should do to improve his or her appearance, and answer your partner's questions. (Remember, for your own tape you are discussing the picture your partner gives you, not the one you brought yourself. Keep the picture your partner gives you in your portfolio.)

2. Record a monologue of your thoughts about *cultural standards of beauty*. Do you think there are any standards of beauty that are universal? If so, what are they? What are some specific standards that vary widely from culture to culture?

Interactive Dictation

Dictate the following to the students. Then have them continue the second paragraph and complete the story. For more information on dictation, see page Txv.

> Charles thought that if he worked out, did a lot of running, and lost some weight, he would be happier and healthier. He wrote about this in his diary: *Dear Diary: I'm going to change my ways. If I start eating right and exercising, I'll be a lot healthier and better-looking. Maybe my friends won't know me. But if that happens, I'll just make some new friends. Maybe I'll be able to find a really pretty girlfriend.*
>
> Six months later, Charles was a new man, with new friends and a new girlfriend. But he wasn't happy. He wrote in his diary again. *Dear Diary: I don't know what happened. I'm really lonely. If . . .*

PROGRESS CHECK
Units 4–6

Progress Checks may be done as homework or may be used in class. As a class exercise, they may be done in several ways:

- as a quiz—students work alone and hand their papers in to you to be corrected

- as pairwork—students work alone and then compare answers with a partner

- as a class exercise—students work alone, and answers are reviewed with the class

GRAMMAR (pages 79–81)

➡ **Using Time Effectively** Have students read the strategy. Remind them that in this kind of exercise, they are looking for errors in grammar and structure. Emphasize that once they are sure they've found an error, they should move on, whether or not they have read and understood the entire sentence.

A Have students read the instructions and do the exercise. For a review of gerunds and infinitives, refer students to Unit 4, pages 46–49; for a review of the passive voice, refer students to Unit 5, pages 57–60; for a review of conditionals, refer students to Unit 6, pages 69–73.

> **Answers**
> **1.** A **2.** B **3.** A **4.** D **5.** B **6.** B **7.** A **8.** C

➡ **Looking for Clues** Have students read the strategy. Emphasize the way in which the question (stem) suggests a certain answer; remind students to look for time expressions, the word *if*, and use of tenses in the question (stem), subject-verb agreement, etc.

B Have students read the instructions and do the exercise. For a review of gerunds and infinitives, refer students to Unit 4, pages 46–49; for a review of the passive voice, refer students to Unit 5, pages 57–60; for a review of conditionals, refer students to Unit 6, pages 69–73.

> **Answers**
> **1.** C **2.** B **3.** D **4.** C **5.** A **6.** D

VOCABULARY (pages 81–82)

➡ **Making an Educated Guess** Have students read the strategy. Review the concept of "educated guesses"—in case the student isn't immediately sure of the correct answer, he/she can eliminate some of the possibilities and compare the ones that are left. Point out that, in many cases, a good test-taking technique is to go through and answer all the "immediate" questions, and then to return to the ones that were difficult and make educated guesses. This will result in the highest proportion of correct answers.

A Have students read the instructions and do the exercise.

> **Answers**
> **1.** C **2.** A **3.** D **4.** D **5.** A

➡ **Answering Word Formation Vocabulary Questions** Have students read the strategy. Review some of the common word formation structures, e.g., adding *–tion* to make a verb into a noun, adding *–en* to make a noun into a verb, adding *–ed*, *–ing*, *–ious*, and *–ive* to make adjectives, adding *–ly* to make adverbs, etc.

B Have students read the instructions and do the exercise.

> **Answers**
> **1.** threatening **2.** validation **3.** emphasis
> **4.** belief **5.** friendly

FEELING LEFT OUT

OBJECTIVES

Students will be able to:
- Talk about handedness
- Describe problems and solutions
- Use relative clauses (identifying and non-identifying)
- Listen and summarize
- Pronounce linked and reduced sounds
- Keep a discussion going
- Identify generalizations and qualifying information in readings
- Analyze concluding paragraphs
- Use expressions with *right* and *left*

GETTING STARTED

Warm Up (*page 83*)

Preview

Ask students how they use their right hands and their left hands differently. What activities do they do with each hand? Do they know? Have them take out a sheet of paper and answer the following questions by writing *L* (left hand) or *R* (right hand). Have students compare their answers with their partners and decide if they are totally, moderately, or not a bit right-handed or left-handed.

    a. Which hand holds your pencil?

    b. Which hand do you use to throw a ball?

    c. Which hand do you use to hammer a nail?

    d. Which hand do you use to hold a book you're reading?

    e. Which hand do you use to slice bread?

    f. Which hand do you use to hold your fork (chopsticks) when you eat?

Presentation

❶ Have students work in small groups to discuss common difficulties left-handed people encounter. Then have students rank the difficulties from most to least serious. Review answers with the class.

Option (for mixed ability students): Tell students that you want them to guess the topic of the unit without looking in their books. Then, using your left hand, write the title *Feeling Left Out* on the board. (If you are left-handed, use your right hand.) You may want to continue to write something on the board or do some other activity, like writing with your pen or shuffling papers, with your "wrong" hand, as they guess.

❷ Have students read the question and discuss answers with a partner. Then have selected pairs share their answers with the class.

❸ Have students read the instructions and work independently. Play the recording or read the audioscript, and have students jot down their answers and discuss them with a partner. Review answers with the class.

Audioscript: The audioscript for Exercise 3 appears on page T139.

> **Answers**
> desks with the arms on the right side, making it awkward and uncomfortable to do school-work; teachers who force lefties to write with their right hand; kitchen utensils/office supplies designed for right-handers; turning the station on a car radio; being stereotyped as naturally accident-prone and generally clumsy

 Workbook: Practice 1

Figure It Out (*pages 83–84*)

Presentation

❹ Give the class two minutes to brainstorm expressions that have to do with left or left-handedness. Put selected results on the board. Tell students they are going to read something about the concepts of "left" and "right." Have students read the instructions and the article independently.

Culture Note: The expressions *Mr. Right* and *Ms. Right* are also used to talk about a person's ideal romantic partner.

Option: Check comprehension by having students take turns asking and answering the following questions with a partner:

1. What is an expression for a person who is a bad dancer? (*two left feet*)

2. What is an expression for a person who is the boss's trusted assistant? (*a right-hand man/woman*)

3. What is an expression for a person who has strange ideas or behavior? (*out in left field*)

4. What is another name for an insult or insincere praise? (*a left-handed compliment*)

Option: Extend the previous option by having students work with their partners to discuss the possible origins of these expressions; for example, *A person with two left feet would be a bad dancer because he/she wouldn't be able to follow the steps properly.* Have selected pairs share their answers with the class.

☑ ❺ **Vocabulary Check** Have students read the instructions and do the exercise independently and then compare answers with a partner. Review the answers with the class.

Answers
1. c **2.** d **3.** b **4.** a **5.** f **6.** e **7.** h

 Workbook: Practice 2

Talk About It *(pages 84–85)*

Option: If you feel that your students need extra help in using relative clauses, you might want to postpone this activity until after the grammar presentation (pages 85–88).

Presentation

Note: This activity is designed to develop fluency. It is best not to interrupt students to correct errors. Make notes of student errors for review with the class after the activity has finished.

❻ Have students read the instructions and the model conversation independently. Have a pair of students read the conversation for the class. Then have students work in pairs to improvise conversations, using the cues and the language in the model. Have students work in groups to discuss potential problems of left-handers or others who may be physically different (very tall, very small, etc.) from the majority and how these problems might be overcome. For example, *They could make reversible guitars, whose strings could be put on either way, so left-handed guitarists wouldn't have such a hard time finding instruments.* Select pairs to present their conversations to the class.

Language Note: A *pollster* is a person who takes opinion surveys, which are sometimes called *polls*.

Culture Note: People who are left-handed are often called *lefties*. Sometimes *Lefty* is used as a personal nickname, like the baseball player Lefty Grove or the country singer Lefty Frizzell. In British English, the term *lefty* is somewhat derogatory and is used to describe supporters of the political left.

Option: Tell students to write their own polling questionnaires and to use these questionnaires to interview people outside of class. Have students report their results to the class.

 Workbook: Practice 3

GRAMMAR

Adjective Clauses *(pages 85–86)*

Preview

Ask students to describe you. Tell them to use characteristics in their description that make you recognizably different from other teachers. Have students describe themselves in the same way with a partner. Ask them what makes them recognizably different from their classmates.

T65

Presentation

Go over the grammar explanations and examples on pages 85–86. Point out that the adjective clauses modify nouns in the sentences, and that they generally *describe* the noun (telling what it's like: *my friend Sam, who is always late*) or *distinguish* it from others (telling which one: *the person who called me yesterday*).

❶ Have students read the instructions and do the exercise independently. Review the answers with the class.

Answers

that reveal bias against all things left; which suggest that left-handers are wrong in some essential way; who has been rejected; whose ideas are considered irrelevant, extreme, or crazy; whom everyone dreads as a partner; which means "evil or threatening"; who is vulgar, tasteless, or lacking grace in social situations; who conducts himself in an exemplary manner; who has read this article

🜨 **Option:** Do the above exercise as a contest, in which students compete to find as many adjective clauses as they can within a time limit. Then review answers with the class.

Presentation

Have students read the explanation and the examples in the boxes on page 86. Point out that when the relative pronoun is the *object* of the clause, it can be omitted. Demonstrate on the board.

❷ Have students work alone and then compare answers with a partner. Review answers with the class.

Answers

a. The company that makes left-handed products has expanded.
b. That man (whom) you saw shopping yesterday owns the factory.
c. That worker who had an accident is left-handed.
d. Power tools that (*or* which) are made for right-handers can be dangerous for lefties.
e. The insurance plan (that) the company has had better be good!

🜨 **Option:** Extend Exercise 2 by asking students to go back through the exercise and omit the relative pronouns in their rewritten sentences wherever possible.

Identifying and Non-Identifying Adjective Clauses (*pages 86–87*)

Preview

Write the following two sentences on the board:

a. *My sister who lives in Seattle got married last week.*

b. *My sister, who lives in Seattle, got married last week.*

Point to **a.** and ask students if they can tell you anything about how many sisters you have. Then point to **b.** and ask them same question. Tell them that the answer to **a.** is *more than one*, and the answer to **b.** is *no one knows*.

Presentation

Write the following on the board:

Which one?

Would you tell me more about him/her/it?

Point out that the adjective clause in **a.** in the Preview above answers the first question, while the adjective clause in **b.** answers the second.

Have students read the explanation and examples in the first box. Point out that identifying adjective clauses do more than just distinguish one thing from another; they can also be used to distinguish one person or thing from all others. Write *the man who wrote Hamlet* on the board, and ask who he is.

Have students read the explanation and examples in the second box. Point out that these clauses are "non-essential" and are placed within commas to separate them from the "essential" parts of the sentence. You can also point out that if we take the commas out of the first example (Tom Cruise), we would be talking about more than one Tom Cruise: we would be distinguishing the left-handed Tom Cruise from another Tom Cruise who isn't left-handed.

❸ Have students read the instructions and then do the exercise with a partner. Point out that the commas have been left out because that would make the exercise too easy; they have to determine from context which type of clause is needed, and then add the commas. Review answers with the class.

Answers

a. I **b.** I **c.** N: Guns, which are dangerous for right-handers too, are a big problem today. **d.** I **e.** N: Children, who are often curious, are the primary victims of hand-guns stored in the home. **f.** I

☸ Option: Have students practice defining relative clauses by writing descriptions of classmates that contain no names. Then have students work in groups. Have them take turns reading their descriptions aloud to each other while the others try to guess who is being described. *"I'm thinking of someone who has long, black hair. . ." "The person I'm thinking of is wearing. . ."*

☸ Option: Have students practice non-defining relative clauses by interviewing a classmate and reporting the results of the interview to another classmate or the class. *"Maribel, who was born on September 6th, perfers autumn to the other seasons."*

☸ Option (for mixed ability classes): Extend the exercise by modeling the pronunciation of the two types of clauses, using appropriate pauses and intonations to show the distinction between those with commas and those without. Then have students work with their partners to do the exercise orally. One partner reads one of the sentences out loud, using pauses and intonation to indicate whether the adjective clause is identifying or non-identifying. The other partner must then respond with the appropriate sentence from among the answer choices. Then have partners change roles and repeat. Finally, have selected students read sentences in a similar fashion to the class, and have the class respond chorally.

 Workbook: Practices 4, 5

Adjective Clauses with *Whose* (*pages 87–88*)

Presentation

Have students read the explanation and the examples in the box. Point out that clauses with *whose* can be identifying or non-identifying, as in the following examples:

*The person **whose book is on my desk** is Linda. (identifying)*

*Jimi Hendrix, **whose guitar playing was inspirational**, was left-handed. (non-identifying)*

❹ Have students read the instructions and do the exercise independently. Then have them compare answers with a partner. Review the answers with the class.

Answers

a. The professor whose research is on handedness gave an excellent lecture.
b. The student whose notes I borrowed took great notes.
c. I thanked the student whose notes I copied.
d. The professor whose class I missed called on me.
e. The professor whose question I answered appreciated my comments.
f. A classmate, whose phone number I have, found my notebook.

Option: Have students work independently to rewrite their combined sentences, using non-identifying adjective clauses wherever possible. Then have them compare sentences with a partner and discuss differences in meaning.

☑ ❺ **Check Your Understanding** Have students read the instructions, do the exercise independently, and then compare answers with a partner. Review selected answers with the class.

Option: Extend the exercise by having students create sentences of their own, following the patterns of each of the sentences they created using the cues. Have selected students share their sentences with the class.

❻ **Express Yourself** Have students read the instructions and then work with a partner to do the activity. Have selected pairs present their dialogues to the class.

Option: As an alternative, assign various situations to the pairs, and then have them create and practice their dialogues. Then mix and match pairs, taking, for example, one student from each of two "Situation A" groups, and having them ad-lib a dialogue for the class.

 Workbook: Practices 6, 7, 8

LISTENING and SPEAKING

Listen: Write Right! (pages 88–89)

Presentation

❶ **Before You Listen** Have students read the questions and then discuss them with a partner. Then have selected pairs share their conclusions with the class.

➡ **Listening to Summarize** Have students read the strategy. Emphasize that a summary doesn't need supporting details. It only reports what the speaker said, not how well he or she said it. Also point out that the goal of a summary is to be as brief as possible while still covering the most important points.

❷ Have students read the instructions and the answer choices. Check to see that everyone understands them. Then play the recording or read the audioscript, and have them select an answer. Have them compare answers with a partner and discuss. Review answers with the class.

Language Notes:

- The expression *what I was getting at* means "the point I was trying to make."

- To *not have a clue* is an idiom for being totally ignorant of something. A more recent variation is to *be clueless*.

- To be *all over the place* is to be confused or unfocused.

Audioscript: The audioscript for Exercise 2 appears on pages T139–T140.

> **Answer**
> c

❸ Have students read the directions and look at the chart. Then play the recording or read the audioscript once more, and have them fill in the chart. Ask them to compare answers with a partner and discuss. Then review answers with the class.

> **Answers**
> **Possible significance of writing in the "hook" position:** Those who write in the hook position do not have the usual left-right hand and brain relationship.
> **Percentage of left-handers who have their language centers in the right hemisphere of the brain:** 40 percent
> *Students will then discuss with a partner what they have learned that helps them understand their own brain.*

Option: As an alternative, ask students to try to fill in the chart before they listen again. Then play the recording or read the audioscript while students check their answers.

 Workbook: Practice 9

Pronunciation (pages 89–90)

Preview

On the board, write the sentence *I never used to use my left hand.* Underline *used to* and say the sentence out loud twice, once naturally and once exaggerating the distinction between the final sound in *used* and the initial sound in *to*. Ask students which sounds more natural.

Presentation

Have students read the introduction. Go over the examples in the grid, pointing out that when the same sounds are put together at the end of one word and the beginning of the next, they run together somewhat, but not completely. In other words, there aren't two distinct sounds, but the single sound is slightly lengthened.

4 Have students read the instructions and do the exercise independently.

🎧 **5** Play the recording or read the audioscript once for them to check their predictions. Then have them compare answers with a partner. If necessary, play the recording or read the audioscript again.

Audioscript: The audioscript for Exercise 5 appears on Student Book page 90.

> **Answers**
> **a.** asked **b.** you **c.** you **d.** you're
> **e.** want

6 Have students work with their partners. Monitor their performance, and have selected students present sentences to the class.

 Workbook: Practice 10

Speak Out (pages 90–91)

Preview

On the board, write the following phrases:

- *keeping a discussion on track*
- *keeping a discussion going*

Ask students if they can explain the difference. Elicit the fact that the first has to do with direction—the discussion might be very active, but not staying on the topic—while the second has to do with activity—the discussion might be slowing down and needs to be stimulated a bit.

Presentation

➡ **Keeping a Discussion Going** Have students read the strategy and the model expressions. Explain that this is the responsibility of the discussion leader, but in an informal discussion, anyone can keep the discussion going. Review the expressions, making the distinction between asking someone to go further with their contribution to the discussion (asking them to *elaborate*, or be more *thorough*) and asking for participation from group members who haven't said anything yet.

7 Have students work alone and then compare answers with a partner and discuss.

> **Answers**
> **1.** E **2.** P **3.** E (or P) **4.** E **5.** P **6.** E
> **7.** P **8.** P **9.** E **10.** P

8 Have students work in small groups. Read through the instructions with the class, making sure everyone understands the goal of the discussion. Appoint a group leader for each group, but tell students that everyone should help keep the discussion moving.

Language Note: *Differently-abled* is a recent and polite alternative term for *handicapped* or *disabled.*

Note: This activity is designed to develop fluency. It is best not to interrupt students to correct errors. Make notes of student errors for review with the class after the activity has finished.

Option: As a follow-up, after groups have reached some conclusions, have each group briefly report its results to the class.

 Workbook: Practice 11

READING and WRITING

Read About It (pages 91–93)

Presentation

❶ Before You Read Have students read the questions and discuss them with a partner. Have selected students share their conclusions with the class.

➡ **Identifying Generalizations** After students have read the strategy, point out that the term *generalization* is usually used negatively, to mean an insufficiently supported statement. Then point out that when making generalizations, writers often protect themselves by using qualifiers like *usually, often, it is believed*, etc.

❷ Have students read the instructions and the passage independently. Have them underline examples of generalizations and qualifiers in the text, or list them on a separate sheet of paper.

Language Note: *Oddballs* are people whose behavior is strange.

Culture Notes:

- On the political spectrum, *left* is often associated with liberalism, socialism, communism, etc., while *right* is often associated with conservatism, capitalism, fascism, etc.

- The *New England Journal of Medicine* is one of the most highly regarded medical journals published in the United States.

- *Louis Pasteur* was a 19th century French biologist famous for, among other things, a process for sterilizing milk. American *John McEnroe* was the top-ranked tennis player in the world from 1981 to 1984. *Martina Navratilova*, who was born in Czechoslovakia and emigrated to the United States, was the top female tennis player in the world from 1978 to 1979 and from 1982 to 1986. *Ty Cobb* was an American baseball star of the early 20th century, starting his career with the Detroit Tigers and finishing it with the Philadelphia Athletics in 1928. *Babe Ruth* is an American baseball

legend, best-known as a member of the New York Yankees from 1919 to 1934. *Oprah Winfrey* is an American television talk show host. She is also known for her Book Club, which reviews and recommends new titles for her televison viewers. *Benjamin Franklin* was an American statesman and diplomat who played a key role in the creation of the *Declaration of Independence. Judy Garland* was the star of many stage and screen musicals, most notably the 1939 film *The Wizard of Oz. Paul McCartney* is an English singer and songwriter, best known as a member of the Beatles. *Albert Einstein*, a German-born physicist of the 20th century, is best known for his theory of relativity. *Bruce Willis* is an actor known for his tough-guy roles in such action films as the *Die Hard* series. *Whoopi Goldberg* is a comedienne and actress who is often seen on television commercials and game shows.

❸ Have students look back at the generalizations they noted as they were reading and discuss the questions with a partner. Have selected pairs share their conclusions with the class.

Answers

Some possible answers:

Generalizations: . . . a disproportionate number of people who are left-handed are more apt to be accident prone . . . (lines 4 – 7), . . . that left-handers are depressed and therefore more likely to . . . (lines 80–85), . . . describing left-handers as oddballs who are at best . . . (lines 47–49).

Qualifiers: Others speculate . . . (lines 79–80), Several studies . . . (line 3), . . . supported by several scientists . . . (lines 5–6).

☑ **❹ Vocabulary Check** Have students work alone and then compare answers with a partner. Review the answers with the class.

Answers

1. e 2. g 3. h 4. d 5. f 6. a 7. b

Think About It (page 93)

Presentation

⑤ Have students discuss the questions with a partner or in small groups. Remind them to support their viewpoints with specific examples.

Write: Concluding Paragraphs (page 94)

Presentation

➡ Have students read the strategy. Tell them that the introduction draws the reader from the outside world into the essay, and the conclusion has to reconnect the reader to the outside world.

⑥ Have students read the instructions and the model conclusion, and then answer the questions independently. Then have them compare answers with a partner and discuss. Have selected students share their results with the class.

> **Answers**
> The author constructs the conclusion by restating the thesis, summarizing the main ideas, and providing closure for the essay. Similar features between a conclusion and an introductory paragraph are the main ideas and the thesis. The author made the ending memorable by posing a question directly to the reader. The last sentence, a play on words, also helps to make the piece memorable.

Write About It (page 94)

Presentation

⑦ Have students read the instructions independently and revise their concluding paragraphs in class or as homework.

☑ **⑧ Check Your Writing** Have students exchange papers with a partner and use the bulleted questions to give written feedback on their partner's paper. Ask students to give feedback on aspects they liked as well as those that need improvement. Have them use feedback from their partner to revise their paper.

 Workbook: Practice 12

Vocabulary Expansion: Expressions with *right* and *left* See page T124.

> **Answers**
> A. 1. h (N) 2. i (+) 3. c (+) 4. d (-)
> 5. b (-) 6. e (-) 7. k (+) 8. f (N)
> 9. j (N) 10. g (N) 11. a (-)
> B. *Answers will vary.*

EVALUATION

See pages Txi–Txii.

Unit 7 Achievement Test

Self-Check See **You're In Charge!**, page 56 of the Workbook.

PORTFOLIO

Writing Revised concluding paragraphs from **Write About It**, Exercises 7 and 8, page 94.

Oral Communication

1. Record a two-minute speech about *handedness*. How much do you think is biological and how much is cultural? For example, why do some cultures drive on the left side of the road (Britain, Japan), while others drive on the right side of the road (the European continent, the Americas)? What do you think causes biological handedness?

2. Work with a partner. Record a brief conversation dialogue on the difficulties that physically different people face, such as being left-handed. For your tape, talk about a specific difficulty you have either had or observed, suggest possible solutions to the problem, and answer your partner's questions. Reverse roles for your partner's tape.

Interactive Dictation

Dictate the following sentences to the students, with the blanks. Then have them rewrite the sentences, filling in the blanks to create adjective clauses. Remind them to use appropriate punctuation. For more information on dictation, see page Txv.

1. Young musicians _____ have some special considerations when deciding what instrument to take up.

2. Instruments _____ for right-handed players, such as the trumpet, aren't a good choice for them.

3. A left-handed trumpet player either has to adapt to an instrument _____, or purchase a custom-made one _____.

4. The piano, however, is an excellent choice for the young leftie.

5. The piano is one of the few instruments _____ design is symmetrical, and it favors a player _____ with both hands.

Then have them write at least three more sentences using adjective clauses, discussing instruments that might be suitable for left-handed players.

YOU'RE NOT MY TYPE

OBJECTIVES

Students will be able to:
- Describe various personality types
- Make general statements
- Use phrasal verbs (separable and non-separable)
- Listen for details and relate them to their own experiences
- Pronounce different stress patterns in phrasal verbs
- Take turns effectively in group discussions
- Read for inferences and tone
- Analyze and recognize point-by-point essay organization
- Use verb phrases that function as nouns

GETTING STARTED

Warm Up (page 95)

Preview

- Ask students to look at the unit title and the picture at the top of the page and predict what they think the unit will be about. Explain that the expression *not my type* usually refers to an unsuitable potential romantic partner. You can remind them that the opposite of this expression would be "Mr. (or Ms.) Right," (see page 84 of Unit 7). Elicit positive and negative vocabulary to describe someone's personality, and place these words on the board.

- Review the categories (*thinkers/feelers, introverts/extroverts*) to make sure that students understand these concepts. Have the class volunteer some other broad personality classifications, such as *night person, day person, cat person, dog person,* etc.

- **Option:** Ask students if they have a "type." Have them form groups of three or four and brainstorm what their "type" is. Ask for volunteers to describe their "type" to the class.

Presentation

❶ Have students read the instructions and do the first part of the activity alone. Tell them to make a multicolumn list that has "myself" and then the names of all the others in the group, and to write three adjectives for each name on the list. Have them compare results with the others in their group and discuss. Ask for volunteers to share their results with the class.

🎧 ❷ Tell the students they're going to hear a conversation about "first impressions" (making judgments about a person you just met based on a first meeting) and how different they can be. Play the recording or read the audioscript. Have students work alone to answer the questions. Then have them compare answers with a partner and discuss. Have selected students share their answers with the class.

🌐 **Option:** As follow-up, ask the students to discuss with a partner if first impressions of people are generally right or wrong. Tell them to think of an example from their own lives and share it with their partner.

Audioscript: The audioscript for Exercise 2 appears on page T140.

Answers

Mari: awfully quiet and kind of uptight; didn't really want to talk to her; shy, cold, and uninterested in the neighborhood; rushed.
Phillip: a great guy; interested in the neighborhood; eager to tell a lot about himself and his family.
Mari bumped into him as he was probably leaving for the airport to pick up his wife and kids, and he was running late.

Language Note: *Uptight* is a slang expression that means tense or nervous.

 Workbook: Practice 1

Figure It Out *(pages 95–97)*

Preview

If students have done Unit 4, remind them of the "pop psychology" questionnaire they took on conflict resolution. Tell them that they are now going to do a questionnaire that is a typical "personality profile," such as is found in popular English language magazines. Elicit adjectives and other vocabulary students might use to describe someone's personality.

Presentation

❸ You might want to check understanding of vocabulary such as **ambitious, strong-willed, stubborn, intuition, spatial, well-structured,** and **objective** before beginning. Have students work alone. Encourage them to use the context to figure out any unfamiliar words, but if they're still stuck, give them hints to elicit the meaning. Then have them calculate their scores and read the conclusions. Have them compare results with a partner and discuss whether they think the profiles (their own and their partner's) are accurate.

> **Example:** *My profile says that I'm articulate, but I can't always express myself well.* Have selected students share their conclusions with the class.

Culture Note: On popular television talk shows in North America, the host asks a celebrity a series of "or" questions that are supposed to help us understand the celebrity's personality. For example: "Dogs or cats?" "Baseball or football?" "Winter or summer?" "Sushi or pizza?" The host then asks follow-up questions to possibly make a conclusion about the celebrity's personality.

🌐 **Option:** Extend the activity by having students work in pairs to do a "celebrity interview" like the one described above.

Have students make lists of "or" questions that they think are significant, then have them ask their partner and discuss the responses. Then either have selected pairs present their interviews to the class, or mix and match students from different pairs and have them ad-lib an interview for the class.

☑ ❹ **Vocabulary Check** Have students read the word list. Point out that these are all phrasal verbs and that the vocabulary in the exercise appears in different phrase combinations than in the questionnaire, although the meanings of the phrasal verbs are the same. Then have students work alone and then compare answers with a partner and discuss.

> **Answers**
> **1.** b **2.** a **3.** f **4.** c **5.** g **6.** d

 Workbook: Practice 2

Talk About It *(page 97)*

Presentation

Note: This activity is designed to develop fluency. It is best not to interrupt students to correct errors. Make notes of student errors for review with the class after the activity has finished.

❺ Set the situation. Discuss different situations in which a personality test might be useful for someone. For example, before people choose a career in North America, it's fairly common to visit a counselor to find out what sort of work best matches their personality. Once the student understands the possible context, go over the functions. Have students work alone. Ask selected students to read the model conversation for the class. Then have students work in pairs to improvise conversations, using the cues and the language in the model. Select pairs to present their conversations to the class.

Option: Have students cover the model conversation. Using only the function column on the right, improvise a conversation with a student to demonstrate variations on possible language. Have the students do the same in pairs, as proficiency permits.

Option: As a follow-up activity, have students work in pairs to create a new type of personality profile. Have pairs make a list of criteria and create a questionnaire or survey activity. Then put pairs together to give and take the surveys and discuss the results.

 *Workbook: Practice 3*

GRAMMAR

Phrasal Verbs *(pages 98–99)*

Preview

Put the phrase *turn down* on the board, and ask students to brainstorm different meanings. Elicit various literal and non-literal meanings, such as *turning down* the blankets before going to bed, *turning down* the heater (or the volume on the radio), and *turning down* someone's offer.

Presentation

Have students read the introduction and the examples in the boxes. Point out that meaning often changes when the preposition is added to a two-word verb, as in *to put someone up* (to give someone a place to stay) and *to put up with someone* (to tolerate someone). Give students some model sentences using examples from the box, such as:

- She **called** me **up** at 7:30 this morning to ask if I had heard the news.

- John **called on** Mary with a bouquet of roses, but she **turned** him **down** because he isn't her type. He was disappointed, but he'll **get over** it.

- We can't **put off** the test because there are only two classes left before the end of the term.

- I was about to go home when Michelle **turned up**.

- I've always **looked up to** Kareem, but I'm afraid he **looks down on** me. I feel like he's just **putting up with** me.

Option: Have students work in pairs to create additional model sentences of their own. Monitor the activity, and have selected pairs share their sentences with the class.

❶ Have students work alone and then compare answers with a partner and discuss. Review answers with the class.

Note: Several of the phrasal verbs in the questionnaire were used in Exercise 4, Vocabulary Check, but there are others. Ask students to find *all* examples of phrasal verbs, not mentioning that some were already used. For mixed-ability classes, you might want to mention the Vocabulary Check; it will give them a headstart on the exercise.

Answers
Phrasal: run into, go with, go over, come to, look at, putting on, feel about, make up, feel about, carried out, figure out, kept to, tend to, opening up, holding back
Verb + Prep: talk to, react to, need to, trying to

---

❷ There are several ways to do this exercise.

- Have students read the article and match each phrasal verb in the box with an italicized word from the article. Have them write the italicized words in the box next to their matching phrasal verbs. (Warn them that the tenses may be different.) Then have them fill in the blanks in the dialogue with phrasal verbs from the box, referring to the italicized words for guidance. (*average difficulty*)

- Have students read through the article for meaning. Then have them fill in the blanks in the dialogue with phrasal verbs from the box, referring back to the article to check their information. (*more difficult*)

- Have students complete the dialogue with phrasal verbs from the box first. Then have them go back and read the article to check their information. (*most difficult*)

Choose one method, and have students work alone and then compare answers with a partner. Review answers with the class. Point out that the phrasal verbs are more commonly used in casual conversation.

> **Answers**
> 1. pointed out 2. look up to 3. figured out
> 4. get along with 5. come across as
> 6. coming up with 7. made up of 8. give up

Language Note: An *icebreaker* is a technique for starting a conversation with a stranger.

 Workbook: Practices 4, 5, 6, 7

Separable and Inseparable Phrasal Verbs (pages 100–101)

Preview

Write the following expressions on the board:

Mari turned down John.

Mari turned John down.

Then write:

Mari turned him down.

Elicit that this is equivalent to the first two sentences.

Then write:

Mari turned down him.

Elicit the fact that this order is unacceptable, and cross it out.

Presentation

Have students read the first introduction and the examples in the first box. Point out that these examples use three-word verbs, which are never separable.

Have students read the second explanation and the examples in the second box. Point out that some two-word verbs are separable and others are not. Also emphasize that when the object is a pronoun, the phrasal verb *must* be separated. Refer them back to the example in the preview.

❸ Have students read the instructions and do the exercise independently. Then have them compare answers with

a partner and discuss. Review answers with the class.

> **Answers**
> 1. b 2. a 3. a 4. b 5. b 6. a

Culture Note: A person who works too much is sometimes called a *workaholic*. It is based on the term *alcoholic* which is a person who is addicted to alcohol. This formation has several other popular variations: *chocaholic* (a person who loves to eat chocolate), *shopaholic* (a person who shops too much), and so on.

☑ ❹ Check Your Understanding Have students read the instructions and do the exercise independently. Then have them compare answers with a partner and discuss. Review answers with the class.

> **Answers**
> 1. out 2. for 3. along with 4. up with
> 5. up with 6. to it 7. out 8. along with
> 9. to

Option: Have students work independently to rewrite the paragraph in Exercise 4, replacing all phrasal verbs with non-phrasal verbs. Then have them compare paragraphs with a partner and discuss. Have selected students share rewritten sentences with the class.

❺ Express Yourself Depending on class size, do this activity in groups, or with the whole class. Give the students a time limit and tell them to first work alone. Encourage them to use phrasal verbs in their descriptions. Then redistribute papers, and have students try to match the description with the person. Tell students that when they think they've figured out whose paper they have, they should approach that person and ask questions to confirm their guess; for example, *Do you get along well with people, or do you usually keep to yourself?*

Option: The Express Yourself activity can be done as a competition if students are asked to count the number of people they approached before they found a match. The student with the lowest number wins.

 Workbook: Practices 8, 9

LISTENING and SPEAKING

Listen: All in the Family (*pages 101–102*)

Presentation

❶ Before You Listen Ask students if they are familiar with the theory that birth order affects personality. Explain that this theory has not yet been proven, but does seem to have some validity. Share your birth order information and thoughts on the subject with the class. Have students work in pairs or small groups to discuss the questions. Open the discussion to the class by having selected students share their answers with the class. Include yourself in the discussion if you wish.

➡ **Relating Information** Have students read the strategy independently, then review it with the class. Point out that this is something we usually do without thinking. By immediately relating details to their own personal experiences, they will be able to remember and interpret the information more easily. Tell them to think about their families as they listen and see if it helps them remember key points.

❷ Have students read the instructions and the questions independently. Play the recording or read the audioscript, and have students answer the questions. Then have them compare answers with a partner and discuss.

Audioscript: The audioscript for Exercise 2 appears on pages T140–T141.

> **Answers**
> 1. c 2. b

❸ Have students read the instructions and the chart headings independently. Ask them to try to fill in the chart before they listen again. Play the recording or read the audioscript again, and have students check their answers. Then have them compare answers with a partner and discuss. Review answers with the class.

> **Answers**
> Mark's brother: first child; strong sense of duty, demanding; yes
> Jeanne: youngest of three; social, a lot of fun, easygoing, not very responsible; yes
> Mark: youngest of five; social, a lot of fun, easygoing, not very responsible; no
> Charles: middle child; gets along with all kinds of people, diplomatic, competitive, especially with the oldest child; yes

❹ Discuss the questions with the class. Refer them back to the chart for the information.

 Workbook: Practice 10

Pronunciation (*page 102*)

Preview

With their books closed, dictate the following sentences to your students, emphasizing the stress patterns:

Let's TALK about it.

Let's TALK it OVER.

Ask for a volunteer to read them aloud. Ask students what they notice about the stress patterns. Elicit and/or model the appropriate stress patterns.

Presentation

Have students read the introduction, and ask volunteers to read the examples in the box. Point out that with three-word verbs, the last word isn't stressed. Recommend that students review the list of stressed particles and try to memorize them in phrasal pairs: *come across, get ahead, go away, come back, fall behind, get into, get off, get on, get over, fall under, come up,* and so on.

❺ Have students read the instructions and do the exercise independently. Then have them compare predictions with a partner.

🎧 ❻ Play the recording or read the audioscript once for students to check their predictions. Have them compare answers with a partner and discuss any differences. Then play the recording or read the audioscript once more for students to confirm their answers.

Audioscript: The audioscript for Exercise 6 appears on Student Book page 102.

> **Answers**
> **a.** figure, out **b.** disapprove **c.** walk away
> **d.** look up **e.** put, work **f.** break out
> **g.** work out **h.** go **i.** throw, away
> **j.** get along **k.** give, back **l.** count

❼ Have students practice their pronunciation with a partner.

 Workbook: Practice 11

Speak Out *(page 103)*

Preview

Review the expression "has the floor," the "floor" being "the right to speak."

Presentation

➡ **Having the Floor** Have students read the strategy independently. Review the context with them: this is a discussion among peers, and people claim and yield the floor themselves. Emphasize that when people refuse to yield the floor, someone (a participant or a group leader) can enforce turn-taking by suggesting that another person be given the floor.

❽ Have students read the instructions and do the exercise independently. Then have them compare answers with

a partner and discuss. Review answers with the class.

> **Answers**
> **1.** T **2.** R **3.** R **4.** G **5.** R **6.** G **7.** T

 Option: Extend the activity by having students practice saying the expressions with a partner. Encourage them to use gestures and other body language (such as extending a hand, palm up, for *Be my guest*).

❾ Review the instructions and the situation with the class. Suggest to the students that they enact the planning stages of the project; they can discuss how they will do their research and what they expect to find. Then have students do the role-play in groups of three. Rotate roles so that each student gets to play each role.

Note: This activity is designed to develop fluency. It is best not to interrupt students to correct errors. Make notes of student errors for review with the class after the activity has finished.

 Workbook: Practice 12

READING and WRITING

Read About It *(pages 103–105)*

Presentation

❶ **Before You Read** Have students work in small groups. Ask them to think about why we classify people by personality type. What do we hope to understand and what will we do when we understand it? Have them read the questions and work in pairs or small groups to discuss them. Have selected groups or pairs share the results of the discussion with the class.

➡ **Making Inferences** Go over the strategy. Review the concept of "reading between the lines."

❷ Have students read the article and make brief notes of inferences they make as they read. Remind them to be aware of tone. You might want to check understanding of the following words: **humiliating** (*deeply embarrassing*), **make it** (*succeed*), **take it in stride** (*accept easily*), **pigeonhole** (*to place in a narrow category*), **flunk out** (*fail*), **expound** (*talk at great length about a topic*), **tagged** (*labeled*), **merit** (*n.-benefit or advantage*).

Answers
Tone: skeptical, humorous, sarcastic. The tone indicates that the author dismisses the idea that there are two kinds of personality traits.

Language Notes:

- *Part and parcel* is an expression that means *an essential part*.

- *Annual and perennial* are two classifications of plants. *Annual*: those that die and must be replanted every year. *Perennial*: those that come up again every spring without being replanted.

Culture Notes:

- *Like Richard Nixon if you made him moon walk:* Richard Nixon was the president of the United States from 1969 until he resigned during the Watergate scandal in 1974. He was known for being self-conscious and uncomfortable in his public appearances. The *moon walk* is an odd, backwards-walking dance step made famous by Michael Jackson.

- *Type A and Type B:* These personality classifications are common in popular psychology and refer generally to people who are intense and driven (A) and those who are relaxed and easygoing (B).

❸ Have students read the instructions and work independently to choose the inferences. Have them use the notes they took while reading, and only refer back to the article if absolutely necessary. Then have them compare answers in a small group and discuss. Review answers with the class.

Answers
1, 2

❹ Have students work in a small group to discuss the questions. Have selected groups share their answers and conclusions with the class.

Answers
a. idea people, feeling people, optimists, pessimists, realists, idealists, animal people, plant people, Type A, Type B
b. He doesn't believe in just two kinds of personalities. He believes there are as many types of personalities as there are people, and each person may be different people at different times. *Students will then discuss whether they agree or disagree with the author, and why.*

Think About It (*page 105*)

Presentation

❺ Check understanding of the factors. Have students do the activity in pairs, then compare rankings with another pair. Compare results and discuss with the class.

☸ **Option:** Poll the class on their choices. (Add the numbers appearing next to each trait in each student's book: the lowest total means that trait was "most important" to the class as a whole.) Put the combined results on the board. Elicit conclusions about the overall attitudes of the class.

Write: Essays of Comparison and Contrast: Point-by-Point Organization (*page 106*)

Have students read the presentation in class or for homework.

☸ **Option:** Tell students to imagine that they are going to compare two people that they know. Ask them what things they would compare. Elicit several points of comparison and put them on the board. Then put the phrase *point-by-point comparison* on the board.

Presentation

➡ Have students read the strategy. Emphasize that this type of organization works very well for essays of comparison and contrast because such essays always have more than one focus point. Review the outline in the box as an example of this.

Write About It *(page 106)*

Presentation

❻ Have students read the instructions and write the essay in class or for homework.

☑ **❼ Check Your Writing** Have students exchange papers with a partner and use the bulleted questions to give written feedback on their partner's paper. Have them use feedback from their partner to revise their own paper.

Note: Students should be encouraged to give both positive and negative feedback to their partners.

 Workbook: Practice 13

Vocabulary Expansion: Verb phrases that can function as nouns See page T125.

Answers

A.
1. putting / on **2.** break up **3.** check up
4. let / down **5.** put / down **6.** broke out
7. turned / over

B. *Sentences will vary. Phrasal verbs as nouns are:*
1. put-on **2.** breakup **3.** checkup **4.** letdown
5. put-down **6.** breakout **7.** turnover

EVALUATION

See pages Txi–Txii.

Unit 8 Achievement Test

Self-Check See **You're In Charge!** page 64 of the Workbook.

PORTFOLIO

Writing Revised essay from **Write About It**, Exercises 6 and 7, page 106.

Oral Communication

1. Work with a partner to record a discussion on "type casting" (giving actors and actresses roles based on the public perception of their "type"). For your tape, describe a standard "type" and name an actor or actress who is an example of it; then give an example of an actor or actress who has successfully broken out of his or her "type." Answer your partner's questions. Then reverse roles for your partner's tape.

2. Record a monologue on finding friends and/or romantic partners. Discuss what characteristics you are looking for in a friend or partner and how you decide if someone has the characteristics you want.

Interactive Dictation

Dictate the following sentences to the students. Then have them go back and write another sentence between each of the dictated sentences, using the phrasal verb provided and making a coherent flow. For more information on dictation, see page Txv.

1. Julius is a real people person; he can get along with anyone.

2. (go along with)

3. His older brother Michael, on the other hand, prefers to keep to himself.

4. (come across)

5. I know them both well, but Michael never keeps in touch.

6. (hear from)

7. Julius and Michael grew up in the same household, but they're completely different.

8. (figure out)

9. Maybe it has something to do with birth order.

10. (put up with)

TECH TRENDS

OBJECTIVES

Students will be able to:

- Talk about technology and ethics, privacy, etc.
- State needs, ask for specifics
- Use articles (definite and indefinite)
- Listen to identify implications and consequences
- Pronounce stress patterns for confirming information
- Manage disruptive behavior in discussion
- Identify stated purpose and actual purpose to improve reading
- Write an essay of point-by-point comparison
- Understand and use computer jargon

GETTING STARTED

Warm Up (page 107)

Preview

- Ask students to look at the picture at the top of page 107. Ask them to briefly discuss with a partner what kind of a future this picture is predicting. Have selected students share their responses with the class.

- Ask students if they are more comfortable with technology than their parents are, or less comfortable. Have them discuss the reasons for their answers with a partner. Have selected students share their responses with the class.

Presentation

Have students read the introduction independently. Briefly review the concepts with the class. What are the dangers that are being hinted at? (*The general point is that technology is changing so fast that consumers can't keep up with it—you practically have to study all the new devices on the market to know what they are and what they do.*)

❶ Have students read the question and make their lists independently. Then have them work in groups to compare lists and discuss. If necessary, review the meaning of *predecessors*—elicit that we are talking about the "ancestors" of these machines; for instance, the record player is the predecessor of the CD player. Have selected groups summarize their discussions for the class.

Language Note: *Technologies*: The word *technology* is usually a singular, collective noun. However, it can be used in the plural, to refer to several distinct disciplines. For example, *DVD technology, e-mail technology, and cell phone technology are just some of the communication **technologies** that have evolved in the last ten years.*

❷ Review the instructions with the students. Emphasize that they are shifting the focus to the future to brainstorm what the new machines will be and do. Have selected groups share the results of their discussions with the class.

🎧 ❸ Have students read the instructions independently. Then have them work with a partner to fill in the chart. Encourage them to think creatively and use detail, such as how many TV sets and how large, what kind of bath fixtures, etc. Then play the recording or read the audioscript one or more times, and have them check their predictions. Have selected pairs share their answers with the class.

Audioscript: The audioscript for Exercise 3 appears on page T141.

Answers

The Reality: Not just a TV, but an underground theater where he watches DVDs; a remote control bath; a sound system that actually follows you throughout the house and lets you listen to music from anywhere in the house; a garage security system which allows only Bill's and Bill's wife's cars into the garage automatically.

 Workbook: Practice 1

Figure It Out *(page 108)*

Preview

Put the word *unethical* on the board. Ask students to give you examples of unethical behavior. Use the examples to draw the distinction between *unethical* and *illegal*. The first is a moral standard, based on common notions of decent behavior; the second is a legal standard, based on written law.

Presentation

❹ Have students read the instructions and fill in the chart independently. Then have them discuss their choices with a partner. Encourage them to discuss their concepts of moral behavior in defending their choices; for example, *I don't see anything wrong with that—it doesn't hurt anyone.* After pair discussion of the responses to Exercise 4, open the topic up to the class. Ask for a show of hands on whether each point is ethical or unethical, and whenever the class seems to be evenly split, ask for representatives of each viewpoint to explain their reasoning.

Language Note: A *blind copy* is an e-mail message sent secretly; there is no indication on the message that the person sent or received a copy of it.

Option: Have pairs or groups write their own questionnaire involving ethics of everyday behavior. For example, screening calls by not answering the phone until someone leaves a message, not replying to personal e-mail messages, or using your company Internet connection to do personal business because it's faster.

 Workbook: Practice 2

Talk About It *(page 109)*

Presentation

Note: This activity is designed to develop fluency. It is best not to interrupt students to correct errors. Make notes of student errors for review with the class after the activity has finished.

❺ Direct students to the picture on page 109. Ask them questions about the picture, such as, *What is the situation?* Then, have students read the instructions, and have a pair of students read the conversation for the class. Then have students work in pairs to improvise conversations, using the cues and the language in the model. Select pairs to present their conversations to the class.

 Workbook: Practice 3

GRAMMAR

Nouns and Articles (page 109)

Preview

Put the following phrases on the board:

a. *a computer*

b. *the computer I bought last week*

c. *computers*

d. *the computers at my school*

Ask students to look at them and think about the differences in meaning.

Presentation

Have students read through the explanation. Review the concept of countability: some nouns have singular and plural forms (most), some have only singular (*water, love*), some have only plural (*pants, eyeglasses*).

Note: These designations of singular-only and plural-only nouns are sometimes disregarded. In some cases, especially in business and commerce, we find examples like the following:

*We have a wide variety of bottled spring **waters**.* (different types)

*We'll be introducing our new cargo **pant** in the spring.* (one style or type)

Specific Reference: The Definite Article (page 109)

Presentation

Have students read the explanation and the examples in the box. Review the concept of *specific reference*: we are designating a certain one (or ones), not just any one (or ones). Point out that the definite article can be used with all types of nouns: singular and plural, count and non-count. Refer students to examples **b** and **d** in the Preview.

Non-Specific Reference: Indefinite Articles (page 110)

Presentation

Have students read the explanation and the examples in the box. Review the concept of *non-specific reference*: we are talking about any one of the many in the world. Point out that we don't use an article when making non-specific references to plural or to non-count nouns. The indefinite article is used only for singular, count nouns. Refer students to examples **a** and **c** in the Preview.

Generic Reference: Definite and Indefinite Articles (pages 110–112)

Presentation

Have students read the explanation and the examples in the chart. Explain that when we are talking generally, the basic rules for definite and indefinite articles are the same. However, we sometimes use the definite article with non-specific reference, as in: *the computer has many uses.* You might point out that this is a formal, almost literary style, and if students don't feel comfortable with it, there is no need to use it.

❶ Have students read the instructions and work with a partner to create example sentences. Have selected pairs share their sentences with the class.

Note: The symbol Ø means *no article is used*.

❷ Have students work with their partners to complete the activity. Put pairs together to compare results and discuss. Then review answers with the class.

> **Answers**
> a. One of many virus protection programs should be installed. b. The question is about any sensitive information. c. You should accept attachments from any sender you trust. d. There is more than one free provider you can start an account with.
> e. You should check the policies of all web-sites. f. All encryption can be figured out.

Language Notes:

- A *virus protection program* is software that protects your computer from programs that are designed to make computers malfunction; these *viruses* are created and sent out over the Internet as a destructive form of a practical joke.

- *E-mail attachments* are electronic documents that are sent along with e-mail messages. They are not part of the main message and must be opened separately. Attachments are often photos, artwork, or large text documents.

- A *dummy e-mail account* is a separate e-mail account that people use for Internet shopping in order to keep Internet "junk mail," or *spam*, from filling up their regular e-mailboxes.

- *Encryption* refers to the encoding and decoding of sensitive information (such as credit card numbers, ID numbers, etc.) when it is sent over the Internet. This keeps it from being read by *identity thieves* and other Internet criminals.

❸ Have students read the instructions and do the exercise independently. Point out that wherever they think no article is needed, they should leave the line blank. Then have them compare answers with a partner and discuss. Point out that there may be some cases where different answers are possible, creating different meanings. Encourage them to find these and discuss the variations in meaning. Review answers with the class.

Answers

Possible answers:
1. Ø 2. the *or* a 3. the 4. a 5. the 6. the
7. a 8. Ø 9. a 10. a *or* the 11. Ø 12. a *or* Ø
13. A 14. the 15. Ø 16. a 17. The 18. Ø *or*
the 19. Ø 20. a 21. a 22. the 23. a 24. Ø
25. the

☑ ❹ **Check Your Understanding** Have students work alone and then compare answers with a partner and discuss. Review answers with the class.

 ❺ **Express Yourself** Have students do the activity in pairs. Monitor their discussions, and have selected pairs present some of their definitions to the class.

♨ **Option:** Have students work in pairs or small groups to discuss the disposable phone as described in Exercise 3. Point out that a little over fifty years ago, the concept of a disposable pen was unknown, and now we are talking about disposable telephones. Have them discuss what other items might soon be made disposable; ask them to brainstorm advantages and disadvantages of various disposable appliances, and of the concept of disposability itself. Monitor the discussions, and have selected pairs or groups share their ideas with the class.

📖 *Workbook: Practices 4, 5, 6*

LISTENING and SPEAKING

Listen: Tech Pets *(page 112)*

Presentation

❶ **Before You Listen** Have students answer the questions in pairs or small groups. When all groups have reached the last question and have had a reasonable amount of time to discuss it, open the discussion up to the class. Make a list of some of the responses to the last question on the board.

➡ **Identifying Implications** Have students read the strategy. Point out that this strategy involves thinking beyond what is being described and imagining what it means for the future.

🎧 ❷ Play the recording or read the audioscript, and have students concentrate on the main ideas. Have them work with a partner to briefly summarize them. Review answers with the class.

Audioscript: The audioscript for Exercise 2 appears on pages T141–T142.

Language Note: To be *in the doghouse* is to be the object of the anger of a family member, usually a parent or spouse. The expression suggests that you are not allowed to sleep in the house, but must sleep outside with the dog.

❸ Have students read the instructions and the list of criteria. Remind them that they are to focus on specific information this time. Play the recording or read the audioscript again, and have them write down the information. Then have them work with a partner and discuss whether they would buy a tech pet and, if so, which one they would buy.

Answers

MUY LOCO
Features: A silver and green robotic chameleon with a pink tongue that talks, sings a few songs, and dances the Rumba and Tango.
Target Age: Not appropriate for younger children. Older children might like it.
Price: $29.95

I-CYBIE
Features: A robotic puppy that wags its tail and shakes its ears when it is petted. It walks around like a live puppy would, and comes up to you to get attention when it feels like it. If you pull its tail, it will squeal or yelp in pain, as a real dog would.
Target Age: Children
Price: At 40% off, it's $150.00.

Option: Extend the activity by having students work in pairs or small groups to discuss the possible implications of tech pets. What is the possible emotional impact of a tech pet on its owner? What is the possible social impact of tech pets in general? Encourage them to think of both advantages and disadvantages.

 Workbook: Practice 7

Pronunciation *(page 113)*

Preview

Put the following dialogue on the board:

> **A:** *I'll have fish and chips, please.*
> **B:** *A dish of chips?*
> **A:** *No—fish and chips.*

Ask for a volunteer to read it with you. Take the **A** part, and model the appropriate stress: *fish and CHIPS* in the first line and *FISH and chips* in the third.

Presentation

Have students read the introduction. Review the example in the box with them. Point out that when one part of the sentence isn't clear to the listener, the listener may ask a question and stress the part that he or she wasn't sure of, and that we answer the question by repeating the sentence with stress on that part, regardless of whether or not it is normally stressed. In other words, we use stress to ask for confirmation and to confirm what was said.

❹ Have students read the instructions and do the exercise independently. Then have them compare predictions with a partner.

❺ Play the recording or read the audioscript once for students to check their predictions. Have them compare answers with a partner and discuss any differences. Then play the recording or read the audioscript once more for students to confirm their answers. Review answers with the class.

Audioscript: The audioscript for Exercise 5 appears on Student Book page 113.

Answers
1. microbots, nanobots **2.** Eighty, eighteen
3. toothbrush, toothbrush, Incredible
4. ROM, RAM

---

❻ Have students read the dialogues aloud with a partner. Monitor their speech and have selected pairs read the dialogues for the class.

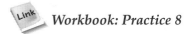 *Workbook: Practice 8*

Speak Out *(pages 113–114)*

Preview

Write *to disrupt* on the board, and ask the students if anyone can define it. Elicit meanings such as *disturb*, *interrupt*, *bother*. Ask them what they would do if they were teachers and were faced with disruptive behavior in a classroom. Have selected students share their responses with the class.

Presentation

➡ **Managing Disruptive Behavior** Have students read the strategy and review the main points with them. Tell them that any participant in a discussion can help to manage disruptive behavior. Point out that this strategy is similar to keeping the discussion on track, but somewhat stronger because it may require criticizing someone's behavior. Remind students that this can be done politely, however.

❼ Have students read the instructions and the dialogue and discuss the answer with the class. Ask what is considered disruptive behavior in their culture, and how this behavior is dealt with. Elicit other things Anne could have said to stop Jeff.

> **Answer**
> By encouraging him to save the jokes until after their work has been completed.

❽ Have students read the instructions. Point out that the term *blocking* refers to disruptive behavior and the term *managing* refers to action taken to stop such behavior. Have students do the exercise independently and then compare answers with a partner. Review answers with the class.

> **Answers**
> **a.** M **b.** B **c.** M **d.** M **e.** M **f.** B **g.** M

❾ Have students read the instructions independently and then work in groups of four or five to discuss the topic. Point out that this role play can be a lot of fun, since it allows them to engage in behavior that wouldn't normally be tolerated in class. You might want to have groups designate some of the participants as "troublemakers." Or you could allow them to ad-lib all the roles, so that a participant might be disruptive one minute and managing disruption the next.

Note: This activity is designed to develop fluency. It is best not to interrupt students to correct errors. Make notes of student errors for review with the class after the activity has finished.

 Workbook: Practice 9

READING and WRITING

Read About It *(pages 114–116)*

Presentation

❶ **Before You Read** Write *genetic engineering* (the science of changing the structure of the genes of a plant, animal, or human—usually to make them stronger or healthier) on the board. Check understanding of the term and ask students to give some examples of genetic engineering. For example, breeding disease-resistant tomatoes. Have students read the instructions independently and then discuss the question in groups of three or four. Monitor the discussions, and have selected students share their answers with the class.

➡ **Assessing Function** Have students read the strategy independently, and then review it with the class. Point out the distinction between function, which is generic, and purpose, which is specific: *persuading* is a function; *informing* is a function; *getting people to vote for Candidate X* is a purpose. A writer may use a variety of functions to achieve one main purpose, so that what looks like multiple purposes is really one. You might want to mention that, as a rule, writers disguise persuasion as information, since readers don't like to be manipulated; they prefer to think they are learning and making up their own minds.

❷ Have students read the instructions and the text independently. Remind them to consider function and purpose as they read.

Language Note: *In utero* means *in the womb*, before the child is born.

Culture Note: *$30,000 dollars a year for injections*: the median household income in the United States in the year 2000 was $42,148.

Note: The writer's strategy in this piece is to provide a lot of factual detail and then ask rhetorical questions designed to raise fears and doubts in the reader's mind. The goal is to lead the reader to the conclusion that genetic enhancement is not a good idea.

❸ Have students work with a partner to answer the questions. Then have them compare answers with another pair and discuss. Review answers with the class.

Answers

a. *Possible answers:* warn the reader about the dangers of intelligence enhancement, persuade the reader that intelligence enhancement could have harmful effects, raise the reader's awareness of intelligence enhancement, and protest against enhanced intelligence.

b. Advantages: treat autism, make one smarter. Disadvantages: unwanted side effects, very expensive, only those who could afford such a treatments would be able to get them.

c. Human growth hormones: intended for children with serious growth deficiencies, but they've come to be used on healthy children who are just unhappy with their short stature (provided their parents can afford the treatment).
Prenatal sex-selection: developed to weed out diseases that affect one gender or the other, such as hemophilia. However, these tests are now being used to allow parents to select the gender of their future children.

d. Only those who could afford such a procedure would be able to get it, possibly creating a new form of discrimination against "normal" unenhanced children with lower IQs.

e. *Answers will vary.*

☸ **Option:** As an alternative method of doing Exercise 3, have students answer the questions independently. Review the answers to the first three questions with the class. Then lead a class discussion on the last two questions. Encourage students to either expand on the author's arguments or to think of counterarguments.

☑ ❹ **Vocabulary Check** Have students read the instructions and do the exercise independently, and then compare answers with a partner. Review the answers with the class.

Answers

Some possible answers:

a. a particular quality in someone's character
b. to fit according to individual expectations
c. attractive d. very interesting e. unexpected result of a situation f. not easily noticed
g. heightened ability h. advanced development of something i. to get rid of something harmful

Think About It *(page 116)*

Presentation

❺ Have students read the question independently and then jot down some of their thoughts. Lead a class discussion on this topic.

T87

🌀 **Option:** As an alternate method of doing Exercise 5, have students discuss the question in pairs. Have pairs report the results of their discussion, and then open the discussion up to the class.

Write: Essay of Comparison (*pages 117–118*)

Presentation

Have students read the introduction. Review the introduction and the diagram with the class, pointing out that the focus is now on the body of the essay, where the actual point-by-point comparisons are to be made. Point out that each body paragraph takes one attribute of pets and uses it to compare the two types of pets.

➡️ Have students read the strategy and the transition expressions in the box. Go over the example sentences below the box, pointing out how the transition expressions are used to show relationships between ideas.

❻ Have students read the instructions and do the activity with their partners. After they have compared results with another pair, have them revise their outline. You may want to collect the outlines and give students written feedback on them.

Write About It (*page 118*)

Presentation

❼ Have students choose a topic and write an essay in class or for homework.

☑ ❽ **Check Your Writing** Have students exchange papers with a partner and use the bulleted questions to give written feedback on their partner's paper. Have them use feedback from their partner to revise their own paper.

 *Workbook: Practice 10*

Vocabulary Expansion: Computer terminology See page T126.

> **Answers**
> 1. chips 2. robot 3. encryption 4. digital
> 5. software 6. scanner 7. virus
> 8. attachment 9. processor

EVALUATION

See pages Txi–Txii.

Unit 9 Achievement Test

Self-Check See **You're In Charge!**, page 72 of the Workbook.

PORTFOLIO

Writing Revised essay of point-by-point comparison from **Write About It**, Exercises 7 and 8, page 118.

Oral Communication

1. Record a monologue on the topic of *useful technology vs. useless technology.* Describe your criteria (standards for judging) and then give specific examples.

2. Participate in a group discussion on "robotic ethics." Discuss these questions with two or three other students: *When we finally create robots that have self-consciousness, will they have emotions? Will they love and hate? Will they be afraid to die? What kinds of rules and laws will we need regarding robots?* Videotape the discussion, or schedule a time when your teacher can attend. (If you use videotape, each participant will need a copy for his/her portfolio.)

Interactive Dictation

Dictate the following paragraph to the students. Then have them complete the second paragraph. For more information on dictation, see page Txv.

We all know that the future is going to be filled with all kinds of high-tech gadgets that we can't even imagine now. But will they be tools, or will they be toys? A tool is something that serves a useful purpose. You might say that a tool's reason for being exists before the tool itself is invented. A toy is another matter. Of course, you can argue that humanity needs toys. But we don't need a specific toy. No one ever sat down and said, "The world would be a better place if we only had the Game Boy."

So how should we classify the PDA, or "electronic organizer"?

PROGRESS CHECK
Units 7–9

Progress Checks may be done as homework or may be used in class. As a class exercise, they may be done in several ways:

- as a quiz—students work alone and hand their papers in to you to be corrected
- as pairwork—students work alone and then compare answers with a partner
- as a class exercise—students work alone, and answers are reviewed with the class

➡ **Lowering Test Anxiety** Have students read the strategy. Point out the value of being thoroughly familiar with any informational material that is available from the test publishers, including sample questions and explanations of the answers. You might also suggest other test-prep materials and courses as a means of improving test performance and reducing anxiety.

GRAMMAR (pages 119–121)

A Have students read the instructions and do the exercise. For a review of adjective clauses, refer students to Unit 7, pages 85–88; for a review of phrasal verbs, refer students to Unit 8, pages 98–101; for a review of articles, refer students to Unit 9, pages 109–112.

Answers
1. C 2. B 3. A 4. D 5. C 6. D 7. A 8. C

➡ **Time Management on Tests** Have students read the strategy. Remind students to be aware of how much time is allotted to each section of the test and to check the time periodically to make sure they are keeping on schedule.

B Have students read the instructions and do the exercise. For a review of adjective clauses, refer students to Unit 7, pages 85–88; for a review of phrasal verbs, refer students to Unit 8, pages 98–101; for a review of articles, refer students to Unit 9, pages 109–112.

Answers
1. A 2. D 3. D 4. B 5. C 6. D

VOCABULARY (pages 121–122)

➡ **Guessing on Multiple Choice Tests** Have students read the strategy. Remind them that on tests that subtract points for incorrect answers, they should **not** guess.

Have students read the instructions and do the exercise.

Answers

Section 1
1. D 2. C 3. D 4. D

Section 2
1. B 2. D 3. A

WRITING (page 122)

➡ **Answering Essay Questions** Have students read the strategy. Stress the importance of taking time at the beginning to plan the essay and leaving time at the end to review the essay for errors in grammar, spelling, and punctuation.

SPACE EXPLORATION

OBJECTIVES

Students will be able to:
- Talk about space and space travel
- Discuss probability and make predictions
- Use the future perfect and the future perfect progressive tenses
- Make personal interpretations while listening
- Pronounce rising-falling intonation
- Use factual support in discussion
- Recognize explicit and implicit comparisons while reading
- Use block-style organization in the body of a comparison-and-contrast essay
- Use expressions for prediction

GETTING STARTED

Warm Up (page 123)

Preview

Ask students to think about the last time they heard a news item about space exploration. Have selected students briefly describe space-related news items they have heard, seen, or read.

Option: Put the expression *the final frontier* on the board and ask students what it means. Elicit something like *Earth has been thoroughly explored; space is the last unexplored area left.* Ask students if they think the phrase is accurate. Point out that this phrase is often applied to space but is sometimes used in other ways. Ask students to brainstorm some other *final frontiers* in pairs and then share their results with the class.

Presentation

Have students read the introduction and the questions independently. Then discuss the questions as a class.

Culture Note: *Sputnik* was the first man-made object to be put into orbit around the Earth. Its launch was a public relations triumph for the Soviet Union and put them ahead of the United States in what was then called *The Space Race*.

❶ Have students read the instructions and choose an answer independently. Compare and discuss answers with the class. You might want to point out that the third option is a *compromise*; it accepts parts of both arguments and offers a "middle path."

❷ Have students read the instructions and review the questions before listening. Then play the recording or read the audioscript twice, and have students answer the questions. Have them compare answers with a partner and discuss. Review answers with the class.

Audioscript: The audioscript for Exercise 2 appears on page T142.

Answers
a. The report is about David Tate. **b.** He is going to the International Space Station on Mars. **c.** He, unlike anyone else, has paid out of his own pocket for a ticket. **d.** He is doing this because it is the ultimate adventure. He's looking forward to just sitting by a window and taking pictures, and he is excited about experiencing weightlessness.

 Workbook: Practice 1

Figure It Out *(pages 124–125)*

Preview

Put the phrase *space tourists* on the board. Ask students what they think of the concept. Do they imagine that they will be vacationing in space someday? Have them briefly discuss with a partner. Have selected pairs share their conclusions with the class.

Presentation

❸ Have students read the introduction and the dialogue independently. Then put the following questions on the board, or copy and distribute them to the class. Have students work on the answers with a partner. Review answers with the class.

1. *According to Sara Chang, what will happen to first-time space travelers once they reach orbit?* (They will be experiencing extreme motion sickness.)

2. *What are four major changes that space travelers' bodies will go through?* (Their hearts will become slightly enlarged, their legs will shrink, their spinal discs will expand, and their muscles will start to deteriorate.)

3. *According to Sara, what will have happened by the end of this decade?* (Commercial space tourism will have become commonplace.)

Language Note: *A piece of cake* is an expression for an activity that is easy and pleasant.

Culture Note: *NASA* is the National Aeronautics and Space Administration. It is the department of the United States government that deals with space exploration.

Option: Extend the activity by having students practice reading the dialogue out loud with a partner. Have them read through it once, then change roles and read through it again. Select one pair to present the dialogue to the class.

☑ **❹ Vocabulary Check** Have students read the instructions and do the exercise independently. Then have them compare answers with a partner and discuss. Review answers with the class.

Answers
1. e   2. d   3. g   4. c   5. b   6. a

 Workbook: Practice 2

Talk About It *(page 125)*

Option: If you feel that your students need extra help in using the future perfect and the future progressive forms, you might want to postpone this activity until after the grammar presentation (pages 126–128).

Presentation

Note: This activity is designed to develop fluency. It is best not to interrupt students to correct errors. Make notes of student errors for review with the class after the activity has finished.

❺ Direct students to the picture and have them describe what is happening. Have students read the instructions and the model conversation independently. Have a pair of students read the conversation for the class. Then have students work in pairs to improvise conversations using the cues and the language in the model. Select pairs to present their conversations to the class.

Option: Expand the activity by having students work in groups to discuss the future of other types of exploration. Prompt them to discuss the sea, deserts, and the polar regions, to make predictions about the future of these areas, and to compare the challenges and potential benefits of exploring these areas to those of exploring space. Have groups summarize their conclusions for the class.

 Workbook: Practice 3

GRAMMAR

The Future Progressive Tense
(*page 126*)

Preview

Ask the question: *What will you be doing tomorrow at this time?* Elicit responses such as: *Tomorrow at this time I'll be sitting on a bus on my way home.*

Presentation

Have students read the introduction and the examples in the box independently. Point out that the contrast between ongoing actions and habitual ones is the same in future progressive as it is in past and present progressive.

❶ Review the instructions, and have students go back to the conversation on page 124 to do the activity independently. Then have them compare answers with a partner and discuss. Review answers with the class.

> **Answers**
> 'll be discussing, will be experiencing, will space tourists be dealing with, will be going through, will soon be deteriorating, won't be taking off

❷ Have students read the instructions and do the exercise independently. Then have them compare answers with a partner and discuss. Review answers with the class, explaining nuances of meaning wherever necessary; for example, in Question #1, future progessive (*I'll be meeting*) is best because the ongoing nature of B's meeting with the scientists is the reason B can't meet with A; the meeting will be in progress, so B has a schedule conflict. The simple future (*I'll meet*) would work if B were making up a schedule: *I'm too busy today; I'll meet with the visiting scientists from Mexico tomorrow.*

> **Answers**
> 1. 'll be meeting 2. will become 3. 'll get it
> 4. won't be taking 5. will need, will have
> 6. 'm going to be floating 7. will probably be sending

The Future Perfect Tense
(*pages 127–128*)

Preview

Put the following sentences on the board:

The final test is tomorrow. Will you be ready?

Then cross out the second sentence and write:

The final test is tomorrow. ~~Will you be ready?~~ Will you have studied enough?

Presentation

Have students read the introduction, and review the examples in the box with them. Ask them to look for time expressions in the examples.

❸ Have students read the instructions and answer the question independently. Review answers with the class.

> **Answers**
> within, by the end of

❹ Have students read the instructions and do the exercise independently. Then have them compare answers with a partner and discuss. Review answers with the class.

> **Answers**
> 1. S 2. D 3. S 4. D 5. S 6. S

🌐 **Option:** Extend the activity by having students work in pairs to create future perfect sentences. One student prompts the other with a time expression, and the other student must complete the sentence using the future perfect.

A: By this time next week . . .

B: . . . I'll have seen *Star Wars VI* forty-seven times!

Then they switch roles and repeat the activity. Have selected pairs present their sentences to the class.

❺ Have students read the instructions and do the exercise with a partner. Ask for volunteers to share the more interesting predictions with the class.

☑ ❻ **Check Your Understanding** Have students work alone and then compare answers with a partner and discuss. Review answers with the class.

Answers
1. will be flying 2. will be traveling 3. arrive
4. will have learned 5. will be enjoying
6. will be dealing 7. will have left
8. will be booking

🌐 **Option:** Ask students to work in pairs to discuss what "cyber postcards" might look like, and how they might be sent from space. Have selected pairs share their answers with the class.

🌐 **Option:** Extend the activity by having students work in pairs to create their own advertisements. Ask them to think of a space-related business of the future (for example, zero-gravity health spas, space funerals, and so on) and write the advertisement, using future progressive and future perfect forms. Have selected pairs read their advertisements aloud to the class.

🖼 ❼ **Express Yourself** Have students read the directions and write their paragraphs independently. Then have them read their paragraphs aloud in groups of three or four and discuss. Have selected students read their paragraphs to the class.

 Workbook: Practices 4, 5, 6, 7, 8

LISTENING and SPEAKING

Listen: Where Is Planet X? (pages 128–129)

Presentation

❶ **Before You Listen** Read through the instructions. Work as a class to come up with a complete list of planets and put it on the board. Then have students work with a partner to answer the last two questions and discuss. Review the results of the discussions with the class.

Note: The English names of the planets are (in order, starting from nearest to the sun): *Mercury, Venus, Earth, Mars, Jupiter, Saturn, Uranus, Neptune, Pluto.*

➡ **Interpreting Relationships Between Ideas** Have students read the strategy independently, and review it with the class. Suggest that students listen for signal words such as *because, believe, predict, so, therefore,* and so on, to help them identify the relationships between ideas.

🎧 ❷ Check understanding of the following terms: *comet, gravity, trillion,* and *the Oort cloud* (a huge orbiting collection of comets which exists at the edge of our solar system). Have students read the questions independently. Play the recording or read the audioscript one or more times, and have students write down their answers. Then have them compare answers with a partner and discuss. Have selected students share their answers with the class.

Audioscript: The audioscript for Exercise 2 appears on pages T142–T143.

Answers
a. Uranus and Neptune don't follow the orbits they're supposed to.
b. A large undiscovered planet; a brown dwarf, a smaller star that never had the mass to shine.

---

❸ Have students work on the answers independently. Then have them discuss their answers with a partner. Review answers with the class.

> **Answers**
> 1. F **2.** T **3.** T **4.** F **5.** F

 Workbook: Practice 9

Pronunciation (pages 129–130)

Preview

Put the following sentence on the board and say it aloud to students:

We're talking about outer space.

Then draw in the intonation arrows, one rising over *outer* and one falling over *space*. Repeat the sentence.

Presentation

Have students read the introduction independently. Review the concept of intonation, and point out that it is used in a variety of ways to show meaning in English. (You might want to point out that intonation is used in speaking to indicate meanings that are indicated in other ways in writing: for example, a rising intonation has the same function as a question mark.) Point out that one of the uses of intonation is to focus on a particular part of a sentence. (You might also point out that intonation and stress are combined in doing this.) In this case, the new information is the focal point.

❹ Have students read the instructions independently and make their predictions by drawing in the intonation arrows. Then have them compare predictions with a partner.

❺ Play the recording or read the audioscript once for students to check their predictions. Have them compare

answers with a partner and discuss any differences. Then play the recording or read the audioscript once more for students to confirm their answers.

Audioscript: The audioscript for Exercise 5 appears on Student Book page 130.

> **Answers**
>
>
> companion star, Nemesis, comets, Oort
>
> Cloud, toward Earth, mass extinctions

❻ Have students practice their pronunciation with a partner. Monitor their speech and have selected students read the sentences for the class.

 Workbook: Practice 10

Speak Out (pages 130–131)

Preview

Write the question *How do you know?* on the board. Tell students that you know there is life on Mars. Respond by telling them that space ships have been found in the Nevada desert. Elicit the question again. Respond with *My friend told me.* Pause, and then say *I heard it on the radio.* Ask them which support they tend to believe more.

Culture Note: On October 30, 1938, a radio adaptation of the H.G. Wells novel *The War of the Worlds* caused a panic in the United States with its realistic portrayal of a Martian invasion of Earth. Listeners who tuned in after the beginning of the program thought they were hearing an actual news report.

Presentation

➡ **Citing Sources for Support** Have students read the strategy. Point out that support is more effective if you not only give the facts but cite the source as well, giving titles, dates, names, and so on.

7 Review the instructions with the students, reminding them to underline the sources of the information as well as the information itself. Then have them do the exercise independently and compare answers with a partner and discuss. Review answers with the class.

Answers
. . . in the last division report, our design was described as "potentially valuable well beyond its cost", . . . Jake Martin, in his column in *Space Today*, said that robotic rovers are clearly providing data more cheaply than any other type of surface-focused vehicle at the current time, . . . nominated for the Robotics Design Award this year.

8 Have students read the instructions and do the exercise independently. Then have them compare answers with a partner and discuss. Review answers with the class.

Answers
a, d

9 Have pairs choose one side of the issue and brainstorm their support. Have them write down fictitious sources and the specific information that they got from these sources. Then put pairs with opposing viewpoints together and have them discuss the issues.

Note: This activity is designed to develop fluency. It is best not to interrupt students to correct errors. Make notes of student errors for review with the class after the activity has finished.

 Workbook: Practice 11

READING and WRITING

Read About It
(pages 131–134)

Presentation

1 **Before You Read** Read through the questions with the class and have students work in pairs to discuss them. Have selected pairs share the results of their discussion with the class.

➡ **Applying Concepts to New Information** Have students read the strategy independently and review it with the class. Point out that essays whose primary purpose is something other than comparison and contrast will still use those techniques in presenting supporting information.

2 Have students read the directions and do the activity independently.

Answers
Sending tourists into space is not far in terms of distance—it's just 100 miles away, straight up, which is less than half the distance between New York City and Washington D.C.

Experts predict, however, that the cost of space travel will ultimately drop, just like that of video cassette recorders.

In contrast, the Apollo lunar program from the 1960s was a fantastic achievement, but it left nothing but a flag on the moon and didn't further space travel in a direct way.

The hotels will be like ocean cruise liners, unhurriedly cruising through the vastness of space. Unlike cruise liners, though, the living accommodations might be closer to those of a base camp on Mount Everest than to those on a cruise ship like *Queen Elizabeth II*.

Sending people to the moon would only take nine days, for example, but a voyage to Mars could take almost three years.

Culture Notes:

- When the Apollo XI spacecraft landed on the moon on July 20, 1969, an estimated 600 million viewers worldwide were watching on television. Since that time, public interest in space exploration has fallen considerably. Shuttle launches have become commonplace and usually merit no more than a casual mention on the evening news.

- *A base camp at Mount Everest*: Extreme adventure travel is becoming more and more popular, with wealthy amateur climbers paying more than $50,000 to be guided to the top of Mount Everest. Space tourism is a logical extension of this trend.

Language Note: *A final frontier*: the use of the indefinite article *a* suggests that there might be many *final frontiers*, and that space is only one of them. The suggestion is that there will constantly be new challenges for mankind.

Option: If you feel your students need help with unfamiliar words before they do the task, you may wish to do the Vocabulary Check exercise on page 134 before the following exercises.

❸ Have students read the instructions and complete the chart independently. Then have them compare findings with a partner. Review answers with the class.

Answers

1. the distance between New York City and Washington D.C. (less than half the distance)
2. the drop in price of video cassette recorders
3. Apollo lunar program
4. a base camp at Mount Everest

---

❹ Have students work with a partner to answer the questions and discuss. Have selected pairs share their answers with the class.

Answers

a. As many as 80 percent of people younger than forty are interested in commercial space travel, and the majority would be willing to pay up to three months' salary for the experience. Ten percent would even pay a year's salary for the privilege of watching Earth from space.

b. Cost. Currently, taking tourists on voyages into space would be in the price range of billions of dollars.

c. 1. The first stage in their proposal calls for a space factory which will be manned by robots, with periodic visits from space crews. 2. Gradually, the factory will expand into a research laboratory which will provide a home for four to six technicians. 3. The next stage will involve the development of a space media center, which will provide services for news organizations, film crews, and meteorologists. 4. Eventually, the space media center will evolve into a "space spa," a place for space crews to stop and recuperate before flying off to other space locations. 5. The final stage of the project foresees the expansion of the recuperation center into a space hotel for guests, with prospects of stunning views of Earth.

☑ ❺ **Vocabulary Check** Have students read the instructions and do the exercise independently, and then compare answers with a partner. Review the answers with the class.

Answers
1. d **2.** h **3.** f **4.** e **5.** a **6.** b **7.** c

Think About It *(page 134)*

Presentation

❻ Ask students to discuss the question in pairs or small groups. Have selected pairs or groups share their answers with the class.

Option: Have students work in pairs to discuss the advantages and disadvantages of a space vacation as compared to one on Earth. Have selected pairs share their results with the class.

Write: Block Organization (*page 134*)

Preview

Put the following two diagrams on the board:

A1 B1		A1 A2 A3
A2 B2		B1 B2 B3
A3 B3		

Tell students that these are two formats for organizing a comparison-and-contrast essay. If they have already done Unit 8, ask them which diagram represents point-by-point organization. Elicit that it is the one on the left.

Presentation

➡ Have students read the strategy and look at the examples in the box. Refer them to the diagram on the right above as a graphic representation of block organization. Letters A and B represent topics, and numbers 1, 2, 3 represent points of comparison.

Write About It (*page 134*)

Presentation

7 Have students write the essay in class or as homework. You might want to point out that Mercury and Pluto correspond to the letters A and B in the diagrams, and the points such as size, temperature, and so on, correspond to the numbers.

☑ **8 Check Your Writing** Remind students to consider the bullet points when they analyze their partner's paper and to give written feedback. Also remind them to revise according to their partner's feedback.

 *Workbook: Practice 12*

Vocabulary Expansion: Expressions for prediction: word families See page T127.

Verb	Noun	Adjective	Adverb
challenge	challenge	challenging challenged	challengingly
develop	development	developed developing developmental	developmentally
	eventuality	eventual	eventually
expect	expectation	expected expectant	expectantly
foresee	foresight	foreseeable	foreseeably
imagine	imagination	imagined imaginative	imaginatively
	potential	potential	potentially
project	projection	projected	
		ultimate	ultimately
	viability	viable	viably

EVALUATION

See pages Txi–Txii.

Unit 10 Achievement Test

Self-Check See **You're In Charge!**, page 80 of the Workbook.

PORTFOLIO

Writing Revised essay of contrast from **Write About It**, Exercises 7 and 8, page 134.

Oral Communication

1. Work with a partner to record a discussion on how problems on Earth (pollution, population growth, dwindling resources, etc.) may raise interest in space exploration in the near future. For your tape, choose one problem and talk about whether you think it will increase interest in space travel and why. Answer your partner's questions. Then reverse roles for your partner's tape.

2. Record a monologue on a science fiction film that involves space travel, comparing the depiction of space travel in the film with what you have learned about the realities of space travel.

Interactive Dictation

Dictate the paragraph below to the students. Then have them write another paragraph using the words and expressions listed in the box. For more information on dictation, see page Txv.

> The question of whether or not manned space travel will be viable in the future is not so much a question of *how*, but of *why*. If you imagine that we will be relying on space to provide us with vital resources, like energy and raw materials, then the answer is probably *yes*. But if you foresee space travel as some sort of cosmic adventure or pleasure cruise, then the answer is probably *no*. We won't be wasting money and risking lives just to see what's out there. It has been more than thirty years since man first set foot on the moon, and we haven''t gone any farther. And thirty, or 300 years from now, we still won't have gone any further, unless we discover some compelling reason to do so.

fuel	explore	distance	commonplace
orbit	crisis	solar	pave the way

ADVENTURE VACATIONS

OBJECTIVES

Students will be able to:
- Talk about adventures
- Describe wishes and regrets
- Use conditionals without *if*, and the expressions *I wish* and *if only*
- Identify tone in listening
- Pronounce thought groups
- Offer support in a discussion
- Recognize explicit and implicit contrasts while reading
- Write a block-style essay of contrast
- Use names and descriptions of geographical features

GETTING STARTED

Warm Up *(page 135)*

Preview

Have students look at the picture and ask them if this is the type of vacation that appeals to them. For those that answer no, ask what types of vacations they prefer. Elicit the distinction between adventure vacations and relaxation vacations. Ask students to brainstorm the activities that correspond with each type, and make two lists on the board.

Presentation

Read through the introduction with the class.

❶ Have students read the instructions and do the exercise independently. Then have them compare answers with a partner and discuss. Review answers with the class.

🎧 ❷ Have students read the instructions and the questions independently. Play the recording or read the audioscript for students to answer the questions. Advise them to just listen the first time and to make notes of their answers the second time. Have selected students share their answers with the class.

Audioscript: The audioscript for Exercise 2 appears on page T143.

> **Answers**
> She was on an adventure vacation (scuba diving trip). While in the Philippines, Paula went diving. She enjoyed herself (after she got out of the water).

 Workbook: Practice 1

Figure It Out *(page 136)*

Preview

Ask students if they read travel brochures when deciding on a vacation destination and whether the information they find there is accurate. If any students answer *no* to the second question, ask them to describe an experience with a misleading travel brochure.

Presentation

❸ Have students look over the brochure for Anasazi Archaeological Adventures. Ask them what kind of experience they would expect to have if they took this type of vacation. Have them read the brochure and work with a partner to make a list of the activities they might do.

Culture Notes:

- The expression *wish you were here* is a cliché of vacation postcards. In popular humor, the typical vacation postcard says *Having a wonderful time, wish you were here*, and nothing else.

- There are several other types of "do it yourself" vacations, including "wind-jammer cruises," where you serve as a crew member on a sailing ship, and "family farm" vacations, where you actually live with a farm family and help them with the farm work.

☑ ❹ **Vocabulary Check** Have students read the instructions and do the exercise independently. Then have them compare answers with a partner and discuss. Review answers with the class.

Answers

1. d   **2.** f   **3.** g   **4.** b   **5.** a   **6.** c

 Workbook: Practice 2

Talk About It *(page 137)*

 Option: If you feel that your students need extra help in using expressions with *wish*, you might want to postpone this activity until after the grammar presentation (pages 137–140).

Presentation

Note: This activity is designed to develop fluency. It is best not to interrupt students to correct errors. Make notes of student errors for review with the class after the activity has finished.

❺ Have a pair of students read the conversation for the class. Then have students work in pairs to create conversations using the cues and the language in the model. Select pairs to present their conversations to the class.

Language Note: The expression *believe me* is used to make what we are saying stronger. It's a way of saying *I'm telling you my true feelings*.

 Option: You might want to do the activity without using all the cues. In that case, have students close their books and put only the cues from the first column (Vacation Plans) on the board. Then have them work in pairs to ad-lib the conversations. Select pairs to present their conversations to the class.

 Workbook: Practice 3

GRAMMAR

Omitting *If* in Conditional Sentences *(pages 137–138)*

Presentation

Have students read the introduction and the examples in the box. Review the structure with them, and point out that this usage is formal, especially when it uses *were*.

❶ Review the instructions and the example with the class. (You might want to point out that the directions say to *restate* the original sentence, but in the example, the new sentence speculates about the past based on information in the original sentence; it is conditional, but the original sentence is not. This is the case in some, but not all, of the items in the exercise.) After students have rewritten the sentences independently and compared their answers in small groups, review answers with the class. See the answer box below for further explanation.

Answers

a. Had Ellen booked her flight in advance, she wouldn't have had to pay a lot of money for a last-minute ticket.
b. Should you ever go on a boat tour of the Amazon, don't forget your mosquito repellent.
c. Had the avalanche been big, the whole expedition would have been swept away.
d. Had the wind been stronger, it might have overturned the raft.
e. Should you see an elephant, take pictures.
f. Had I known how to ski, I could have taken the same slopes as you.

 Workbook: Practice 4

Wish *(pages 138–139)*

Presentation

Have students read the introduction and the examples in the boxes. Review with the class. Point out that the main clause (containing the word *wish*) is in the present tense, and the wish clause (containing "what we wish for") is in various tenses depending on the time frame of "what we wish for"—a past condition, present condition, or future condition.

Note: You might want to also point out that *wish* in the main clause can be used in various tenses. For example:

> He **will wish** that car **got** better gas mileage. (I am predicting his wish about the present.)

> He **will wish** he **hadn't eaten** that. (I am predicting his wish about the past.)

In the example above, the tense in the main clause indicates when the wishing happens, and the tense in the wish clause indicates the time frame of "what he is wishing for" in relation to when the wishing happens. The exception to this is wishes about the future, which almost always take place from a present time frame.

In reviewing the examples involving ability, you might also want to point out that the expression *had been able to* can replace the expression *could have*. Advise students that in formal speech and in writing, the verb *be* becomes *were* (subjunctive) in all past tense *wish* clauses: (*I wish*) *I were, you were, he/she were, we were, they were.*

❷ Have students read the instructions and do the exercise independently. Then have them compare answers with a partner and discuss. Review answers with the class.

 *Workbook: Practices 5, 6*

If Only *(pages 139–140)*

Presentation

Have students read the introduction and the examples in the box. Point out that the expression *If only* is not a clause because it has no subject, but that it takes the place of the main clause *I wish*. Also point out that in casual speech it is sometimes used by itself as an exclamation, as in:

A: Someone told me you're going skiing in the Alps this winter.

B: **If only!** (I wish that were true, but it isn't.)

❸ Have students work independently. Then have them compare answers with a partner and discuss. Review answers with the class.

Answers

Some possible answers:

a. If only we had taken enough oxygen with us.

b. If only it hadn't been cold last night.

c. If only the assistant guide weren't so rude!

d. If only I weren't completely exhausted.

e. If only my legs weren't completely numb from the cold.

f. If only the cell phone would work.

g. If only the guides had brought a spare compass.

 Workbook: Practice 7

☑ ❹ **Check Your Understanding** There are two ways to do this exercise. One is to have the students use the cues to create three sentences of approximately equal meaning that could be used interchangeably in the situation. The other is to have them create three independent sentences with a logical flow, as in:

Had I known this trip would be so dangerous, I wouldn't have come.

I wish I had read the brochure more carefully.

If only I had bought travel insurance!

Choose a method and have students complete the sentences independently and then share answers with a partner. Have selected pairs share their sentences with the class.

Option: Extend the activity by having students work in pairs to prompt each other with a situation, to which the second partner must respond with an expression using *I wish, should,* or *if only.* Monitor the activity, and have selected pairs share their sentences with the class.

❺ Express Yourself Have students do the activity in groups of three or four. Have students take turns opening a topic with the appropriate expression, such as *I wish I had traveled more when I was younger.* After a discussion period, have them rotate and let the next student open a new topic. Monitor the discussions and have selected students present their "openers" to the class.

LISTENING and SPEAKING

Listen: Newsworthy
(*page 141*)

Presentation

❶ Before You Listen Have students read the questions and then discuss them in pairs or small groups. Have selected students share their answers with the class.

Culture Note: One such major event is the festival of San Fermín, which takes place in Pamplona, Spain, in the second week of July each year. During the festival, bulls are herded through the streets of the old section of the city, and tourists and local people run in front of them, risking their lives and proving their courage.

➡ **Identifying Tone** Have students read the strategy independently and then review it with the class. Point out that speakers often use tone to project an opinion or judgment on a neutral statement of facts.

❷ Have students read the instructions and look at the pictures. Then play the recording or read the audioscript for them to answer the questions. Review answers with the class.

Audioscript: The audioscript for Exercise 2 appears on pages T143–T144.

Answers
Announcer 1: Bottom right; Announcer 2: Bottom left; Announcer 3: Top left

❸ Have students read the instructions independently. Play the recording or read the audioscript again, and have students answer the questions. Then have them compare answers with a partner and briefly discuss. Review answers with the class.

Answers
a. 2   b. 1   c. 3

 Workbook: Practice 8

Pronunciation
(*pages 141–142*)

Preview

Say to the students, *Let's talk about thought groups.* Write it on the board. Then say it again, and put a slash between *about* and *thought.* Then ask them to work with a partner and briefly discuss what a thought group is.

Presentation

Have students read the introduction and review the examples in the box with them. Model the example sentences by reading them out loud. Have students work with a partner and practice saying the sentences with appropriate pauses and intonation.

4 Have students read the instructions and do the exercise independently. Tell them to divide thought groups with a vertical line. Then have them compare predictions with a partner and discuss.

5 Play the recording or read the audioscript and ask students to check for division into thought groups. Have them compare answers with a partner and discuss any differences. Then play the recording or read the audioscript once more for them to confirm their answers. Review answers with the class.

Audioscript: The audioscript for Exercise 5 appears on Student Book page 142.

Answers

A: Have you heard about *Kon-Tiki*?

B: No, what is that?

A: It's the name of a famous raft | built by Norwegian scientist Thor Heyerdahl | in the 1940s.

B: Why is it so famous?

A: Because Heyerdhal and his crew | sailed from Peru to Polynesia | on that raft.

B: Wow, that's about 5,000 miles! | Why did they do it?

A: The crew wanted to demonstrate | that people could have sailed | from South America to Polynesia | hundreds of years ago.

B: Well, | he sure made his point! | By the way, | who or what is Kon-Tiki?

A: Kon-Tiki is an ancient Sun god.

Culture Note: Thor Heyerdahl wrote a best-selling book about his trip, called *Kon-Tiki*. However, many archaeologists still don't accept his premise that the Polynesian islands were settled by seafarers from South America.

6 Have students practice reading the dialogue with a partner. Monitor their speech, listening for pauses and intonation. Select one or two pairs to read the dialogue aloud for the class.

 Workbook: Practice 9

Speak Out   (pages 142–143)

Preview

Write the expression *Good idea!* on the board, and point out that it is an informal expression of support. Ask students to think about what they say when they want to show support for someone's ideas in a more formal context.

Presentation

➡ **Providing Support** Have students read the introduction independently. Tell them that they will be looking for expressions of support in the next two exercises.

7 Have students read the instructions and do the exercise independently. Then have them compare answers with a partner and discuss. Review answers with the class.

Answers

Well, I find Bill's suggestion to be the best in terms of efficiency.

I'm for Bill's solution too.

---

8 Have students read the instructions and do the exercise independently. Then have them compare answers with a partner and discuss. Review answers with the class.

Answers

a, c, e, g, h, i

---

❾ Assign each pair one of the two positions on the issue, and have students brainstorm their supporting reasons and examples. Then put pairs with opposing positions together and have them discuss the issue. Suggest that while they should begin by supporting their partner to vote for the assigned position, they are allowed to change their mind at some point in the discussion, if they wish, and start supporting the other side. Ask each group to come to some sort of resolution, and have groups report their results to the class.

Note: This activity is designed to develop fluency. It is best not to interrupt students to correct errors. Make notes of student errors for review after the activity has finished.

 *Workbook: Practice 10*

READING and WRITING

Read About It
(pages 143–145)

Presentation

❶ **Before You Read** Have students read the questions independently and then discuss them with a partner. Elicit qualities of a successful explorer, and make a list on the board.

➡ **Recognizing Comparisons and Contrasts** Have students read the strategy independently and review it with the class. Point out that comparisons and contrasts may be implicit, requiring the reader to make inferences; the writer simply presents a set of facts and lets the reader make the judgment.

❷ Have students read the article. Ask them to make notes of comparisons and contrasts that they find (or infer) by marking them in the text or noting them on a separate sheet of paper by line number.

Culture Note: Another Japanese woman, Yasuko Namba, died on Everest in 1996 while trying to duplicate Junko Tabei's feat and become the second Japanese woman to

conquer the Seven Summits. The story of the disastrous Everest expedition of 1996 is told in Jon Krakauer's bestselling book *Into Thin Air*.

🌐 **Option:** If you feel your students need help with unfamiliar words before they do the task, you may wish to do the Vocabulary Check exercise on page 145 before the following exercise.

❸ Have students complete the chart independently. Remind them to use the notes they took as they read to help them. Then have them check answers with a partner and discuss. Review answers with the class.

Answers
1. The author compares the difficulty of the climb with making the preparations for the climb. E
2. The author compares Tabei's short height with the highest mountains. I
3. The author compares Tabei's raising of money by teaching piano lessons with the idea of receiving money from corporate sponsors. E

🌐 **Option:** Extend the activity by having pairs discuss any additional comparisons and contrasts that they found as they read the article.

☑ ❹ **Vocabulary Check** Have students read the instructions and do the exercise independently, and then compare answers with a partner. Review the answers with the class.

Answers
1. j   2. d   3. f   4. h   5. a   6. i   7. k
8. c   9. g   10. e

Think About It *(page 146)*

Presentation

❺ Have students read the instructions and do the exercise independently. Then have them compare answers with a partner and discuss. Have selected students share their answers with the class.

Write: Essay of Contrast
(page 146)

Preview

Write *block style* on the board and review it with students. Ask for a volunteer to sketch a diagram on the board.

Presentation

Point out that in block-style organization, each item being compared has its own paragraph. Remind students that each paragraph of a block-style essay of comparison deals with all the points of comparison for that item.

❻ Have students work with a partner to come up with three points of comparison between educational vacations and adventure vacations, and outline the essay, including a thesis statement. After students compare their outlines, have selected pairs put their outlines on the board.

➡ Have students read the strategy and look at the list of transition words and expressions in the box. Review the example sentences below the box, pointing out that in block-style essays, the transition expressions tend to occur more often in the second of the two body paragraphs, where the comparison is actually being made.

Write About It *(page 146)*

Presentation

❼ Have students choose a topic and write the essay, either in class or for homework.

☑ **❽ Check Your Writing** Remind students to consider the bulleted points when they analyze their partner's paper and to give written feedback. Also remind them to revise according to their partner's feedback.

 Workbook: Practice 11

Vocabulary Expansion: Geographical features: names and descriptions See page T128.

Answers
A.
1. e **2.** g **3.** f **4.** a **5.** d **6.** b **7.** c
B.
dense forests, rolling hills, fertile grasslands, snow-capped mountains, barren deserts
(*the last two phrases can be reversed*)

EVALUATION

See pages Txi–Txii.

Unit 11 Achievement Test

Self-Check See **You're In Charge!**, page 88 of the Workbook.

PORTFOLIO

Writing Revised essay of contrast from Write About It, Exercises 7 and 8, page 146.

Oral Communication

1. Work with a small group to discuss proposals for new types of adventure vacations. First, come up with your own proposal. Then meet with a group of two or three other students, present your proposal, and hear their proposals. Discuss all the proposals and try to select one that the whole group agrees on. Videotape your discussion or schedule it when your teacher can attend. (If you use videotape, each participant will need a copy for his/her portfolio.)

2. Record a monologue on the recent popularity of "extreme" adventure travel. Why do people want to risk their lives "in their spare time"? Do you think these activities should be more strictly regulated? Why or why not? Use specific examples.

Interactive Dictation

Dictate the following sentences to the students. Have them complete the even-numbered sentences in such a way as to comment on or expand on the information in the odd-numbered sentences. For more information on dictation, see page Txv.

1. I used to take my vacations close to home; I never went anywhere that you couldn't drive to in one day.

2. I wish . . .

3. Once I was offered the chance to spend a week on a sailing ship in the Caribbean.

4. Had I . . .

5. Several of my friends went trekking in the Himalayas last summer.

6. . . . I could have . . .

7. I guess I've missed a lot of opportunities for excitement.

8. If only . . .

9. Maybe it's not too late for me to start. I read that someday they're going to have "space resorts."

10. Should I . . .

A WAY WITH WORDS

OBJECTIVES

Students will be able to:
- Talk about translation and mistranslations
- Use reported speech
- Ask for and give interpretations
- Listen for implicit information and draw conclusions
- Change meaning with intonation
- Summarize and close a discussion
- Analyze style and language choice while reading
- Edit their own writing
- Use literary terms

GETTING STARTED

Warm Up (page 147)

Preview

- Put the phrase *English only!* on the board. Whether or not this is your actual classroom practice, ask students what they think of it. Ask them if there are classroom situations where they think translation is acceptable, and if so, what they are.

- Point out the unit title, *A Way with Words*, and ask if anyone can explain it to the class. Elicit something like *It means that someone is skillful with language.*

Presentation

Have students read the introduction independently.

❶ Ask students to discuss the questions with a partner, focusing on experiences outside of the classroom as well as in it, and refer to specific incidents. Have selected students share their experiences with the class.

❷ Have students work independently to answer the questions. Then have them compare answers with a partner and discuss. Have selected students share their answers with the class.

❸ Have students read the questions independently. Play the recording or read the audioscript twice, and have students answer the questions. Then have them compare answers with a partner and discuss. Have selected students share their answers with the class.

Audioscript: The audioscript for Exercise 3 appears on page T144.

> **Answers**
> The book is called *Translating Lies*. It is a discussion of the problems that translators always encounter.

 Workbook: Practice 1

Figure It Out (pages 148–149)

Preview

Put the expression *It loses something in the translation* on the board, and ask students what they think it means. Elicit the fact that translations are never completely faithful to the original.

Presentation

❹ Have students read the dialogue and then work with a partner to answer the following questions:

1. What did John F. Kennedy mean to say when he went to Berlin? (*I am a citizen of Berlin.*)

2. What did he actually say? (*I am a pastry.*)

3. What was the English meaning of the message on the souvenir t-shirts? (*I saw the potato.*)

4. What was it supposed to be? (*I saw the Pope.*)

5. What did people in Africa think when they saw the labels on the baby food jars? (*They thought the jars contained parts of real babies.*)

Culture Notes:

- In a speech in Berlin, John F. Kennedy said "Ich bin ein Berliner." ("I am a Berliner.") There is some controversy about what that sentence actually means. Some say that in German the indefinite article *ein* is not used for describing a person's place of origin: *Ich bin Berliner* would be the normal construction. According to this viewpoint, what Kennedy actually said was that he was a type of pastry called a *Berliner*. It seems that the construction is ambiguous in German, and not everyone agrees that Kennedy made an error.

- The T-shirts promoting the Pope's visit to the United States referred to *La Papa* rather than *El Papa*. Since the gender of the noun in Spanish is indicated by the definite article, this mistranslation points to the wrong meaning of *Papa*, referring to "the potato" rather than to the "Pope."

- A well-known American soft drink company used an inaccurate translation to advertise its products in Taiwan. The English slogan used the idiom *come alive*, meaning to become excited and invigorated; the translation referred to the dead coming back to life.

☑ ❺ **Vocabulary Check** Have students read the instructions and do the exercise independently. Then have them compare answers with a partner and discuss. Review answers with the class.

Answers

1. g   2. d   3. e   4. b   5. f   6. h   7. a

Workbook: Practice 2

Talk About It *(page 149)*

🌀 **Option:** If you feel that your students need extra help in using reported statements, you might want to postpone this activity until after the first grammar presentation (page 150).

Presentation

Note: This activity is designed to develop fluency. It is best not to interrupt students to correct errors. Make notes of student errors for review with the class after the activity has finished.

❻ Have students read the instructions and the model conversation independently. Have a pair of students read the conversation for the class. Then have students work in pairs to improvise conversations, using the cues and the language in the model. Select pairs to present their conversations to the class.

Culture Notes:

- *Mohandas K. Gandhi*, known for his advocacy of non-violence and civil disobedience, was one of the leaders of the movement for Indian independence from Britain in the 20th century.

- *François, duc de La Rochefoucauld*, was a French nobleman of the 17th century who was known for his moral sayings.

- *Confucius* was a Chinese philosopher of the 4th and 5th centuries B.C., whose work was the basis of the Chinese educational system for more than 2,000 years.

- *Miguel de Cervantes* was a Spanish writer of the late 16th to early 17th century. His best-known work is *Don Quixote*.

- *Socrates*, a Greek philosopher of the 5th century B.C., passed his thinking down through the writings of his student, Plato. He was executed as a danger to the state by the Athenian government.

- *Molière* (the pen name of Jean-Baptiste Poquelin) was a 17th century French playwright who is known for his social satires.

Workbook: Practice 3

GRAMMAR

Reported Statements (page 150)

Preview

Select two student volunteers. Write the question *What did she say?* on the board. Then say to the class *There will be a test next week.* Elicit the question, from one student to the other, and listen to the response. It should be something like *She said that there would be a test next week.*

Presentation

Have students read the introduction. Review the introduction and examples with them, pointing out that when the reporting verb is in the past tense, the verb or modal in the next clause shifts tense: from present to past, from past to past perfect, from *will* to *would*, from *can* to *could*, and so on.

❶ Review the instructions and the examples with the students. Point out that in some cases, the signs will not contain a verb, in which case they should use context to determine the appropriate verb when they report what the sign meant to say. Have selected pairs share their results with the class.

Answers

Some possible answers:

a. Teeth extracted by the latest methods
b. Specializes in women's diseases and other diseases
c. Women's fitting rooms are upstairs.
d. Children are not allowed in the bar.
e. Order your summer suit. Because in a big rush, it is first come, first serve.
f. Just for today, there's no ice cream.

 Option: Extend the activity by having students report the original meanings of the mistranslated signs, for example, "The sign in the Norwegian hotel said that women weren't allowed to give birth in the bar."

Workbook: Practice 4

Reporting Verbs (page 151)

Preview

Write the expressions *say something* and *tell me something* on the board and ask students the difference. Elicit the fact that the second one has an indirect object, *me*, and that *me* in this case represents the listener. Point out that, in some cases, we are interpreting the speaker's state of mind when we choose a reporting verb, but in many cases the appropriate reporting verb is determined by the context or by the manner of speaking. One *confesses* to having done something wrong, one *whispers* so as not to be heard too loudly, and so on.

Presentation

Have students read the introduction and the verbs in the boxes independently. Review the meanings of the verbs in the boxes, and give a few example sentences, such as:

*He **confessed** that he was the one who had stolen the car, but the police **informed him** that they had alredy arrested someone else.*

*Kerry **whispered** that she was ready to leave, but I **persuaded her** to stay just a little bit longer. At the party, Julio **announced** that he and Caroline were getting engaged, but we **informed him** that we already knew about it.*

❷ Have students read the instructions and do the exercise independently. Then have them compare answers with a partner and discuss. Review answers with the class.

Answers

Some possible answers:

She explained that she had been working on translating Chinese poetry into English last year. She informed me that she was also translating a book about the Ming Dynasty, which is due to appear in this country next year. She pointed out that this was not the first work she had translated from Chinese. She said that her translation of *The Chinese Diaries* sold here and in Asia last year. She complained that it didn't have as many sales as they had expected because it didn't get enough publicity. She explained to me that having knowledge about the culture behind the language is just as important as knowing the words of the language. She mentioned that the Chinese title of the film *The English Patient* was *Don't Ask Me Who I Am* because Chinese audiences weren't familiar with the book and would not have gone to a movie with the translated title *The Sick Englishman*.

Culture Note: The Ming Dynasty (1368–1644) was the period in Chinese history when the Han Chinese regained control of the country from the Mongol invaders who had ruled for almost 100 years.

 Workbook: Practice 5

Reporting Questions (pages 152–153)

Presentation

Point out that the rules for reporting questions are different from those for reporting statements. Have students read the introduction and the examples, and review both with them. Emphasize the word order in reported questions, as well as the use of *if* and *whether*. You may also want to point out that the verb *wonder* is sometimes used in indirect questions, which are reported like statements rather than questions: *I wonder if Jane has enough time to finish the job.* = *He said that he wondered if Jane had enough time to finish the job.*

❸ This exercise can be done in several different ways:

- Partners can work on each line together, discussing the structure as they write.
- Partners can do alternate lines and then compare their results when they have finished.
- Partners can work separately to rewrite all the lines and then compare results when they have finished.

Choose a method and have pairs do the exercise. Review answers with the class, having selected students put sentences on the board and eliciting corrections or alternatives from the class.

Answers

Some possible answers:

Student A asked what the difference was between a translator and an interpreter. Student B said the difference was that translators generally work on written text, and interpreters translate simultaneously what a speaker is saying, usually at a conference or business meeting.

Student A wondered what the typical rate for translation per 1,000 words was. Student B said it was hard to say because it depends on the languages involved, the subject matter, the complexity and length of the text, as well as the time available for translation.

Student A wanted to know how long it would take to get about fifty pages translated. Student B said that it depends on the subject matter and the complexity of the text, but that in general, a translator can produce about ten to twelve pages a day.

Student A asked what a "source text" and "target text" were. Student B said that a "source text" refers to the text in the original language requiring translation, and "target text" is the text after it has been translated into the second language.

Student A wanted to know if there were automated translation systems that work. Student B informed Student A that more and more translation software is appearing on the market. However, Student B doesn't think that it will ever take the place of an actual translator because there is just too much translation that depends on human judgment.

☑ ❹ **Check Your Understanding** Have students work in pairs. As each partner reports the joke, have the listener read along in the text. At the end, the listener should offer comments and alternatives. Have selected students share their answers with the class. Then write several possible answers on the board.

Answers

Some possible answers:

Joke 1: Two translators on a ship were talking. One translator asked the other translator if he could swim. He replied that he couldn't, but could shout for help in nine languages.

Joke 2: Two software developers were talking. One developer told the other developer that the phrase *out of sight, out of mind* had been translated by automatic translation software from English into Japanese and back into English again. The other developer asked what the final product was. The developer answered, "*The invisible idiot.*"

☯ **Option:** As an alternative method of doing the activity, assign one joke to each partner. The listener should close his or her book while the joke teller is "reporting" the joke. The listener should then try to write the speech of the character in the joke; the partner can then compare what the listener has written to the actual text of the joke. Review answers with the class.

🔲 ❺ **Express Yourself** Have students read the instructions and write in their answers independently. Then have them discuss their answers in groups of three or four, and take brief notes of the discussion. Finally, either have groups get together and report on the content of their discussion, or have each group report to the class.

 *Workbook: Practice 6*

LISTENING and SPEAKING

Listen: One World, One Language? (*page 154*)

Presentation

❶ **Before You Listen** Have students read the questions independently and then discuss them in groups of three or four. Then have groups report the results of the discussion to the class.

➡ **Drawing Conclusions** Have students read the strategy independently, and then review it with the class. Point out that if one is to take some sort of action based on the information or argument, one has to reach some sort of conclusion: making judgments, accepting or rejecting arguments, or selecting one particular aspect as worthy of further inquiry, are all forms of conclusions.

🎧 ❷ Have students close their books. Play the recording or read the audioscript, and have students take notes on key ideas. Have them compare answers with a partner and discuss. Then have them open their books and answer the true/false questions. Have them compare answers with a partner, and then play the recording or read the audioscript again for them to confirm their answers.

Audioscript: The audioscript for Exercise 2 appears on pages T144–T145.

Answers
a. T   b. F   c. F   d. T

---

❸ Have students read the instructions and the questions independently. Play the recording or read the audioscript again, and have them answer the questions. Then have them compare answers with a partner and discuss.

Answers

a. It has regular grammar, without all the many exceptions that frustrate learners of English. Every word is pronounced exactly as it is spelled. There are no "silent" letters or spelling exceptions. The vocabulary was chosen to be immediately recognizable to large groups of people around the world.

b. The vocabulary is immediately recognizable to large groups of people around the world. It is a completely neutral language with no political or economic ties that dictate its use for the convenience of whatever group is dominant. In terms of effort, it is much more equitable.

c. *Answers will vary.*

4 Have students read the instructions and do the exercise independently. Then have them compare answers with a partner and discuss.

 Workbook: Practice 7

Pronunciation *(page 155)*

Preview

Put the expression *That's exciting* on the board, and ask for a volunteer to read it. Most likely, the reading will be an "excited" one, with the intonation rising and falling over *exciting*. Then model an alternate reading, with the intonation rising and falling exaggeratedly over *That's* and rising slightly over *exciting*. Ask students what your tone is. Elicit things like *sarcastic, humorous, ironic*.

Presentation

Have students read the introduction and the example in the box. Model the sarcastic intonation, and point out that the speaker's meaning is directly the opposite of the literal meaning of the words: the speaker thinks that translating poetry must *not* pay very well.

5 Have students read the instructions and do the exercise independently. Then have them compare predictions with a partner.

6 Play the recording or read the audioscript once for students to check their predictions. Have them compare answers with a partner and discuss any differences. Then play the recording or read the audioscript once more for students to confirm their answers.

Audioscript: The audioscript for Exercise 6 appears on Student Book page 155.

Answers
kidding, way, no

7 Have students practice their pronunciation with a partner, focusing on intonation for excitement. Monitor their speech, and have selected students read the dialogue for the class.

 Workbook: Practice 8

Speak Out *(pages 155–156)*

Preview

Ask students if they've ever attended an "endless" meeting, one that stretched well past its scheduled time but still didn't accomplish its goals. If possible, have a few students share experiences of such meetings with the class.

Presentation

➡ **Closing a Discussion** Have students read the strategy. Review it with them, pointing out that while many discussion strategies (managing disputes, keeping a discussion moving) can be practiced by any participant, officially closing a discussion or meeting is usually left to the chairperson or discussion leader. Review the examples in the box, and have students practice saying them with a partner.

❽ Have students read the instructions. Review the distinctions among the three functions. Then have students do the exercise independently, compare answers with a partner, and discuss. Review answers with the class.

Answers
1. T   2. P   3. S   4. T   5. T   6. S   7. P
8. S

❾ Have students read the instructions independently and then work in groups of three to choose a topic and do the activity. Suggest that they choose several topics and take turns being discussion manager.

Note: This activity is designed to develop fluency. It is best not to interrupt students to correct errors. Make notes of student errors for review with the class after the activity has finished.

 Workbook: Practice 9

READING and WRITING

Read About It
(pages 156–158)

Presentation

❶ **Before You Read** Have students read the instructions and the questions independently and then discuss them with a partner. Have selected students share their responses with the class.

Have students read the introduction independently, and review it with the class. Point out the image of the window: it's often said that the best translation is "transparent" because it lets the reader see through to the original meaning. Ask students if they think that it's possible for language to be transparent and, if so, what makes one word or sentence structure more transparent than another.

➡ **Focusing on Language Choice and Style** Have students read the strategy. Remind them of the example from the dialogue in the Warm Up. *Viernes trece* means *Friday the 13th* in Spanish, but it doesn't have the sense of bad luck and evil in Latin culture that it does in Anglo culture. Point out that literal translation is often not the most "transparent" translation.

❷ Read the two translations of the Rilke poem out loud to the class, or ask for a student volunteer to read it while students follow along in their books.

Language Note: *Pupil*, as used here, is the hole in the eye through which light enters.

Culture Notes:

- *Rainer Maria Rilke* was a German poet of the late 19th and early 20th century whose work often depicts the contrast between spiritual and material aspects of existence.

- The *Jardin des Plantes* (Botanical Garden), in the Fifth Arondissement of Paris, contains a small zoo that dates back to the late 18th century.

☑ ❸ **Vocabulary Check** Have students read the instructions and do the exercise independently and then compare answers with a partner. Review the answers with the class.

Answers
Version 1:   1. h   2. f   3. b   4. e   5. d
6. i   7. c   8. a   9. g
Version 2:   1. b   2. d   3. a   4. f   5. c
6. e

❹ Have students do the activity with a partner. Have them make two lists, one for each poem, and discuss the questions. Then put pairs together into small groups, and have them discuss the poems. Finally, discuss the issues as a class.

Think About It *(page 158)*

Presentation

❺ Have students read the questions independently and then discuss them in groups of three or four. Have groups report on their discussions to the class.

Write: Self- and Peer Editing *(page 158)*

Preview

Write the expression *my own worst critic* on the board and ask if anyone knows who that is. Elicit the meaning that one is one's own worst critic. (The key word is *own*.)

Presentation

Have students read the introduction and point out that we often practice self-editing as students but that peer editing is less common. Point out the value of having an objective, non-judgmental person advise us on the creation of a piece of writing.

➡ Have students read the strategy. Review it with them, pointing out the various levels of editing, from global concerns of meaning to particular points of punctuation.

Emphasize the value of a series of questions (*a rubric*) as a means of being thorough and of maintaining objectivity. Have students read the questions in the box. Suggest that when they peer edit or self-edit, they sit down with a copy of these questions and answer every one, and then go back to every question with a *no* answer and rephrase it as a suggestion, for example, *Needs more variety of sentence structure: too many simple sentences, not enough compound or complex.*

Write About It *(page 158)*

Presentation

❻ Have students write the essay contrasting the two translations of Rilke, either in class or as homework. Suggest to them that they think about whether their thesis would be better supported using point-by-point or block organization.

☑ ❼ **Check Your Writing** Remind students to go through all the questions of the rubric when they analyze their partner's paper and to give written feedback. Also remind them to revise according to their partner's feedback.

Vocabulary Expansion: Literary and linguistic terms See page T129.

EVALUATION

See pages Txi–Txii.

Unit 12 Achievement Test

Self-Check See You're In Charge!, page 94 of the Workbook.

PORTFOLIO

Writing Revised essay of contrast from Write About It, Exercises 6 and 7, page 158

Oral Communication

1. Translate a short poem from another language into English. Then record yourself reading the original and the translation, and discussing your specific word choices, how literal they are, and why you made them.

2. Choose an interview from a magazine, newspaper, or book, or from radio or television, that was originally done in a language other than English. Select the highlights of the interview, and record a monologue in English, describing what questions were asked and what the responses were.

Interactive Dictation

Dictate the dialogue verbatim to the students. Then have them rewrite it in paragraph form, reporting what was said. Tell them to use a variety of reporting verbs, and not to use *said* more than twice. For more information on dictation, see page Txv.

Marta: When I was traveling in France, I had a lot of trouble being understood.

Louis: I don't know why—your French is so good! (*sarcastically*)

Marta: You're being sarcastic. I hate it when you're sarcastic.

Louis: Not at all. OK, maybe just a little. So, when did you go to France?

Marta: Right after high school. I had a lot of fun, in spite of the language barrier.

Louis: On my trip, I never had to worry about the language barrier.

Marta: Why is that? Because your French is so good? (*sarcastically*)

Louis: Who's being sarcastic now? No, it's because I speak the international language of love!

PROGRESS CHECK
Units 10–12

Progress Checks may be done as homework or may be used in class. As a class exercise, they may be done in several ways:

- as a quiz—students work alone and hand their papers in to you to be corrected

- as pairwork—students work alone and then compare answers with a partner

- as a class exercise—students work alone, and answers are reviewed with the class

GRAMMAR (pages 159–161)

➡ **Identifying Distracters** Have students read the strategy. Point out to students that if the correct answer to a multiple choice question isn't immediately obvious, they can begin by eliminating incorrect answers. This will improve their chances of selecting a correct answer.

A Have students read the instructions and do the exercise. For a review of the future perfect and the future progressive, refer students to Unit 10, page 126–128; for a review of *wish* expressions, conditionals without *if*, and *if only* expressions, refer students to Unit 11, pages 137–140; for a review of reported speech, refer students to Unit 12, pages 150–153.

Answers
1. C   2. C   3. D   4. C   5. B   6. C
7. B   8. B

➡ **Look for Time Expressions** Have students read the strategy. Point out that the grammar sections of tests often deal with tenses, and that time expressions are one of the clearest ways of identifying correct tense usage.

B Have students read the instructions and do the exercise. For a review of the future perfect and the future progressive, refer students to Unit 10, page 126–128; for a review of *wish* expressions,

conditionals without *if*, and *if only* expressions, refer students to Unit 11, pages 137–140; for a review of reported speech, refer students to Unit 12, pages 150–153.

Answers
1. B   2. B   3. B   4. A   5. C   6. B
7. C   8. D

VOCABULARY (pages 161–162)

➡ **Dealing with Unfamiliar Vocabulary** Have students read the strategy. Remind them that eliminating wrong answer choices and making an "educated guess" is a valuable technique. Point out that context and keywords in the question can help rule out certain answer choices.

Have students read the instructions and do the exercise.

Answers
1. C   2. B   3. B   4. B   5. D   6. A

WRITING (page 162)

➡ **Answering Essay Questions** Have students read the strategy. Remind them that organization and accuracy will be the major criteria by which the essay will be judged. Emphasize the importance of "playing it safe" in essay test situations.

Unit 1

FOOD FOR THOUGHT

Compound adjectives

There are several types of compound adjectives. Here are some examples:

- A *five-ounce cup* is a cup that can hold five ounces.
- A *mouthwatering treat* is one that makes your mouth water: it's delicious. An *–ing* ending means that the noun (*treat*) does something.
- *Full-flavored beans* are beans that are full of flavor. An *–ed* ending means that the noun (*beans*) is in a certain condition, or that something happens to the noun.

Note: Some compound adjectives, such as *mouthwatering*, are not hyphenated.

A. *Read the sentences below. On the line, write a phrase using the boldfaced* **noun** *from the sentence and a compound adjective using the words in parentheses.*

    Example: Those coffee **beans** have a rich aroma. (*full, flavor*) <u>full-flavored beans</u>

1. The sweet flavor comes from something that we put on the **ham** before we baked it. (*honey, glaze*) _____

2. The **dressing** that was on the salad was interesting; it was both sweet and sour. (*honey, mustard*) _____

3. Nowadays, designers are creating more fashions for **women** who are not slim. (*full, figure*) _____

4. That ice-cream parlor had such an **assortment** of flavors that I couldn't believe it! (*mind, boggle*) _____

5. I like the **chicken** that they serve in this restaurant; it's not as greasy as fried chicken. (*oven, roast*) _____

6. We had some wonderful **desserts**. We couldn't help making noises as we were eating them. (*lip, smack*) _____

B. *Match items from all three columns to make adjective + noun phrases. Use* *–ed or –ing forms as necessary. Then write a sentence using the phrase.*

Column 1	Column 2	Column 3
half	rhubarb	liquid
pie	eat	contest
dish	wash	pie
strawberry		apple

1. _____

2. _____

3. _____

4. _____

Unit 2

MEMORABLE MOMENTS

Idioms of emotion

The expression *to have butterflies in one's stomach* means to be nervous or afraid. It's easy to understand the image: it is the physical feeling we have when we experience the emotion of fear. There are many idioms that express emotional states. Some of them, like *butterflies*, refer to physical feelings; others are based on objects, colors, or other things that can represent our emotions.

A. *Look at the list of idioms below and put them in the appropriate columns in the chart.*

- to be down in the dumps
- to go ballistic
- to be all choked up
- to be on cloud nine
- one's heart is in one's throat
- to hit the ceiling
- to be walking on air
- to be petrified
- to have chills down one's spine
- to be blue
- to blow a fuse
- to be on top of the world

Fear	Sadness	Anger	Happiness

B. *Choose one idiom from each column and use it in a sentence.*

1. Fear: _____

_____

2. Sadness: _____

_____

3. Anger: _____

_____

4. Happiness: _____

_____

Unit 3

THE FUTURE OF FILM

High-tech idioms

Users of computers and of the Internet are adding a lot of new expressions to the English language. In most cases, these are expressions that didn't exist before but are based on pre-existing words and expressions, combined and used in new ways to describe things that didn't exist before.

Fill in the crossword puzzle below with words related to high technology and the Internet, or to the film industry.

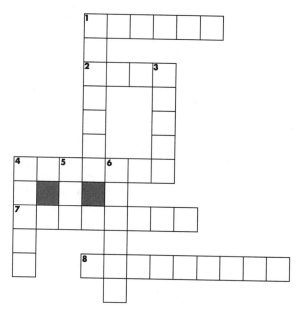

ACROSS

1. Needed for a webcast
2. Record a CD
4. _____ reality
7. Get from the Net
8. Two machines in one

DOWN

1. Like TV on the Net
3. Basis for many films
4. Not audio
5. Uncooked or unedited
6. Put on the Net

Unit 4

I BEG TO DIFFER

Idioms of confrontation

Unfortunately, conflict and confrontation are part of daily life. For this reason, there are many idioms that refer to confrontation. Fortunately, conflict resolution is also part of daily life, and there are idioms to deal with that, too.

A. *These idioms refer either to conflict or to conflict resolution. Check the appropriate box next to each idiom. Then match it with one of the meanings below.*

		Conflict	**Resolution**
_____ **1.**	to lose face	❑	❑
_____ **2.**	to smooth things over	❑	❑
_____ **3.**	to be at odds	❑	❑
_____ **4.**	to be called onto the carpet	❑	❑
_____ **5.**	to work things out	❑	❑
_____ **6.**	to lay down the law	❑	❑
_____ **7.**	to face off	❑	❑
_____ **8.**	to give someone the cold shoulder	❑	❑

a. to make a strong statement of your position

b. to be criticized by a superior

c. to engage in a one-on-one confrontation

d. to resolve problems or issues

e. to be embarassed in an encounter

f. to be in general disagreement

g. to ignore someone on purpose

h. to get rid of bad feelings

B. *Write a paragraph describing a conflict and a resolution. Use at least five of the expressions above.*

_____

_____

_____

_____

_____

_____

Unit 5

ODD JOBS

Job names and titles

Some job names describe exactly what the person does, such as *salesperson*, *mechanic*, etc., and are well known to the general public, while others refer to specialized jobs that not everyone knows. Titles identify rank in addition to area of speciality, such as *vice-president for project development* or *sales manager*.

Use one phrase from each column to create a sentence that describes the jobs. Some verbs from the middle column can be used more than once; some might not be used.

1. A network administrator	directs	people with disabilities.
2. A home health aide	organizes	a company's actions to the public.
3. A software engineer	reviews	accounting procedures.
4. A public relations manager	explains	celebrations.
5. A human resources assistant	works with	information systems.
6. A restaurant critic	prepares	people with health problems.
7. A loan underwriter	supervises	computer applications.
8. A wedding planner	advises	the food at restaurants.
9. A residential counselor	creates	the employees of a company.
10. A comptroller	designs	applications from people who want to borrow money.
	develops	

1. _____

2. _____

3. _____

4. _____

5. _____

6. _____

7. _____

8. _____

9. _____

10. _____

Unit 6

BEHOLDING BEAUTY

Describing physical characteristics

- In English there are many common adjective-noun phrases used to describe physical characteristics, such as: *She has a **heart-shaped face** and **silky skin**.*
- Body types are usually described only with an adjective: *He is **tall**.*
- Some body characteristics can also be described with a phrase: *She has a **slim figure**.*

A. *Write as many phrases as you can using adjectives from the left column and nouns from the right. Use the indefinite article (a, an) wherever necessary.*

	almond	hair
That person is . . .	shiny	shoulders
	smooth	skin
	thick	eyes
	stocky	legs
	sparkling	eyebrows
	bushy	figure
That person has . . .	sturdy	face
	high	cheekbones
	slender	forehead
	broad	ears
	oval	eyes
	high	hair
	pointy	
	short	

B. *Write a brief description of a person you know, using expressions from the box above.*

Unit 7

FEELING LEFT OUT

Expressions with *right* and *left*

Some common expressions in English use the direction words *right* and *left*, such as *my right-hand man* and *out in left field*. There are also some words that are derived from other languages, such as *sinister*, meaning *evil* or *unlucky*, from the Latin for *on the left side*. In general, expressions with *left* are negative, and expressions with *right* are positive.

A. *Match these expressions with their meanings. Then circle* [+] *for* positive, [-] *for* negative, *or* [N] *for* neutral.

_____ **1.** ambidextrous + - N   **a.** in a state of confusion

_____ **2.** adroit + - N   **b.** very reluctant to do something

_____ **3.** dexterity + - N   **c.** skill

_____ **4.** gauche + - N   **d.** rude; unsophisticated

_____ **5.** I'd rather give my right arm + - N   **e.** unaware; unconscious

_____ **6.** out in left field + - N   **f.** political conservative

_____ **7.** right-hand man + - N   **g.** person who is left-handed

_____ **8.** rightist + - N   **h.** "two right hands"—skilled

_____ **9.** leftist + - N   with both hands

_____ **10.** lefty + - N   **i.** skillful

_____ **11.** the right hand doesn't know what   **j.** political liberal
          the left hand is doing + - N   **k.** trusted assistant

B. *Write five sentences, using expressions from Exercise A.*

1. _____

   _____

2. _____

   _____

3. _____

   _____

4. _____

   _____

5. _____

   _____

Unit 8

YOU'RE NOT MY TYPE

Verb phrases that can function as nouns

Some phrasal verbs in English can be joined together and used as nouns:

> *Jennie and I **broke up** yesterday. I'm kind of sad,*
> *but I saw this **breakup** coming a long time ago.*

Some of these nouns are hyphenated, but most are only one word.
In general, the noun is one word, unless the spelling makes pronunciation confusing.

A. *Use one word from each column to complete the sentences with phrasal verbs. You may have to change tenses.*

1. I don't believe what you're saying; I think you're _____ me _____.	turn	
2. They were supposed to get married, but I heard that they are going to _____ _____.		down
3. I'm going to the doctor and have him _____ _____ on my heart and a few other things.	put	on
4. I had high hopes for that movie, but it really _____ me _____. I was so disappointed.	break	off
5. Jackie said she didn't like my type. She really _____ me _____.	check	over
6. Have you heard? Seven prisoners _____ _____ of the county jail yesterday!	let	out
7. In 1997, Great Britain _____ Hong Kong _____ to China.	put	up
	come	

B. *Write a sentence paraphrasing each of the sentences in A., using the phrasal verb in that sentence as a noun.*

Unit 9

TECH TRENDS

Computer terminology

The growth of computer technology has created the need for new words; we need names for things that never existed before. People naturally tend to use names for things that they are familiar with that are similar to the new objects. For example, automobiles were originally called *horseless carriages*.

Read the following definitions and choose computer terms from below to complete them.

virus	scanner	digital
software	chips	robot
processor	encryption	attachment

1. Older electronic devices contained circuit boards, which were flat pieces of stiff material covered with wiring. Computers contain miniature versions, made of silicon. They are like small wafers or slices of something. Instead of *boards*, they are called _____.

2. In the 1930s, scientists and science fiction writers were getting interested in the concept of humanlike machines that could do our work for us. A Czech writer named Karel Capek wrote a book about such machines, and he named them using a Czech word that means "forced labor." We still use that name today: _____.

3. A Greek word that means "secret" is the root for two words that we use in English. One means "burial place;" the other, which refers to encoding information to "keep it secret," is _____.

4. Computer code is based totally on numbers: alternating ones and zeroes; this is why anything that is controlled by a computer or uses information in the same way is called _____.

5. English already had a word for tools and machines; for computers, another word was needed for the information that a computer uses to do its tasks. That new word is _____.

6. There is a machine that can "look over" a picture and turn it into digital code to be used by a computer. The name of the machine is the same as the word for a person who "looks over" something: a _____.

7. Something that enters a computer's operating system and makes it function badly is named after something that enters our bodies and makes us sick: a _____.

8. In old-fashioned offices, business mail sometimes came with a picture or another document stapled or paper-clipped onto it. The same word is used for something that comes with an e-mail message: an _____.

9. A word that simply means "someone who does something" is also used for the central part of a computer that does all the work: a _____.

Unit 10

SPACE EXPLORATION

Expressions for prediction: word families

In English there are many "word families"—different parts of speech based on a common root. Let's look at some of the different forms of words that we use in discussing the future and making predictions.

Verb	Noun	Adjective	Adverb
predict	prediction	predicted predictable	predictably

Complete the chart using as many forms of the word as you can. (Some words may not exist in all forms.) Then use a dictionary to check your answers.

Verb	Noun	Adjective	Adverb
	challenge		
	development		
		eventual	
expect			
foresee			
imagine			
			potentially
	projection		
			ultimately
		viable	

Unit 11

ADVENTURE VACATIONS

Geographical features: names and descriptions

Some names of geographical features are well known, like *mountain*, *river*, and so on. Others, like *isthmus* and *strait*, are not as well known. Additionally, the names of geographical features often appear with adjectives as commonly-used noun phrases. It is helpful to be familiar with these when describing landscapes.

A. *Here are some place names that indicate the type of geographical features of the place. Using your knowledge of world geography (and an atlas, if necessary), match the specific examples on the left with the generic descriptions on the right.*

_____ **1.** the **Isthmus** of Panama
_____ **2.** the **crevasses** on the slopes of Mount Everest
_____ **3.** Bikini **Atoll**
_____ **4.** The Nile River **delta**
_____ **5.** the Great Barrier **Reef**
_____ **6.** the Philippine **Archipelago**
_____ **7.** Stavanger **Fjord**

a. area where a river flows into a larger body of water, usually very fertile
b. a group of islands
c. a narrow, steep-sided inlet of the sea
d. an underwater coral or rock formation
e. a narrow strip of land connecting to larger areas of land
f. a circular reef partly above water, creating an island and sheltered bay
g. a deep crack in the ice or earth

B. *Complete the sentences by choosing words from the box below to create adjective-noun combinations.*

Adjectives		Nouns	
snow-capped	dense	deserts	forests
fertile	rolling	grasslands	mountains
barren		hills	

Moving across the United States from east to west, we can see a great variety of terrain. The Eastern Seaboard, although now mostly developed, was once covered with _____ _____, which still remain in pockets. The Midwest is characterized by _____ _____, which gradually flatten out into the _____ _____ that supply wheat and other grains to the rest of the nation and much of the world. Then come the two great barriers: the _____ _____ and the _____ _____ that for so many years blocked easy passage to the West Coast.

A WAY WITH WORDS

Literary and linguistic terms

In discussing language and literature, we often find that there are opposing viewpoints and various ways of looking at an issue or a literary work. These common "opposites" are often expressed in pairs of adjectives or nouns:

a. **literal** vs. **interpretive** translation

b. **literal** vs. **figurative** language

c. **interpretation** vs. **translation** of language

d. **one interpretation** vs. **another interpretation** of literature

e. **style** vs. **substance** in language and literature

f. **broad meaning** vs. **nuance** in language and literature

g. **sound** vs. **sense** in language and literature

Match each description below with the set of viewpoints it represents from the list above.

_____ **1.** Someone who is very good at expressing written Japanese in written English might not be able to do the same thing with the spoken language.

_____ **2.** You can translate the movie title *Friday the 13ᵗʰ* into Spanish as *Viernes trece* (Friday the 13ᵗʰ), but to convey the same meaning that it does in English, you should really call it *Martes trece* (Tuesday the 13ᵗʰ).

_____ **3.** A translator of poetry may have to decide between a word that makes a good rhyme and one that is closest to the true meaning of the original.

_____ **4.** You think the main character of a new novel is motivated by her hatred for her father; your friend thinks she is motivated by her love of humanity.

_____ **5.** An ugly event can be described beautifully, or a good idea expressed awkwardly; there's a difference between *what* is said and *how* it is said.

_____ **6.** *I'm on fire* can mean that *I'm burning to death*, or *I'm in love.*

_____ **7.** She said *Thanks* instead of *Thank you* when I held the door for her. I wonder what that means?

Student Book Audioscript

UNIT 1: Food for Thought

Page 3, Exercise 3

Penny: Well, we've finally decided what videos to rent, so now it's time to get some comfort food. Who wants pizza?

Julia: Not me. I've already eaten pizza three times this week! If I eat anymore, I'm gonna look like Margherita herself! How about some doughnuts? I could kill for glaze.

Lisa: Doughnuts as a movie snack? No way! They're too sweet. Doughnuts are good in the morning with coffee, not at night, on the couch. I say we get some popcorn.

Penny: I could go for some popcorn. I just read in the *Times* today that popcorn has been around for some six thousand years.

Julia: Really? That must be some stale popcorn!!!!

Penny: Very funny, Julia! No really. Popcorn was grown in Mexico and in the American Southwest thousands of years ago.

Julia: How do they know that?

Penny: I can't remember now, but the article had a lot of interesting facts about food and why we eat what we eat.

Julia: Well, I eat according to my mood. If I want pizza for breakfast, I have it. And if I feel like nothing but fruit for a week, then bring on the fruit baskets.

Penny: You'd better start eating right, Julia, or you're gonna have problems when you get older. Have you ever heard about something called a balanced diet?

Julia: Look who's talking! You're the one who's suggesting pizza!

Lisa: Is it OK if we finish exchanging health tips next year sometime? Let's get the popcorn. Three cups' worth is only a hundred and twenty calories. And then if we get hungry, we can order pizza and doughnuts for dessert.

Penny: But make sure you get diet soda, OK? Regular soda is fattening!

Page 10, Exercise 2

Student 1: So, maestro, are we gonna learn about New York-style pizza today?

Maestro: Nothing good comes of starting in the middle! First, you have to savor the long and appetizing history of pizza—from when pizza began as a simple peasant dish to the time when it became famous and a favored dish of a queen.

Student 1: Well, let's begin with the birth of pizza, in Italy.

Maestro: So pizza comes from Italy?

Student 1: Maestro, don't joke with sacred things! Everyone knows Italy is the birthplace of pizza.

Maestro: I see. Well, don't tell the Greeks.

Student 1: The Greeks?

Maestro: Yes. Centuries ago, the Greeks came up with the idea of using flat round breads called *plakuntos* as plates. They baked them in ovens with simple ingredients like oil, garlic, onion, and herbs. Now, does that sound familiar?

Student 2: Well, yes and no! We use all those ingredients, but they didn't use tomato! So, to me, it's not pizza.

Maestro: Tomatoes weren't always used, you know. In fact, Italians didn't even know the tomato existed until the Spanish brought it back from Mexico and Peru in the sixteenth century. And even then, they didn't use it right away, because many people thought it was poisonous.

Student 2: You mean the Italians didn't discover the tomato? That's the weirdest thing I've ever heard.

Maestro: Well, it may seem strange now, but tomatoes didn't really become a pizza ingredient until the eighteenth century. That was about the same time people started using mozzarella cheese on pizzas. Mozzarella is another key ingredient. It used to be made only from the milk of the water buffalo. In fact, when you buy authentic mozzarella cheese it's called "buffalo mozzarella." Nowadays, there are all kinds of people making cheese from other types of milk, and they have the nerve to call it mozzarella! This is shameful!

Student 2: But you said that in the Campania region, people have always followed tradition. Right?

Maestro: Yes. And Naples is still the pizza capitol of the world. So, in my pizzeria, only the true buffalo mozzarella, the best tomatoes, and the freshest basil top my pizzas. Can anyone tell me what kind of pizza those ingredients are used in?

Student 1: Those are the ingredients of the classic Pizza Margherita, right?

Maestro: You've got it! The first Pizza Margherita was made to honor King Umberto the First and Queen Margherita when they came to visit Naples in eighteen-eighty-nine. The pizza looked very patriotic, like the Italian flag, because of its red tomatoes, white mozzarella, and green basil. It was named after the queen, who, naturally loved that pizza.

Student 2: Maestro, who made that pizza for the queen? Was it the chef at the royal court?

Maestro: Not at all. It was a simple baker, Raffaele Esposito of Naples. And the pizzeria where he made it is still turning out pizzas even today. OK, enough of history, let's move on. Who can tell me about the Associazione Verace Pizza Napoletana?

Student 1: I can. It's the professional association of the best pizza makers. And all its members agree to obey the association's guidelines and rules to maintain the quality of Neapolitan pizza.

Maestro: You've got it! That's right. For example, the only ingredients allowed in pizza dough are flour, yeast, salt, and water. And, they must be baked in a wood-burning oven on a volcanic stone surface. And remember, it's very important that the temperature be seven hundred fifty to eight hundred degrees Fahrenheit.

Student 1: Do you think that's how they do it in New York?

Maestro: Who knows, these days? But when Italians immigrated to America in the second half of the nineteenth century, pizza went with them—pizza made in the traditional way. Enough talk, now. Let's go to make some dough.

Student 2: Yeah, enough dough to roll in.

Maestro: Don't get smart. You make the pizza first, and the millions later.

UNIT 2: Memorable Moments

Page 15, Exercise 3

A: Hey, I've got a survey from *Time* magazine about the most significant events of the twentieth century. They asked people all over the country to vote. Wanna see how you do? You tell me what you think the top three events are, and I'll compare them to the survey. Deal?

B: You're on.

A: OK, what do you think was the number one significant event of the twentieth century?

B: Hmm . . . Hard to say. I guess maybe, the creation of the Internet?

A: Good guess. The Internet has had a big

impact, but, believe it or not, it's only number eight in the survey.

B: Only eighth place? Let's see . . . OK. Was it World War II?

A: Well, you're getting closer, but that's not quite number one. People voted World War II as the fourth most important event. I'll give you one. Number three was Gandhi's civil disobedience in nineteen-fifteen.

B: How interesting! I never would have thought of that. So, what're numbers one and two?

A: Well, the second most important event is the first—

B: Wait, let me guess. Is it the first landing on the moon?

A: You got it! And event number one was Elvis teaching teens to rock'n'roll.

B: No way! You gotta be kidding me. What could possibly make Elvis Presley so important to history?

A: I don't know. I'd guess it's probably not just about rock'n'roll, though. It's probably about how teens became the big consumers, and started to have a lot of influence on culture.

B: Yeah, but still, I'll bet you most of the people voting were American.

A: And women over fifty-five!

Page 21, Exercise 2

Andy: Listen, have you ever done something really stupid or dangerous just to impress someone?

Rob: What? You mean like bungee jumping? Sure.

Smita: Bungee jumping! It must have been so scary!

Rob: You better believe it! The only reason I didn't chicken out is because my girlfriend was there and I didn't want to look like a coward.

Andy: So, what was it like?

Rob: First, I had to sign a waiver form saying basically that it's all my responsibility if I die! That's when I got chills down my spine.

Smita: And what happened after you signed your life away?

Rob: Then they weighed me.

Andy: Weighed you? What for?

Rob: Yeah, I know. I thought it was kind of odd too. But it's for a good reason. 'Cause your weight determines how long the bungee cord will be. So you don't hit the ground.

Smita: Ouch! Sounds painful.

Rob: And very dangerous. Some people have actually died that way. But anyway . . . So, they weighed me and put all this gear on me, like ropes and straps.

Andy: Did you get nervous watching the people ahead of you jump?

Rob: Oh, yeah! And I got butterflies in my stomach with every one. Just looking down was pretty scary too. I'm not afraid of heights, but even for me looking straight down two hundred feet was pretty disheartening.

Smita: And you still jumped?

Rob: Yeah, in a moment of insanity. So, when my turn came, they put the cord around my legs, but—get this —they didn't tie it. They just wrapped the cord around my legs a few times and said, "OK, you're ready." I really thought I was going to die.

Andy: I'm not surprised!

Smita: How did it feel to be jumping off into thin air with just a rope around your ankles?

Rob: Well, I summoned all my courage and tiptoed to the edge of the platform. As I was stepping toward the edge, it seemed that the cord around my ankles was getting looser. And that was unbelievably scary, I'll tell you! Then I jumped and I plummeted straight toward the ground. I have to say, I thought I was a goner. But then, I felt the tug of the cord and I realized that the scariest part was over, and I was still alive! And there's really not much more to tell, except that I can brag about that jump for the rest of my life!

Smita: Sounds so terrifying! I don't think I could ever go bungee jumping.

Andy: Me neither!

Smita: Wanna hear about something scary I did?

Rob: Sure. We're all ears!

Smita: OK. It's when I went whitewater rafting.

Rob: Whitewater what?

Smita: Whitewater rafting. You know, it's when you go down a raging river in a rubber raft. They call it whitewater rafting because the water's all foamy from constantly smashing into rocks and there are lots of rapids and whirlpools in the river.

Andy: You know, I've always wanted to try that. What was it like?

Smita: Oh, it was fabulous! Just fabulous!

Although the first time is the worst because you don't know exactly what to expect. But if you've ever been hit in the face with a bucketful of freezing water, then you have a pretty good idea of what it's like.

Rob: Cool!

Smita: Yeah, well, it was the absolute thrill of my life!

Rob: And you weren't afraid of the rapids?

Smita: Well, yeah, I was pretty scared at first, but that's what made it exciting.

Rob: Were you alone on the raft?

Smita: No, there were six people per raft, plus the guide. Before we got into the raft we had to first put on wet suits and then we had to learn how to paddle in unison.

Rob: And then they just let you go down the river? Must have been hard for people without any rafting experience.

Smita: Yeah, it was pretty rough at the beginning, but we managed to get our act together pretty quickly, and started paddling as a team. It was really exhilarating to make it through rapids together and not turn over. Everybody had to pull together. It was literally sink or swim.

Andy: Did anybody fall out of the raft?

Smita: Yep, uh, I did. The river sucked the back of the raft down, and I went with it. I went down, came up, went down again, and then came back up. Finally, my buddies pulled me into the raft. It felt like the river had just chewed me up and then spat me out.

Rob: Did you think you might not make it?

Smita: Oh, of course! There have been quite a few casualties, you know, in whitewater rafting.

Rob: How did it feel when you finished?

Smita: Well . . . I was soaked, freezing, and absolutely exhausted. But at the same time, I was really happy and proud of myself. I felt on top of the world!

Rob: Sounds great! We should all go!

Andy: OK. But only as long as there's no bungee jumping afterwards!

UNIT 3: The Future of Film

Page 27, Exercise 2

A: Hey, I'm thinking about signing up for a film class next term. You guys are taking that class, right? How's it going?

B: It's great! Right now, we're analyzing *Citizen Kane.* You know, the American Film Institute says it's the best movie ever made.

A: Really? You know, I saw it years ago, and I don't remember it being anything special. Why's it supposed to be so good?

B: Well, to begin with, the story's really complex. All the events are like a puzzle with pieces that don't fit together until the final scene, so there's lots of suspense.

C: Also the direction's awesome. It's full of new ideas and the images are brilliantly put together. Plus the characters are really nicely blocked.

A: Wow! I guess I missed all of that when I saw it. I just focused on the acting. I did think the performers were really believable. I liked Mr. Bernstein, Kane's partner at the paper. I thought he was fantastic.

B: Absolutely! And the camerawork was incredible. All those long shots and tight close-ups and the use of light and shadow?

A: Wait, wait! Don't tell me too much now or there'll be no reason to take the class.

Page 32, Exercise 2

Sarah: Good evening everyone, and welcome to *Thoughts on the Future*. Tonight's topic is the future of cinema. Our guests for the round-table discussion are: film director Igor Batchvarov, film critic Valerie Mitchell, and noted professor of film history, Frank Weinstein. I'm Sarah Lee. Welcome to the show.

Igor: It's a pleasure to be here.

Valerie: Thank you for inviting us.

Frank: Thank you.

Sarah: Lately I've heard the term "digital revolution" a lot. What does digital revolution mean exactly? Frank?

Frank: Well, basically, it refers to digital technology that is being developed and, which I believe, will radically alter the way movies are made and distributed. In fact, the process is already well under way.

Sarah: I see. Could anybody give us an example? Yes, Igor?

Igor: Take the camera, for example. It used to be big, cumbersome, and very complicated. As technology advanced, it became lighter and easier to operate. The new digital cameras are tiny and relatively easy to use. The technical side of filmmaking has become a lot less challenging.

Sarah: So, you might say that technology has advanced so much that even technophobes like me will be able to use it, right?

Igor: Right. And this means that practically anybody who can buy a digital camera can make a movie. Getting the right equipment will no longer be an obstacle for the new talents out there.

Frank: Exactly. It will no longer stand in the way of the creative process!

Sarah: Yes, but what about cost? These new digital cameras might be easy to use, but aren't they still expensive?

Igor: Well yes, they are not cheap, but they are far more affordable than professional cameras of the past. As I see it, if the cost of cameras keeps on dropping, almost everybody will be able to afford one.

Sarah: So, you're saying you believe that filmmaking is going to be a lot less expensive than it used to be. And how is that going to influence the industry?

Frank: Well, for one thing, I think that it will remove the economic limitations on cinema. Right now, you need a lot of money, as well as talent, to make a good film. As I see it, in the future, talent alone will be enough.

Sarah: So as movie production becomes cheaper, a whole lot more movies are going to be produced. Don't you think that will saturate the market?

Valerie: Not at all. The fact that most people can afford to buy a pen doesn't make them world-class writers, does it? The same fact goes for filmmaking: even when everybody is able to afford a camera, not everybody will be producing award-winning movies.

Igor: I agree completely. There will always be an audience for quality films. Talent will prevail.

Sarah: OK. So, let me make sure I understand. You're saying you believe filmmaking will become cheaper and easier to use. This will make it possible for many more talented filmmakers to express themselves, so more quality films will be produced. Am I getting this right?

Igor: Precisely.

Sarah: OK, going back to our topic . . . Are there any other important changes that the digital revolution is going to bring about in the movie industry?

Frank: Yes, definitely. In my opinion, one of the most important changes is that it will free cinema from political censorship. You probably know that there are still several countries where movies have to pass an ideological screening before they can be distributed.

Sarah: Yes, I am aware of that. But how will digital technology help with this situation?

Frank: The magic words are: *the Internet*.

Sarah: I think I'm going to need more help here. Can you explain further?

Frank: Let me try again. The new cameras record images on disks or computers, right? So, a movie will be a computer file and it will be very easy to upload it to the Internet, where anybody can watch it. And if you ask me, there's no way governments will be able to control that!

Igor: That's right. Frank has a point there. The digital era will bring more freedom of expression and perhaps even end censorship. And I must say I think that's wonderful.

Valerie: Well, I'm definitely against political censorship. But you have to admit that not having *any* kind of censorship could let anybody—including children—watch anything. And that could get out of control. Just think of all the violent images that are already on the Internet!

Sarah: Maybe so, but if governments censor what can or can't be published, where does this leave the freedom of speech? It's a very thorny issue, right? But I guess we'll have to leave that for our next session. Let's take a short commercial break now.

UNIT 4: I Beg To Differ

Page 43, Exercise 3

A.

Mother: Look, I've told you a thousand times. If you stay out so late with your friends, you're not going out at all.

Daughter: But Mom, eleven o'clock isn't all that late. Not on a Saturday night.

Mother: It's late in *my* book.

Daughter: But all my friends can stay out till one.

Mother: I don't care about your friends. They're not *my* children. As long as you live in this house, you follow my rules. When I was your age, I had to be in bed by ten.

Daughter: That was so long ago they probably didn't even have clocks back then.

Mother: What did you say?

Daughter: Nothing!

B.

A: Excuse me, but that was *my* parking space. I had my turn signal on.

B: What do you mean *your* parking space? I'm already parked there.

A: I was just about to back up in there, you know. And then you showed up out of the blue, and without even a blinker just pulled in.

B: Sorry, pal. You snooze, you lose!

C.

A: Hey, Bob, can I talk to you for a second? I'm sorry, but this is the third time this week I've seen you surfing the Web. And I don't recall that being one of your duties in the office.

B: But I was just checking the weather! It takes two seconds! It's not as if I was on the Web for hours or something.

A: That may be so, but if I see you check the weather during office time again, you may find there's a storm at work!

Page 50, Exercise 2

Lecturer: Hello, everybody. Today we're going to discuss conflict resolution. More specifically, I'd like to focus on conflict resolution strategies. In other words, these are the ways in which we handle conflict. But first, let me start with a question. Would you say that you've had a conflict with someone in the last month or so? (*students murmer in agreement*) So, tell me, what's the first thing that comes to your mind when you think of an interpersonal conflict?

Alberto: A battle, a fight?

Stella: I think of a communication breakdown.

Alberto: Suppressed anger, high blood pressure!

Lecturer: Interesting. I'd say these are all pretty negative reactions. I'd like to propose, however, that conflict does not have to be all negative. There are both negative and positive dimensions to interpersonal conflict. I believe that conflict serves important purposes in relationships. Can you think of any positive aspects of conflict?

Alberto: Yeah, I suppose conflict leads you to find new ways of looking at things. And that's always positive.

Lecturer: Absolutely. So, in a way, there's no progress without conflict.
Before I move on to conflict resolution strategies, let me reinforce once again the point that conflict is inevitable. It can be positive or negative, constructive or destructive, depending on what we make of it, but our fights and differences are part of life, and it is a mistake to avoid conflict.
OK. Now, let's move on to conflict styles and strategies. Let's see. Ask yourselves, when you are in a conflict, do you withdraw? Do you stop talking? Storm out of the room? Give the other person the cold

shoulder? All of these behaviors are ways of avoiding conflict and withdrawing from it.

Stella: Sorry to interrupt, but can you give us an example of this?

Lecturer: Sure. Imagine that you have a conflict with a roommate over, hmm, let's say, not doing your part of the housework. If your roommate confronts you about this, and you say, "Look, I don't want to talk about it," then you're withdrawing from the conflict.

Stella: Thanks.

Lecturer: I'd like to emphasize that withdrawing or avoiding a conflict can cause it to grow out of proportion. Now, the next strategy is "accommodating." Basically, accommodating is preferring to smooth things over and refusing to acknowledge the fact that a conflict exists. Sometimes accommodating is the sensible option. Can anyone think of an example?

Stella: Is it when there's a slight disagreement and bringing it up would put too much unnecessary pressure on the relationship? Like when my husband talks more to the dog than to me.

Lecturer: Yeah, right, something like that. Or when you may choose to not bring up a certain topic, and you choose tact over brutal honesty. Such as when your best friend asks you if you like her new haircut! Suppressing a serious conflict, however, means that you don't want to talk about it. OK. The next conflict style is called "competing." Does anyone want to guess what this style involves?

Stella: Is it when you set out to prove that the other person's wrong?

Lecturer: That's it, Stella. This is a so-called "win/lose" approach, and it's often a power struggle in which one person comes out on top. Generally, this is not a good solution to the problem because one person gains at the other's expense. And the loser's not going to be happy about that!

Alberto: But what about cases when someone in authority has to lay down the law for everyone's sake? For example, a teacher keeping order in a classroom.

Lecturer: That's an excellent point. In some situations, a competitive style may be useful. OK. Let's move on to the fourth strategy, which is "compromising." In other words, adopting a middle-of-the-road approach. This can be the fairest approach to take, as dividing things equally is often accepted as the fairest thing to do because everyone shares what's available.

Stella: So, are you saying that compromising is also the best conflict resolution style to take?

Lecturer: Well, what do the others think?

Alberto: I think it can be good, but sometimes when you compromise you feel that you gave in more than the other person, and that's *not* good. I remember when Andrew and I were working on an assignment for our economics class and we both had to compromise about what topics we should cover. We finished the assignment, but we didn't feel happy with it because we didn't really like all the topics.

Lecturer: That's an excellent example, Alberto. Keep in mind that often whichever conflict style works best depends on the situation. Compromise is usually better than conflict, but there are cases when it isn't the best solution. So, to summarize, avoidance, accommodation, competition, and compromise are four of the most common conflict management styles. But there is one more strategy to add to your collection— the collaboration approach, or also called the "win/win" approach. People usually believe that if there's a winner, there's a loser. This is true in sports, but it is not always true in life. In many circumstances, everyone involved can win something. The advantages of collaborating are that people develop mutually satisfying solutions.

Stella: But how do you make win/win work in real life?

Lecturer: It's hard, I admit. But imagine this situation: You are in the kitchen with two people and they both want the last orange. What would you do?

Stella: Cut it in half.

Alberto: Toss a coin.

Lecturer: All of these are possible, but the win/win approach requires that you find out more about the situation first and explore options before you come up with a final solution. So, imagine that you decided to ask the two people why they want the orange, and one said, "Because I'm thirsty." The other said, "Because I want to make a cake." What would you do then?

Stella: A-ha! I would give one person the orange juice and the other the rind.

Lecturer: Precisely.

Alberto: But what if both people are thirsty and want the juice? What would you do then?

Lecturer: Well, what do you think? What are some possibilities?

Alberto: I guess they could share the juice, but that would be a compromise.

Stella: What about if they add sugar and water? Or buy more oranges? Or drink something else as well?

Lecturer: Exactly! In a win/win situation, you can think of new solutions if you treat the other person as a partner and not as an opponent. The point is that you look together for win/win situations and acknowledge each other's needs.

Stella: Well, class ended five minutes ago. If we all leave now, we can have a win-win situation!

UNIT 5: Odd Jobs

Page 55, Exercise 2
Conversation 1

A: So, you just play videogames all day, every day?

B: Well, not exactly all day. I also have reviews to write. But I do play whatever game I'm writing about for about an hour or so every day.

A: And you get *paid* for that?!

B: Yeah!

A: Do you ever get tired of videogames?

B: No, I love games. Playing them, writing about them, learning about new ones. The whole deal.

A: You've got to be the luckiest guy on the planet! Does your company need any more videogame reviewers? I'd love to send my resumé. I've got years of experience playing videogames!

Conversation 2

A: Hey, what do you say we go get some punch?

B: Great idea! How do you like the punch bowl?

A: It's exquisite.

B: It's made of ice, you know. I made it!

A: You're kidding me! From ice?

B: Yeah, I'm an ice sculptor. That's what I do for a living.

A: You know, you're the first ice sculptor I've ever met.

B: Yeah, I hear that a lot!

A: Is it real ice that's actually used? What about when it melts?

B: That's part of the uniqueness of the sculpture. It's not permanent. It melts before your eyes.

A: But doesn't it bother you when the sculpture melts?

B: No, not at all. I think of it as an added challenge, and not a problem.

A: How interesting. So, let's go get that punch before the punch bowl melts!

Conversation 3

A: I must say, you have the most unusual job I've ever heard of.

B: Maybe it's unusual for you, but in Tokyo, subway pushers are a common sight.

A: Yeah, I guess you need subway pushers because Tokyo's subways are so packed. Riding the train in the morning must be quite a challenge.

B: It is! We have to cram three hundred people into cars built for one hundred.

A: Don't you feel awkward, though? I mean, the Japanese are so respectful of personal space, and here you are, pushing them into subway cars.

B: It's strange, but we Japanese are very tolerant of the situation. People just accept it because Tokyo has so many people. And subway pushers do wear white gloves, when we push.

A: Well, I guess the white gloves make all the difference!

Page 60, Exercise 2

Ronald: Hello, everybody and welcome to *Offbeat Jobs*. Today on our show we have Mark Warren, who is a storm chaser. Mark, welcome.

Mark: Thank you.

Ronald: Is it true that you are the world's only full-time professional storm chaser?

Mark: Absolutely. At least the only one I know of. Most people who chase storms do so as a hobby or for research reasons. I do it full time, for a living.

Ronald: Year 'round?

Mark: Yes. In the spring I chase tornadoes, in the summer I go after lightning storms in the desert. And during the late summer and early fall I follow hurricanes. And if there's a nice blizzard out there in winter, I'll go after that, too.

Ronald: Let me get back to your comment that a lot of people chasing storms do it as a hobby. So, are there different types of storm chasers?

Mark: There are, actually. I'd say there are about four basic categories of storm chasers: First, you have the scientists, who chase storms as part of their research; then there are the so-called recreational chasers who photograph or videotape severe weather for their records.

Ronald: So, in a way, that's their hobby?

Mark: Right.

Ronald: What a hobby! And which are the other groups of storm chasers?

Mark: You also have the spotters. Their job is to observe and report threatening weather. These guys are often the unsung heroes of storm chasing. They often risk their life when they perform their valuable services. There are also "yahoos" or thrill seekers. They only chase storms for the thrill of it. And I'm sorry to say that they often do it in an irresponsible manner. Often they just compete with each other to see who can get the most extreme video but, in the process, place themselves and others in danger.

Ronald: So, you have a whole range of storm chasers.

Mark: Yes.

Ronald: What do you think the effect of the movie *Twister* was on storm chasers? The movie is about people chasing tornadoes, right?

Mark: Right. Well, so much excitement was generated by it that there were yahoos all over the place, trying to chase tornadoes. And that's really dangerous.

Ronald: Do you have any stories of storm chasing to share with us?

Mark: Oh, there are lots. Let me see . . . My experiences with tornadoes are the most interesting and dangerous. Hurricanes are difficult, but at least you can predict when and where they are going to hit. Tornadoes, on the other hand, are moody. Chasing tornadoes requires not just to be at the exact place, but also to do a lot of thinking and planning. If you mess up, you are not only going to miss the picture but also might end up in big-time trouble.

Ronald: Any specific tornado stories?

Mark: There was that time when I was driving like mad down a highway in Kansas, trying to outrun a tornado roaring behind me. It sailed over my car and sucked stacks of papers out of it in no time. During my getaway, I passed scraps of farm equipment and pieces of houses that the tornado had ripped up and dumped on the road. I did a U-turn at seventy-five miles an hour and managed to get away from the twister. Now, *that* was scary!

Ronald: I bet! It's obvious, Mark, that you really love your job. And you're also very successful. Major newspapers and magazines have published your photographs. But let's look at the other side of things. What is the price of success?

Mark: Very good question. The price of success? I think it's the danger I have to face every time I'm chasing a tornado or a hurricane or a storm. Many of the decisions in my line of work are often life-and-death.

Ronald: And yet, you are a storm chaser.

Mark: It's really thrilling to be out there, chasing a tornado. To feel the adrenaline. To be so close to one of the most powerful forces in nature. I guess it's a bit like going up Mount Everest.

Ronald: Do you have any future dreams connected to storm chasing?

Mark: Oh, absolutely! For me, one of the secrets of life is to always have one goal that you haven't attained yet.

Ronald: And what's yours?

Mark: I have yet to get the perfect tornado shot!

Ronald: It sounds very exciting. I have to say, though, I'm glad *my* job only takes me to this radio studio and not into a tornado! Mark, this is all we have time for. Thank you very much. And the best of luck!

Mark: Thank you.

UNIT 6: Beholding Beauty

Page 67, Exercise 3

Grandson: Wow! Grandpa, look at the model in this ad! She's really hot!

Grandpa: Hmm . . . I suppose she would be quite attractive if she gained about thirty pounds.

Grandson: What do you mean?! She's perfect. Look at that nice, slim figure, those long, slender legs . . .

Grandpa: Well, she may be considered beautiful by today's standards, but forty years ago people would have thought she was too skinny to be attractive.

Grandson: You're kidding! Really?

Grandpa: Yes, when I was young, the ideal woman had to have a little more meat on her bones. A small waist was all right, but in those days, the preference was for a healthy-looking woman. You know, like Marilyn Monroe. Think about it—if Marilyn

Monroe were alive today, she would be considered overweight.

Grandson: Yeah, I see what you mean. You know, I read something about that in some magazine . . . you know, like how different cultures can have really different ideas of what's beautiful. I guess the same's true for different generations, huh?

Grandpa: Absolutely! So tell me, what else did that magazine say?

Grandson: Well, it said that in some countries people prefer to have bodies that would be considered overweight in Western cultures. Oh, yeah, and get this—it also talked about how a long time ago women in Japan used to dye their teeth black because they didn't like white teeth back then.

Grandpa: Now that's one I'd never heard.

Grandson: Oh, yeah, and then there are people in West Africa, I forgot the name of the tribe, but the *men*, not the women, put on makeup, and then they dance and make faces to get the women to notice them. It's a kind of beauty contest, and the women choose the best-looking men for their husbands. But if you want, I'll find that magazine for you.

Grandpa: Thanks, I'd like that. Maybe I could get a few pointers on how to make myself a little more attractive to the ladies.

Grandson: But I think you'll need a lot more than make-up, Grandpa.

Page 73, Exercise 2

Professor: Good morning, class. Today we are going to examine the concept of symmetry, specifically the relationship between symmetry and attractiveness. Just to be sure we all have the idea, let's start by defining symmetry. Yes . . . Allen?

Allen: Uh, I think symmetry is . . . well, you know, when both sides of something match, like, if you draw a line down the middle or fold it in half.

Professor: Well, yes. You could say that symmetry is being the same, or almost the same, on both sides. It goes beyond that, however. There are different types of symmetry. For example, there's bilateral symmetry and there's radial symmetry.

Now the type of symmetry you described, Allen, is what's known as bilateral symmetry. In bilateral symmetry, a flat object is divided into two mirror images. Now, in radial symmetry, an object with more than one dimension divides an object into two mirror images.

Allen: Excuse me, could you repeat what you said about the second type of symmetry?

Professor: Of course. The second type is called radial symmetry. That is an object with many surfaces divided into two mirror images.

Francine: Sorry, I still don't get it. Could you give us an example?

Professor: OK. For instance, imagine a big ball and you want to cut it in half. You could begin cutting anywhere to cut it in half as long as you make only one cut. You'll divide it into two mirror images. That's radial symmetry.

Francine: OK, got it. Thanks.

Professor: Now, if we look around us, we see that symmetry of one type or another is everywhere. Think of nature. What comes to mind as examples of symmetry?

Allen: Well, snowflakes. And sunflowers, and starfish, and . . .

Francine: And crystals, right?

Professor: Why, yes. The atoms in a crystal are arranged in a regular repetitive pattern. Good example, Francine. But I'm really thinking of a more obvious example. If you think about it for a second, it will come to you.

Francine: Do you mean . . . humans?

Professor: Right you are. Most people have two eyes, two ears, two arms, two legs, and so on. Now the interesting thing about this is that studies show humans and animals both prefer symmetrical members of their species. Why is that?

Allen: Maybe for reasons of survival? An animal with four legs runs away from an attacker faster and better than one with three legs.

Professor: Well, that's certainly true . . .

Francine: What about symmetry as a sign of health? The first thing parents want to know about their newborn baby is if it has all its little fingers and toes, and that everything looks OK.

Professor: Right. And babies care about symmetry, just as their parents do. Babies prefer to look at faces. Of course, babies need to recognize their caregivers to survive, but they specifically prefer looking at symmetrical faces over asymmetrical ones. And what goes for babies goes for college men and women, too. In studies, adults have rated symmetrical faces and bodies as much more attractive than those that are not symmetrical.

Allen: But surely, uh, personality and other things entered into it.

Professor: Actually, the people in the studies never met, and so personality was not a factor. The same is true of animals, too. For example, female scorpion flies prefer mates with symmetrical, same-sized wings. And bees prefer symmetrical flowers over asymmetrical ones, if the flowers have nectar.

Francine: Could we get back to humans for a minute? Are you saying that we're biologically programmed to be attracted to symmetry?

Professor: Well, yes, that's one way of putting it. Symmetry appears to be a sign of health and fertility, and so we are attracted to it. And, of course, if we are attracted to something, we find it desirable, and therefore, if I may say so, beautiful.

UNIT 7: Feeling Left Out

Page 83, Exercise 3

Jenny: Kate! I'm so glad I ran into you! I sent you a card, but I want to thank you again in person for your gift. I can't believe you found a pair of scissors especially for left-handers!

Kate: My pleasure. I know how much you've wanted some.

Jenny: You wouldn't believe how much easier my life is!

Kate: Does it really make that much of a difference?

Jenny: Oh, Kate, believe me, it does. You can't imagine how being left-handed complicates things!

Kate: Well, I know many left-handers have a tough time in school.

Jenny: I certainly did when I was little. For one thing, all the school desks were the kind that had arms on the right side. It was awkward and uncomfortable to do schoolwork. And my teachers were forever trying to make me use my right hand! It drove me crazy.

Kate: Gee. At least that's over with.

Jenny: Yeah. But nobody thinks of left-handers. My kitchen utensils are all designed for right-handers, and so is all of the office equipment. And try managing to find a station on your car radio while you're driving! Do they always have to be located on the right side? No wonder some people think left-handers are naturally accident-prone and generally clumsy! It's so unfair!

Kate: I know. But you're proof it's not true, so relax!

Page 89, Exercise 2

Professor: Break's over, class. When you settle down, we're going to look at the relationship between handedness, the brain, and writing.

Now, we discussed earlier that many left-handers remember learning to write as one of their biggest difficulties. For example, left-handers put more physical effort into writing. Because they're working from left to right, they have to push, rather than pull, the pen or pencil. These awkward hand postures can cause them to tire sooner and write less neatly. Yes, David?

David: I'd like to comment on that. I'm left-handed myself, and I think the main reason left-handed people have so much trouble learning to write neatly is really the fault of the schools.

Professor: What do you mean by that?

David: Well, there are the desks, for one thing! Look around this classroom. There's only one left-armed desk in this room, and there are three of us here who are left-handed. Shouldn't the school provide equipment *all* their students can use? When I was in elementary school, there was never a desk for left-handers! It was incredibly hard to write. My arm and hand used to cramp after fifteen minutes, or so.

Professor: Well, that's what I was getting at . . .

Marie Louise: But most *teachers* are right-handed, and they don't have a *clue* how to teach a left-handed child to write! Even today!

Professor: Good point. Well, new research is providing some interesting information on the relationship between the brain and handedness. As you know, we've been aware for some time now that the two sides of our brain control different parts of our bodies. The *left* side of the brain usually controls language—things like speaking, reading, and writing. This left side also usually controls the movements of the right side of the body. The right side of the brain controls the movements of the *left* side of the body.

Marie Louise: So, professor, does that mean the brains of left-handed people are the exact opposite of right-handed people?

Professor: Well, actually, most left-handers' brains are not just mirror images of right-handers'. Their brain organization is different, yes, but about 60 percent of left-handers have their language centers in the left hemisphere, the same as right-handers. Only about 40 percent seem to have control centers for language in the right hemisphere.

David: So what does that mean?

Professor: Basically, it means that the brain functions of left-handers are distributed more evenly between both sides of the brain—that is more than right-handers.

Marie Louise: I think I've read that it's the same for women—that they are more likely to have their language skills located on the right side of their brain or even on both sides. So as a left-handed woman . . .

David: You're all over the place!

Professor: Well, that's a topic for another day! Let's look at writing and hand position for a minute. Left-handers who write in the upside-down position known as "the hook" are the 60 percent with their language centers in the left hemisphere, just like right-handers. The other 40 percent, those who write in a mirror image of right-handers, generally have their language centers in the right hemisphere of the brain.

David: So now we know!

Professor: Don't jump to conclusions, David. Research rarely comes neatly wrapped like a present! Other research shows that even some *right-handers* write in the hook position. So, we can only conclude that whoever writes in the hook position does not have the usual left-right hand and brain relationship.

UNIT 8: You're Not My Type

Page 95, Exercise 2

Mari: I just met our new neighbor.

Phillip: Oh, really? I met him yesterday. He seems like a great guy.

Mari: You think so? He seemed awfully quiet and kind of up-tight to me. I got the impression he didn't really want to talk to me.

Phillip: No kidding? That's not the impression I got. He seemed really outgoing. He came right up to me and introduced himself. He seemed to be really interested in the neighborhood. He wanted to talk about restaurants, find out about shopping, the area, and all that.

Mari: Hmm. Well, he might be interested in the neighborhood, but I couldn't get him

to say anything about himself. Maybe he's just shy.

Phillip: Shy? He didn't strike me that way. Actually, he told me quite a lot about himself and his family. We must have talked for at least an hour. He's a lawyer with two kids. His wife's from Costa Rica and she's there with the kids now. In fact, I think they're coming back today.

Mari: Really! Are we talking about the same man—tall, with brown hair . . . ?

Phillip: . . . and a mustache, right? Richard. Yep. That's the same guy.

Mari: I wonder why he was so cold to me.

Phillip: I don't know. Maybe you remind him of someone he doesn't like. Wait a minute. Did you say you just met him?

Mari: Yes. Why?

Phillip: What was he doing?

Mari: Well, he was just getting into his car.

Phillip: That explains it. He told me he was picking up his wife and kids from the airport at three this afternoon. Look, it's two thirty now. He must have been running late and didn't have time to talk.

Mari: Now that you mention it, he did act rushed. I take back what I said about him.

Page 101, Exercise 2

Jeanne: Hey, Mark, did you know that some people believe your personality is affected by your birth order position in your family?

Mark: What? What are you talking about?

Charles: Birth order. You know, people who are the first child in a family tend to have certain personality characteristics, and people born last tend to have certain other characteristics.

Jeanne: That's right, Charles. It says here in this book, for example, that first children have a strong sense of duty. They can also be very demanding.

Mark: Boy, that's my oldest brother, all right! He expects me to do whatever he says! And it seems like he always disapproves of me when I don't!

Jeanne: It also says here that first children are very responsible because their parents expect them to take care of the younger children.

Mark: You know, that must be why he calls every week or so. He's checking up on me! That's really interesting.

Charles: Now find out about yourself, Jeanne.

Jeanne: OK—I'm the youngest of three.

Mark: I'm the youngest too—of five. What does it say about us?

Jeanne: Let's see. Well, Mark, we're described as social, and a lot of fun and easygoing.

Mark: Wow. That does sound like you—but I'm a lot quieter.

Jeanne: I guess it does sound like me. I love meeting new people and trying out new things. Whoops! It also says here we may not be very responsible.

Mark: Oh, that's certainly not true for me!

Jeanne: That's right. That's why you're always the one who takes out the garbage, washes the dishes, cleans up after everyone else . . .

Charles: I'm a middle child. Here—let me look it up.

Jeanne: OK, Charles.

Charles: Let's see. It says I know how to get along with all kinds of people. I'm diplomatic.

Mark: Does that description fit you?

Charles: Well, I do act as a negotiator between my older and younger brothers. It also says here that middle children can be competitive—you know, trying to catch up with the older child.

Jeanne: So, do you believe in all this?

Mark: Well, I have always felt that I had to do better than my big brother. I guess it does seem accurate. What do you think?

Charles: I believe parts of it.

Mark: Which parts?

Charles: The ones where it says what a great person I am, of course!

UNIT 9: Tech Trends

Page 107, Exercise 3

A: I was just thinking about a profile on Bill Gates' house I saw on *Dateline* Friday. Did you see it?

B: They did a whole story on his house?

A: Yeah. He has a smart house.

B: Smart?

A: You, know, totally computerized. You wouldn't believe all the things it does.

B: Like what, for instance?

A: Well, for starters, instead of a just a TV, he has an underground theater where he watches DVDs. It's state-of-the-art of course. And there's a sound system that lets you listen to music anywhere in the house. It follows you all over the house, even right into the pool.

B: Cool!

A: Yeah. And then he's got all these great things he can use by remote control. For example, he can actually turn on his bathtub from his car, fill it up to just the right level, and it'll be ready and waiting for him when he pulls into the garage. The front gate and the garage door are supposed to sense when his car is driving up and open automatically. He has two garages: one that holds four cars, and another one underground that holds six. But the remote will only work for his car or his wife's. That's part of the security system.

B: I bet he's got some complicated security system to protect all this, right?

A: You bet! Not only does he have security cameras everywhere in the house, but he even has a pressure-sensitive floor that tracks where people are at all times.

B: Oh, man! I wouldn't like that. Can you imagine security cameras watching you all the time, and having your movements monitored in your own home?

A: I don't think I'd like it too much either—but for that remote control bathtub, I'd put up with a lot.

Page 112, Exercise 2

Matt: Hey, cool. Sylvia, Daisy, get a load of these. They're "smart toys." You know, the kind that has computer chips and interactivity and stuff.

Sylvia: Oh, yeah, the kind that flashes lights, buzzes and beeps, asks stupid questions, and runs all over the house! They're so annoying!

Daisy: Well, I don't think so. Especially the latest ones—you know, pets.

Sylvia: Computerized pets? You've got to be kidding, right?

Matt: No, they really exist. Come on. I wanna get one for my nephew's birthday.

Daisy: Well, let's take a look at them and we'll help you decide.

Matt: So what do you think of this one?

Sylvia: What *is* that thing?

Matt: It's called the "Muy Loco." It's a robotic chameleon!

Daisy: Oh yeah? I've never seen a silver and green chameleon with a pink tongue before!

Sylvia: What is that little silver thing on its side?

Matt: Let's see. The box says it's a little fly that the chameleon can catch on its tongue!

Daisy: Is that what it does? Eat a fly?

Matt: No! Look, it talks, sings a few songs, and dances the rumba and tango, too! And the price is right: it's twenty-nine ninety-five.

Sylvia: Well that's okay for you, but what makes it a *pet*? It's not cuddly or soft or anything! I don't think Bobby would stay interested very long. Unless he's interested in learning to dance, what does it *teach* him? Think about it Matt, he's only going to be five years old. I don't really think it's age-appropriate.

Daisy: That's a good point, Sylvia. A good toy encourages intellectual, social, and emotional development. And tech pets are also supposed to teach responsibility and caring.

Matt: What about this one then—I-Cybie Puppy.

Sylvia: Look, Daisy! It does look like a puppy!

Matt: Listen. It sounds like a puppy too!

Daisy: That is the cutest thing I've ever seen. And, look! It wags its tail and shakes its ears when I pet it!

Matt: Put it down on the ground. It just starts walking around like a live puppy would do! And it comes up to you to get attention when it feels like it!

Sylvia: Here, let me try something. Oh my gosh!

Daisy: You pulled its tail! Wow! It reacts just like a live dog would. That's brilliant!

Matt: Why?

Daisy: Don't you see? It will teach Bobby that it needs to be treated properly, not violently! And that way, Bobby will understand his responsibility in caring for a pet.

Matt: Well, it looks like I should get Cybie, then. And look—it's on sale for 40 percent off. It's only . . . a hundred and fifty dollars???!!! That can't be right. For that price I could buy him a real puppy. In fact, I think I will.

Sylvia: Talk to your sister first, though, OK? If you get Bobby a puppy without her permission, *you'll* be the one in the doghouse.

UNIT 10: Space Exploration

Page 123, Exercise 2

News broadcaster: . . . And finally tonight, we have a short report on David Tate, the first tourist to Mars. Mr. Tate, a California multimillionaire, tonight is on the space shuttle *Quest* on his way to the International Space Station. His goal is to spend a week at the Space Station, which circles Mars two hundred twenty miles above its atmosphere. Although several non-astronauts have journeyed into space over the years, never before has someone paid out of his own pocket for a ticket. The cost for this most exotic of getaways is forty million U.S. dollars and six months of grueling training at a space camp, alongside the astronauts. When asked what motivated this trip, Mr. Tate responded that for him it's the ultimate of all adventures. He also added that he looks forward to just sitting by a window and taking pictures of Mars. And, of course, he is very excited about experiencing weightlessness. Bon voyage to Mr. Tate. By tomorrow, Mr. Tate will have already arrived at the International Space Station. He has promised us a live interview! This is Andrew Mitchell for *Eyewitness News*. Good night.

Page 129, Exercise 2

Professor: Good morning, class. Throughout man's existence people have speculated about the sky. In the early nineteen hundreds, an American astronomer named Percival Lowell noticed that the planets Uranus and Neptune did not follow the orbits they were supposed to. He thought that a large undiscovered planet, the so-called Planet X, might be responsible for these inconsistencies. And he was right—at least he was right there was an undiscovered planet. In nineteen-thirty, one of Lowell's followers, Clyde Tombaugh, discovered Pluto. However, Pluto does not have the size or mass to be Planet X, and so it doesn't explain these discrepancies in planetary orbits.

Pat: Are scientists still looking for Planet X today?

Professor: They certainly are. For instance, the English scientist John Murray thinks he is very close to finding the missing planet. He describes it as a giant dark object about three trillion miles from the sun. He believes it is ten times larger than Jupiter, and a thousand times more distant than Pluto. He says he will be concentrating on parts of the Oort cloud to find it as he photographs the sky through giant telescopes.

Ken: If it's that big, why hasn't someone seen it yet?

Professor: It's not that easy, Ken. If Planet X is in fact in the Oort cloud, it is buried in an enormous group of comets at the very end of our solar system. It's so far away that Murray thinks Planet X will have completed only one orbit around the sun in five million years!

Ken: Wow.

Professor: But Planet X may not in fact *be* where Murray thinks it is or even *what* he thinks it is. There's another group of scientists that envision Planet X differently, Whitmire and Matese among them. Whitmire and Matese think Planet X is probably a brown dwarf, a smaller star that never had the mass needed to shine. They describe it as very dark, cold, and about two trillion miles from the sun.

Pat: That sounds pretty much like Murray's description.

Professor: Yes, in some key ways. But there is one big difference. Whitmire and Matese place Planet X in a completely different part of the sky! They say it is somewhere within what they call a "great circle" that cuts across the sky at a right angle to the band of the Milky Way galaxy.

Ken: So who is right?

Professor: There's no telling. Whitmire and Matese accept no evidence for Murray's theory, and Murray supports no evidence for their theory! And there are still other scientists, who doubt both theories. And, anyway, the kind of telescope needed to find a giant planet or other body that distant is still on the drawing board, so we won't know anything for a while longer. But who knows? Maybe by the time you're my age, someone will have proven the existence and location of Planet X!

UNIT 11: Adventure Vacations

Page 135, Exercise 2

Steve: Let's hope the food comes soon. Say, Paula, where'd you get that great necklace?

Paula: In the Philippines, believe it or not.

Steve: The Philippines? What were you doing there?

Paula: Uh, I was on an adventure vacation.

Steve: No kidding! That's one thing I would never expect you to do!

Paula: I know. It was a scuba diving trip, actually, but . . .

Steve: Scuba diving? That's great. Boy, I wish I could do that.

Paula: See, I was at this travel fair, and there was this diving company that was having a contest, and you had to guess how many

pearls there were in this jar. The person who guessed the closest number won, and well, I won. The prize was a diving trip to the Philippines.

Steve: No way! You *won* the whole trip? Wow. That's fantastic! I wish I were that lucky!

Paula: You wouldn't have felt lucky if you had been me. See, there's a small problem. I don't know how to dive!

Steve: You've got to be kidding!

Paula: No, I'm not. I don't swim very well, and what's more, I don't even like the water much. But I had always hoped I could see the Philippines one day, and so I went.

Steve: So, was it all you expected it to be?

Paula: We were there for just ten days. I wish I could have stayed longer, but I had no choice in the matter. We stayed on three islands: Luzon, Cebu, and Bohol. We traveled around by bus, small plane, and boats called banqua, sort of like canoes.

Steve: That's so cool. So did you go diving in all the places you visited?

Paula: Let's say the *other* twelve people went diving! I *wish* you could describe what I was trying to do as diving!

Steve: What went wrong?

Paula: Oh, a lot. You know, you have to wear a lot of heavy equipment, and you have to practice in shallow water before you try the deeper water. But the waves were really high, and they kept knocking me down, and I couldn't get back up!

Steve: How terrible.

Paula: It was scary. I kept hoping someone would help me, but no one even noticed I was having trouble. I *did* finally get out in the deep water, but it got worse, not better. There were all these little biting fish you couldn't even see!

Steve: That's really too bad. So you had a horrible time, huh?

Paula: Not after I got out of the water! I spent the rest of my time relaxing on the beach and eating the incredibly delicious food! It was fabulous!

Steve: Speaking of food, I wish ours would come. I'm starving!

Page 141, Exercise 2
Commentary 1

Announcer 1: What an incredibly close finish this will be! If only you could see this, folks! The two remaining teams in this whitewater rafting competition are true professionals! I never expected to see the kind of raw courage they have exhibited! The water has been presenting even more of a challenge than usual after the recent rains. Not to mention the icy wind blowing as we speak. Oh, Team One almost had a nasty spill trying to get around that big rock on the left side. Team Two forges ahead! Victory! Ladies and gentlemen, this year's whitewater rafting winner is Team Two!

Commentary 2

Announcer 2: We're standing in front of St. Joseph's Hospital waiting for Mayor Sabatini to appear to congratulate the five adventure vacationers who were rescued from Harrod's Cave early this morning. They were exploring the northern end of the cave when the cave partially collapsed, leaving them trapped for six days with few provisions and little air. I'm sure, during that time, they wished they had chosen to stay home like the rest of us!

Well, Mayor Sabatini has just arrived. Let's follow her into the hospital to see what words she has for the survivors.

Commentary 3

Announcer 3: Thanks for that update, Ed. Well, listeners, I'm still here at the site of our local cross-country ski event. I wish I could bring you some good news, but I can't. For the second day in a row, I have to report that the event will not take place as planned because of unfavorable weather conditions. Let's hope we have better luck tomorrow.

UNIT 12: A Way with Words

Page 147, Exercise 3

Host: . . . And we're back. In case you just joined us here on *Book Talk*, we're talking to Bret Robinson, author of *Double Standard*, *At the Top of the Tower of Babel*, and *Translating Lies*. Now Bret, back to your new book, *Translating Lies*. Why did you choose precisely that title?

Bret: It really pinpoints the heart of the matter. The book is a discussion of the problems that translators always encounter. The fact is that no translation, no matter how good, can truly convey every nuance of the original text and still be faithful to it.

Host: What do you mean by that exactly?

Bret: OK, well, let's start with one of the decisions any translator has to make. Take, for example, something as simple as a movie title. One of the most popular horror movies in English is entitled *Friday the*

Thirteenth. Now, imagine you're going to translate that into Spanish.

Host: Hey, I studied Spanish at one time. Wouldn't that translate as viernes trece?

Bret: Right—and wrong. That is the literal translation of Friday the thirteenth, but to many Spanish speakers, that wouldn't have the same meaning. You see, in English-speaking countries, Friday the thirteenth is the traditional day of bad luck, but in many Spanish-speaking countries, to indicate the same sense of danger or bad luck, you would have to say "martes trece," *Tuesday* the thirteenth.

Host: I see. So, the translator would have to decide between using the Spanish word for Friday, viernes, and another word that carries the same meaning of bad luck in Spanish.

Bret: Right. And, as you can see, if the translator chooses Friday, the feeling of danger or bad luck is lost in Spanish. But if he chooses to use Tuesday, then he isn't being true to the literal, original English word—Tuesday just isn't Friday.

Host: So it's a kind of "lie" either way!

Bret: Indeed it is. Now, let's look at an example with English and Japanese.

Host: Bret, we'll do that after another commercial break, if you don't mind. Don't go anywhere, listeners. We'll be right back.

Page 154, Exercise 2

Moderator: And with the introductions of our distinguished panelists done, we're ready to begin our discussion. Dr. Barnes, if you don't mind, we'll start with you.

Barnes: Thank you. Before beginning, I'd just like to say that while much of what we will be discussing is true for any number of constructed languages, I will be using Esperanto as my example, as it is currently the most widely spoken artificial language.

Moderator: Perhaps a brief overview is in order.

Barnes: I was just getting to that. Esperanto is an artificial language created by Dr. Zamenhof of Poland in eighteen-eighty-seven to be used for international communication. When he published his work, he used the name, "Dr. Esperanto," which means "one who hopes." This then became the name of the language, and it's known as Esperanto to the approximately *two* million people who speak it and to the rest of the world as well.

Grant: Dr. Barnes, if I may interrupt, isn't the figure of two million speakers questioned? Dr. Faike said there were perhaps only a hundred thousand regular speakers of Esperanto.

Barnes: You're quite right, for pointing that out, Dr. Grant. We don't know *exactly* how many people speak Esperanto. However, I believe the two million figure cited by Dr. Culbert and this research contains the most accurate information available.

Moderator: Thank you. Please continue. I was wondering if you could comment on the belief that Esperanto should replace English as a global language.

Barnes: Of course. First, let me say that English is not really the global language that many people think it is. About 11 percent of the world's population spoke English in nineteen-fifty, only about eight and a half to nine percent speak it today. But, I want to stress that Esperanto was not developed to take the place of any language, including English. It is supposed to be a second language, a supplemental language that people use when they are from different cultures and do not know each other's first languages.

Moderator: But don't you think that's why people use English?

Barnes: It's different. Currently, English is used because of the current political and economic impact of English-speaking countries. But we should remember that *all* the countries that have held power throughout history have seen their languages take over for a time. It's a cyclical process, and right now English just happens to dominate.

Moderator: Yes, Dr. Hochman?

Hochman: I was just thinking about how unfair this is. Imagine two people, one say, from Korea, and one from England. Why does the Korean have to make all the effort to learn English? English, as everyone knows, can be a very hard language to learn. Now this poor Korean has had to make an enormous effort, while the person from England has made no effort at all, except to perhaps correct the Korean's mistakes!

Barnes: But that's exactly why Esperanto is ideal! It is a completely neutral language. In fact, if more people used Esperanto, it would help protect the existence of endangered, minority languages. These languages would stand a better chance of surviving in a world dominated by the language of the current power. And in terms of effort, which you mentioned, Dr. Hochman, it is much more equitable. Both your Korean speaker and your English speaker would have to make the same amount of effort to learn Esperanto. And Esperanto is relatively simple, unlike English, so they would meet on neutral ground.

Moderator: Dr. Barnes, you said that Esperanto was easier to learn than English. In what way?

Barnes: Well, in several ways. First, Esperanto has regular grammar, without all the many exceptions that frustrate learners of English. Second, in Esperanto, every word is pronounced exactly as it is spelled. Again, this is not the case with English. And, finally, the vocabulary was chosen to be immediately recognizable to large groups of people around the world. Around 75 percent of Esperanto vocabulary comes from Romance languages, mostly French and Spanish. Less than a fourth comes from German and English, and even less from Russian, Polish, and Greek.

Hochman: Interesting. Are there any well-known people or large groups committed to using Esperanto?

Barnes: A number of Nobel Prize winners speak Esperanto, including the nineteen-ninety-four Economics prize winner, Dr. Reinhard Selten. And, Esperanto is very popular in Hungary, Estonia, Finland, Vietnam, Japan, and China, among other places. In fact, China was the host of the nineteen-eighty-six Esperanto Congress, which was the most attended international conference in five thousand years of Chinese history!

Moderator: Indeed. Dr. Barnes, you'll have more time later, but it is now time for us to hear from Dr. LaPorte, who is going to discuss one of Esperanto's rivals, as it were, the language Interlingua.

Workbook Audioscript

UNIT 1: Food for Thought

Page 6, Practice 8

Host: That's a great story, Myra. And now, let's talk a little about today's topic, pasta.

Myra: One of my favorite things, as you know.

Host: All the world loves pasta, including me. Do we actually know where pasta was first made? Is it a very old food?

Myra: Good questions. It isn't clear, really, where pasta originated because it popped up in different parts of the world.

Host: Oh, so even though the word "pasta" is Italian, it didn't originate in Italy?

Myra: Pasta has roots among the Arab, Chinese, Roman, and Etruscan civilizations.

Host: Etruscans? Who were they?

Myra: The Etruscans were a very early Italian civilization—they dated back to the eighth century B.C. The oldest known evidence of pasta was found in an Etruscan tomb near Rome, dating from pre-Roman times.

Host: What kind of evidence did they find?

Myra: There are murals of pasta-making tools on the walls of this tomb.

Host: Wow. That's some ancient pasta!

Myra: There was ancient pasta in China too. The use of it there goes back to five thousand B.C. And pasta was carried on Arab ships during the Islamic expansion of eleven-fifty A.D.

Host: How did people eat this pasta? With a fork and knife?

Myra: No, my dear. Pasta was eaten with the hands.

Host: That gets kind of messy, doesn't it? Tomato sauce up to your elbows, I would imagine.

Myra: Well, tomatoes didn't reach Europe until the Spanish explorer Cortez brought them from Mexico. And it was a lot longer before someone got the bright idea to make spaghetti sauce with tomatoes.

Host: No fork. No tomato sauce. Well, just how did people like to eat their pasta?

Myra: Before the eighteenth century, people liked to eat their pasta cooked with milk or broth, and mixed with sugar, butter, and sweet spices!

Host: Fascinating. I never knew all these things about pasta. I'm so glad you came to talk with us, Myra.

Myra: So am I. I like to think of pasta as a simple food with a complicated history.

Host: Stay tuned. After this commercial break, Myra's going to share some delicious recipes. We'll be right back.

UNIT 2: Memorable Moments

Page 13, Practice 8

Bill: Thanks for joining us today, Huff, on *Memorable Moments in Sports History,* as we celebrate Jackie Robinson's birthday. It's today isn't it?

Huff: Yes, that's right, Bill. Jack Roosevelt Robinson was born on this date, January thirty-first nineteen-nineteen in Cairo, Georgia. I sure wish he were still around today. He was quite a character and a courageous man, too.

Bill: Well, not everyone is a sports nut like you and me, so could you tell us a little bit about him?

Huff: Sure, Bill. Jackie was my idol when I was growing up. He was a baseball player in the nineteen-forties and fifties. I'm kinda giving away my age here, folks, but if you grew up in that era, you know that baseball was racially segregated until Jackie Robinson came along.

Bill: What do you mean segregated?

Huff: Obviously, you're too young to remember those days, but during those times, there was absolute racial segregation in baseball. There were black baseball teams and white teams, and they played in different leagues.

Bill: Well, how did Jackie Robinson get into baseball? Did he start out as a kid?

Huff: No, he didn't. While Jackie was attending the University of California, he starred in four college sports. He played track and field, football, basketball, and baseball with outstanding results.

Bill: So then he went into professional baseball after college?

Huff: No, actually he went into the army after college. That was in nineteen forty-two. When he got out of the army, he joined a Negro League baseball team known as the Kansas City Monarchs, in Kansas City, Missouri. Team owners started taking notice of Jackie. The next year, he joined the minor league team in Montreal, Canada, that was affiliated with the Brooklyn

Dodgers. It was an all-white team until Jackie came along.

Bill: So that was a historic moment.

Huff: I suppose it was, but the really courageous and memorable moment came on April fifteenth when Jackie Robinson joined the Brooklyn Dodgers as the first black player in the major leagues. Then the world took notice.

Bill: Was he easily accepted?

Huff: Are you kidding? Jackie suffered in silence as he received insults, death threats, and other kinds of abuse. He had to hold his anger inside and not speak out because he had promised his manager he wouldn't.

Bill: And how was he as a player for the Brooklyn Dodgers?

Huff: Great! He was Rookie of the Year in nineteen-forty-seven and Most Valuable Player in nineteen-forty-nine. He also led the National League in stolen bases.

Bill: Did Jackie enjoy a long career in baseball?

Huff: Long enough. He played ten seasons with the Dodgers and retired in nineteen-fifty-six. They voted him into the Baseball Hall of Fame in nineteen-sixty-two.

Bill: That's awesome. Well, even if I wasn't around during Jackie's baseball days, I do remember when he died in nineteen-seventy-two.

Huff: Yeah, he was only fifty-three years old, but he left quite an impact on the sport of baseball and he won't be forgotten.

UNIT 3: The Future of Film

Page 20, Practice 6

Conversation 1

A: Good morning. Motion Picture Studios, may I help you?

B: Yes, can you tell me what time you open?

A: We open at nine Monday through Saturday and at noon on Sunday.

B: OK, and what time do you close?

A: We're open until six every evening, except on Sundays, when we stay open until eight.

B: OK. Thank you very much.

Conversation 2

A: Good evening. Movie House Restaurant.

B: Hi, yeah. I'd like to make a reservation for a table tomorrow night.

A: Sure. For how many people?

B: Six.

A: Would you like a table near the screen or farther back?

B: Farther back, if you have one.

A: Which show do you want it for, sir?

B: The second show at eight o'clock.

A: And your name is?

B: Spacey.

A: OK, Mr. Spacey, we'll see you tomorrow at eight. Bye.

B: Thanks. Bye.

Conversation 3

A: Good morning. This is The Electronics Outlet. Can I help you?

B: Yes, could you tell me if you sell multi-system video players that are able to show European as well as American videos?

A: Yes, ma'am we do.

B: And do you also sell TVs that are compatible with these video players?

A: You tell us the combination you want and we'll fix you up, ma'am.

B: Good. I'll try to get down there tonight. You're open until nine, aren't you?

A: That's right.

B: Thanks. Bye.

Conversation 4

A: Hello. Could I speak to the manager please?

B: Could I ask what it's about?

A: Yes. I have a complaint. Your outdoor movie last night wasn't over until very late. I want to speak to the manager about that.

B: I'm really sorry that it bothered you, sir.

A: I thought your movies were always over by ten.

B: They're usually over by ten, but not last night. And tonight our movie's going to last until twelve.

A: So, it's going to be just the same tonight?

B: That's right, sir.

A: Oh, fantastic!

Conversation 5

A: Can I have two tickets to the late show tonight?

B: Yes, ma'am. Where would you like to sit?

A: Oh, not too far back.

B: How about in Row F?

A: Sure, that'll be fine.

B: It starts at nine thirty.

A: Can you tell me what time the show finishes tonight?

B: About twelve o'clock.

A: OK. My credit card number is six-nine-two-four-one. . .

Page 21, Practice 7

Lloyd: So, Hal, you're saying that we're going to see a lot of changes in the movie industry in the next few years?

Wood: That's right. I'm sure you'll find the American film audience gradually moving away from the standard commercial movies that have been so popular in the past thirty years.

Lloyd: H-m-m-m-m, that's interesting. So, what kind of movies will take their place?

Wood: I think we'll see a lot more films from other countries. People are getting tired of the same old thing in movies. Foreign films will take viewers to new places and new cultural experiences. Take Pedro Almodóvar, for example.

Lloyd: You mean the Spanish director?

Wood: Yes, well, his films have already had tremendous international success. They're very popular in the U.S. too, even though they're different from typical American movies. And look at the Italian director, Roberto Benigni. His masterpiece, *La Vita è Bella*, or *Life is Beautiful*, earned an amazing fifty-seven million dollars in the U.S.

Lloyd: Wow! I can see the potential as foreign films take off in North America. And what about that Iranian director, that young twenty-year-old woman?

Wood: Samira Makhmalbaf? She'll surely have a lot more success. The list could go on and on.

Lloyd: Where else do you see filmmaking leaping forward?

Wood: Well, we've seen wonderful movies come out of China in the past few years, and as China continues to open up to the West, we're going to discover more great Chinese directors, actors and movies.

Lloyd: Can you say more about that?

Wood: Sure. We've already discovered the Taiwanese director, Ang Lee. Look at what a hit he's had with *Crouching Tiger, Hidden Dragon*. He's going to keep rising in popularity based on his record so far.

Lloyd: Wow, Hal, listening to you, I'd say it's going to be a very exciting time for movie goers. And I agree with you. In fact, tonight I'm seeing the Chinese-French production, *Beijing Bicycle*, for the second time! It's subtitled. I really prefer that. I want to hear people speaking Chinese in a Chinese movie!

Wood: I couldn't agree with you more. In many countries, subtitled movies have been the standard for years, but in the U.S., people have been slow to accept them. Today, however, with *Crouching Tiger, Hidden Dragon*, I think we have seen a change. After that exciting film experience, more and more people are going to be open to viewing subtitled movies. I'm sure they'll see the advantage now of always hearing the original language.

Lloyd: I hope you're right. I've certainly been won over. Don't you think the fact that so many people travel to other countries today has changed people's attitudes, as well?

Wood: Oh, yes! Seeing a movie today that takes place in Japan, for example, and everyone is speaking English makes the movie seem unreal. Movie audiences are becoming more sophisticated. North American directors are going to realize they also need to change their mindset and have native dialogue in their films.

Lloyd: Some already have, haven't they?

Wood: Yes, that's true. Many directors have already put short dialogues in other languages in their films to add authenticity to them.

UNIT 4: I Beg to Differ

Page 29, Practice 7

Conversation 1

A: Excuse me, sir. Would you mind moving the back of your seat forward a bit? You have it all the way back, and I can't use my laptop computer. I have some important work to do on this flight.

B: I'm sorry. I need room. I'm very tired and I've got to relax. If I don't put my seat back, I feel cramped and I can't sleep.

A: Well, could you only move it halfway? The way you're sitting now, *I'm* very cramped. I don't want to do the same to the person behind me.

B: Well, I wish I could help you out, buddy, but I bought a ticket, and I have the right to sit back the whole trip if I want to, and I do. You have no guarantee you can work on the plane when you buy a ticket.

A: That's true, but there is such a thing as consideration.

B: You should be in first class if you want consideration. I'm keeping my seat like this!

Conversation 2

A: Excuse me, sir. I think you're in my seat.

B: Yes, ma'am. I know this isn't my seat, but my wife here doesn't speak English. I'd like to sit with her.

A: Well, I understand and I'd like to help, but I specifically chose this seat. It wasn't just *assigned* to me.

B: Well, actually I was bumped up to business class so you could take my seat. I just want to be with my wife.

A: Oh, uh . . .

B: It's an aisle seat like this one. If you still prefer this seat, I certainly won't prevent you from having it.

A: Oh, I'm sorry for jumping to conclusions. I should have asked you where your seat was. I don't need to look at it first. It'll be fine. You're doing me a bigger favor than I'm doing you!

B: Thanks a lot. Enjoy the flight.

Conversation 3

A: I can't believe the way you acted at that party! You just couldn't wait to sit down next to that new girl!

B: Oh, you won't believe what I found out about the new soccer coach.

A: Don't change the subject!

B: Oh, let's talk about it later. I'm tired. I want to see what's on TV.

A: I can't believe you can sit there and talk about being tired and watching TV and everything else but what you were doing at the party.

B: I'm hungry. Got anything to eat here?

UNIT 5: Odd Jobs

Page 37, Practice 7

Student 1: We're so thrilled you could come and visit our program, Mr. Yu. Are you going to tell us exactly what you do?

Mr. Yu: Yes, I'm hoping to. You see when we refer to a master tap water taster, which is my job, we're not thinking of tasters of bottled water, although they're also water tasters. We're talking about people who taste *tap* water, the stuff that comes out when you turn on the faucet in the kitchen or bathroom of your home.

Student 2: What does great tap water taste like?

Mr. Yu: Well, the answer is easy. Water should have no taste. Water is tasted to see what flavors it has, but the goal is an absence of taste.

Actually, water tasters are taught to start with smelling the water. Here again, an absence of smell is the ideal. The smell of chemicals, minerals, metal, or chlorine is unwanted. The tasters have been instructed to reject any water sample that smells.

Student 3: I know what you mean. I've smelled some pretty foul water in cities I've visited.

Mr. Yu: Me too. So after the smelling process is complete, water with an odor is eliminated, and the rest is selected for further testing.

In the next phase of the process, water tasters are encouraged to follow the example of coffee tasters: to swish the water around in their mouths and then spit it out.

Student 1: Why don't they just swallow it?

Mr. Yu: One reason is the taste. Some of the water doesn't taste very good. Also, a taster could drink over sixty samples of water in a session. That would be a fair amount of water to swallow, don't you think?

Anyway . . . as with smelling, the water taster is told to look for a taste. Some tastes, like chlorine or sulphur are worse than others. And it also depends on how strong or mild the taste is. Points are given to water with little to no taste. When the water samples with a strong taste have all been eliminated from the competition, the remaining water sample with the lowest points is chosen as the best water of the group.

Student 3: Is that all there is to it?

Mr. Yu: No there's one more step. A final comparison is made with some of the best bottled waters. Really good tap water is often found to taste as good as, or even better than, very good bottled water.

Of course, there can be impurities and bacteria in water that can't be tasted, so tasting the water isn't a guarantee that the water is good; however, it's certainly more pleasant to drink when it tastes good.

Teacher: Thanks so much, Mr. Yu. Does anyone have more questions? If not, we're going to do some water tasting of our own.

UNIT 6: Beholding Beauty

Page 45, Practice 9

Panelist 1: Well, I think a good place to start talking about female beauty in history would be with Helen of Troy. She was one of the great beauties of classical Greek myth.

Panelist 2: What about Nefertiti or Cleopatra?

Moderator: As the moderator, I can say we'll be talking about them too a little later.

Panelist 1: As I was saying, Helen of Troy was one of the most controversial figures of ancient times. In fact, even the famous Trojan War that she was involved in is still under debate.

Panelist 3: Yes, while most experts agree that the Trojan War really happened, over time the war heroes and their acts have become more and more exaggerated.

Panelist 2: And at some point, the gods got involved, too. And the gods, of course, had everything to do with Helen.

Moderator: Can you tell us more about that?

Panelist 2: Supposedly, Zeus, the king of the gods, was her father, and the beautiful Leda, a mortal woman, was her mother.

Panelist 1: So her beauty was a combination of the human and the immortal.

Panelist 2: And that was the reason men from all over Greece came to Sparta to ask for her hand in marriage.

Panelist 3: Well, there is, of course, that view. But many feel that Helen, in spite of her beauty, was simply being used in a political game.

Panelist 1: Yes, and in that view, Helen's being forced to marry Menelaus was a political move, due to his wealth, power, and connections.

Panelist 2: That really backfired though, didn't it? Because Menelaus, brought the handsome Paris, Prince of Troy, back to Sparta, and the minute Paris saw Helen, he fell passionately in love with her.

Panelist 3: And she with him. So she ran away with Paris back to Troy, leaving her husband and children. Once she was in Troy, the royal family there agreed to protect her. They refused to give her up to the envoys from Greece that Menelaus sent, and so the Trojan War began.

Panelist 1: Before we finish this discussion, I'd like to say a little about Helen of Troy's character because there are different views on that as well. Some critics feel she was evil and indifferent to all the suffering caused in her name. Others believe that her perfect exterior beauty reflected her inner beauty, and that she was a victim of the gods, her fate essentially beyond her control.

Moderator: Thank you, panelists. That was very informative. Let's move on to Cleopatra now . . .

UNIT 7: Feeling Left Out

Page 53, Practice 9

Saleswoman: Good morning, *We're Left*, may I help you?

Caller: Yes, good morning. I'm calling to find out about your products. I didn't even know your store existed!

Saleswoman: Oh, yes. We've been around for seven years already.

Caller: That's fantastic! My friend who gave me your number told me she'd found lots of great things at your store.

Saleswoman: I'm glad to hear it. People who are left-handed usually appreciate finding things that make their lives easier.

Caller: I'm sure that's true. I have a son who's left-handed and I'd like to buy some things for him—especially things to help him at school.

Saleswoman: Uh-huh. Sure. The parents I've talked to say their kids seem to do better in school because of our products. So that's encouraging.

Caller: You bet it is! So, do you suppose you could give me some examples of the kind of things these parents have bought?

Saleswoman: Of course. I'd be happy to. And I can mail you our catalogue too, if you'd like. We also have a Web page that shows and explains all our products.

Caller: Oh, just a minute. Let me write that down.

Saleswoman: Sure. It's www dot we're left dot com.

Caller: Got it, thanks.

Saleswoman: OK, now back to your question. For children we have several books on handwriting for young left-handed learners. How old is your son?

Caller: Truman is six. So that sounds ideal.

Saleswoman: Oh, good. Well, we also have a learning-to-read series with two funny characters, Alfie, who is right-handed, and Betty, who is left-handed. It's a big hit. The kids love it!

Caller: Yeah, that sounds very nice! Oh, yes, I wanted to mention that we bought Truman a left-hand guitar. Do you have any books or accessories for that?

Saleswoman: Oh, we certainly do. We have instruction books for the guitar from beginner to advanced. We also have a special instrument section.

Caller: This sounds great! I can't wait to see

all your stuff. I'll go to the store tomorrow. Where is it, exactly?

Saleswoman: We're in the Westside Mall. You go to the third floor and it's number fourteen, on your left, as you get off the elevator.

Caller: Great! Can I pick up a catalogue from the store?

Saleswoman: You sure can. The latest ones have just arrived.

Caller: Wonderful. See you tomorrow then. And thanks so much for your help.

Saleswoman: My pleasure. Thank *you* for calling! Good-bye.

Caller: Good-bye.

UNIT 8: You're Not My Type

Page 62, Practice 10

Margaret: OK, group, they've asked us to put our ideas together and come up with some conclusions. Let's quickly go over the various personality theories.

Elton: Well, let's see, we have the blood-type group, the thinkers or feelers . . .

Elizabeth: And don't forget those who are outgoing or reserved . . .

Elton: Yes, the extroverts and introverts, and . . . oh, yeah, the food preference theory.

Margaret: Well, there's the favorite season group, as well.

William: Oh, and the color preferences, types of pets, and order of birth in a family, the zodiac sign, the shape of the face . . .

Elizabeth: And the Type A and Type B theory. This one makes the most sense to me. I mean the rest are so illogical. I can see almost everybody I know as an A or a B. Take Elton, for example.

William: Wait, it's not that simple, Elizabeth. I think . . .

Elizabeth: I haven't finished yet, William. We can apply the A/B thing to all of us and it works.

Margaret: I think we need to hear what other people think before we go directly to a conclusion. Is there one theory you think is more accurate, William?

William: Well, I identify most with the order-of-birth theory. I think it has a more scientific and sociological . . .

Elton: No more than astrology.

William: Could I just finish up here, first, Elton? . . . Well, yes, I think it is more scientific. I mean, people have studied

behavior patterns of oldest, middle, and youngest children in families.

Margaret: Uh-huh.

William: Let's face it, most of us can see those same tendencies in ourselves and in people we know.

Margaret: OK, Elton, now what's your theory?

Elton: I'm a zodiac man. I think people almost always fit their astrological description, whether it is really scientific or not.

Elizabeth: Oh, how *sixties*, Elton! People make excuses for things just to fit into a particular zodiac sign. If they don't sound right, they can blame it on their rising sign or moon sign. Get real! The A/B thing is much simpler and more accurate.

Elton: You've made your point, Elizabeth, and we know how you feel, but the rest of us don't have to agree with you.

Margaret: *That's* very true. And wild as it may seem, I really go for the blood type idea. I don't know if I find it more accurate, but it certainly is interesting. Now, when I meet new people, I can say, "What's your blood type?" What fun!

UNIT 9: Tech Trends

Page 68, Practice 7

Advertisement 1

Announcer: Does your cell phone connect to the Internet? Can you get weather and traffic reports? Can you listen to music and send e-mail messages and faxes? Well, if you can't do all these things, it's time you got a new cell phone—a Cellex cell phone, that is. Available exclusively at all PMC Electronics stores, it comes in every color and it's only sixty-nine-ninety-five ($69.95) plus tax. Don't miss this great offer. Remember, ask for Cellex, and accept no other.

Advertisement 2

Announcer: Great news, folks! That portable DVD player you've been waiting for is here! You can now listen to hours of music or watch your favorite movie on its amazingly clear viewing screen. The movie images have wonderfully high definition, and the sound system is state-of-the-art. Now on sale at most electronics stores, you can get this awesome DV-MAN. All this technology for only four-hundred-ninety-nine-ninety-five ($499.95). Get yourself a DV-MAN today!

UNIT 10: Space Exploration

Page 77, Practice 9

Host: And now, listeners, it's time for "Frequently Asked Questions." Our guest is Dr. Carla Fuentes, who will answer your call-in questions about today's topic, black holes. . . . Yes, caller one, what is your question?

Caller 1: I'm embarrassed to ask this, but what exactly *is* a black hole?

Host: There are probably many others with that same question. Dr. Fuentes?

Fuentes: Yes, black holes are very complex. They're caused, we think, by a star running out of fuel and collapsing into itself. It then has such a huge concentration of mass that nothing near it can escape its gravitational pull, not even light.

Caller 1: How's that possible?

Fuentes: Well, scientists will be arguing the details of that question for years to come, but we do have a general idea. As an example, imagine that you're going to send a rocket up into space. For the rocket to escape the pull of Earth's gravity, it has to go a certain speed, what we call "escape velocity."

Host: And the larger the mass of the planet or whatever, the stronger its gravitational pull, right?

Fuentes: Correct. The Moon, for example, has a smaller mass than the Earth, and so its escape velocity is also less than that of Earth. A rocket would have to travel about five thousand three hundred miles per hour to leave the Moon, but it would have to travel about twenty-five thousand miles per hour to leave the Earth. The stronger the gravity, the faster the rocket or any other object has to go to escape the gravitational field. And the fastest anything can go is, as we know, the speed of light.

Caller 1: How does that relate to a black hole?

Fuentes: Well, think about it. Remember, a black hole has an incredibly huge mass concentrated in a relatively small space. The mass is so enormous that its escape velocity is more than the velocity of light. And, since nothing can go faster than the velocity of light, nothing can escape the black hole's gravitational pull.

Caller 1: So even light can't escape from a black hole. Now I get it. Thank you very much, Dr. Fuentes.

Host: Now let's go to caller two.

Caller 2: Are black holes just theory, or is there any real evidence they exist?

Fuentes: Well, you can't just "see" a black hole, since light can't escape from it. We have to depend on indirect evidence, such as measurements of how much mass there is in a certain region in space. Astronomers have identified eight galaxies with black holes in their centers.

Caller 2: What about white holes?

Host: White holes? Are there such things?

Fuentes: Well, mathematicians have theorized about them, but there's no evidence, direct or indirect, that they really exist. The idea behind white holes is that instead of drawing everything into its center as a black hole does, a white hole would allow everything to escape. Nothing could fall into it.

Host: Fascinating. Well, Dr. Fuentes, it's time for a commercial. We'll continue our question-and-answer session right after the break.

UNIT 11: Adventure Vacations

Page 86, Practice 8

Yoko: Ellen! You're back from vacation! How nice to see you.

Bobby: You look wonderful!

Ellen: Thanks. Yes, I'm back home, but let me tell you, I wish I weren't!

Yoko: The vacation was that good, huh?

Ellen: Absolutely the best. And who would've thought I would spend a week shipwreck diving!

Bobby: And loving every minute of it?

Ellen: Yes. I loved the Dominican Republic, and the ships we explored were incredible. Most of them were just off the northern coast of the island.

Bobby: Did you just visit them or did you actually get to help in search and recovery?

Ellen: I got a little training, and then I actually operated both a metal detector and a water dredge. It was so exciting!

Bobby: What did you like best?

Ellen: Well, the first sight of the wreck of a two-hundred-year-old wooden ship was just incredible. As I swam closer, I could begin to make out the shapes of some of its metal cannons, covered in coral growth.

Yoko: That must have been really exciting.

Ellen: It was! Other things, though, were very hard to identify because they were partially buried or so covered in coral that I couldn't tell what was actually underneath.

Yoko: Wow! If only I had done something that adventurous!

Ellen: So what did you do, Yoko?

Yoko: I went to visit my cousin in Philadelphia. It was nice, but I wish I had planned something more exciting now!

Bobby: I'd love to hear more about your trip, Ellen. Where are the photos? I'm sure you took some.

UNIT 12: A Way with Words

Page 92, Practice 7

José: . . . so anyway, the first time I came to the United States, I thought I knew a lot of English until I had a couple of embarrassing incidents. Now, when I look back on them I can laugh, but it wasn't funny then.

Tom: Oh, I know what you mean, José. There were a few pitfalls I learned about when I went to Mexico.

Julia: Do either of you remember any funny experiences?

José: Well, I remember the time I went on a fishing trip. When I bought my ticket for the trip, the guy asked me if I wanted to go in on the pool. I said I hadn't brought my bathing suit with me, and he looked at me kind of weird and chuckled.

Julia: *I* know why.

José: I bet you do. Later I found out there's another kind of pool. The people on the fishing trip put their money together and it goes to the person who catches the biggest fish of the day. The money collection is called a pool. How do you like that?

Tom: That's a good one. What about you Julia? You lived in Japan.

Julia: Let me think. Oh, I've got one. Hot chocolate is very popular in Japan. We call it cocoa and they pronounce it ko-ko-a. So I went to the supermarket to buy some and I asked for what I thought was ko-ko-a, but I guess it sounded like ko-ko-wa which means "Where is here?" They certainly gave me strange looks. Then they started pointing to the supermarket sign as if I didn't know where I was.

José: Okay, Tom. It's your turn. What happened in Mexico?

Tom: I asked a friend, in Spanish of course, to go grocery shopping with me. Only I said something like, "Let's buy some *grocerías*" because I didn't know how to say groceries in Spanish. My friend laughed hysterically and then told me that *grocerías* means bad or vulgar words. Was I embarrassed!

Julia: Oh, wait. I've got another story . . .

Workbook Answer Key

UNIT 1: Food for Thought

Practice 1
Answers will vary.

Practice 2
1. blends
2. traced back to
3. mouthwatering
4. savor
5. desirable
6. delights in
7. resembles
8. range

Practice 3
A, B. Answers will vary.

Practice 4
1. follow
2. are . . . getting
3. 'm or am
4. comes or is coming
5. are looking
6. Are
7. add or are adding
8. happens
9. form or are forming
10. drop or are dropping
11. fry or are frying
12. smells
13. decorate or are decorating
14. pour or are pouring
15. dust or are dusting
16. 'm dying or am dying
17. 'm begging or am begging

Practice 5
Action verbs

cook	boil
fry	roast
grow	steam

Stative verbs

know	belong
need	look like
see	want
seem	hear

Can be both

think	appear
feel	taste

Practice 6
1. She still has more pasta to make.
2. Bill began working out and continues to do so.
3. Kim didn't like cooked carrots in the past and doesn't like them now.
4. Sam is still living above the restaurant.
5. She watches a show and then tries a recipe.

Practice 7
1. belongs
2. know
3. comes
4. measures
5. needs
6. cultivate or have cultivated
7. account for or have accounted for
8. have produced
9. has . . . been
10. is
11. contains
12. are
13. has not heard or hasn't heard
14. has
15. combines
16. have made
17. have gained
18. is

Practice 8
B. 1. The show was about pasta.
2. Not sure. Possible origins are from the Arabs, Chinese, Roman, and Etruscan civilizations.
3. They found murals of pasta-making tools on the walls of an Etruscan tomb near Rome.
4. Pasta was originally eaten with the hands.
5. Pasta used to be cooked with milk or broth and mixed with sugar, butter, and sweet spices.

Practice 9
/s/
ingredients
secrets
amounts
/z/
derives
means
includes
kinds
/ɪz/
spices
dishes

Practice 10
Answers will vary.

Practice 11
A. If there is such a thing as a wonder food, the creamy milk product known as yogurt would surely earn that name. Associated everywhere with long life, yogurt is nutritionally superior to ordinary milk in many ways. In fact, in many parts of the world such as southeastern Europe and Asia Minor, this is the only form in which milk is consumed.

Used by many as a health food, the benefits of yogurt are almost limitless. Yogurt is an important source of calcium and vitamins, and if one to three cups of yogurt are eaten daily, some kinds of infection clear up quickly. Yogurt also aids in the digestion of iron. As a face mask, yogurt's astringent qualities are a help to oily skin.

Yogurt has become increasingly popular, and more and more people are interested in learning how to make it at home. To do so, heat one quart of fresh milk to "hand hot," about 90° to 100° F (32° to 37° C). To this very warm milk, add about three tablespoons of yogurt from a previous batch that contains live cultures (usually *lactobacillus bulgaricus* and *streptococcus thermophilus* or *lactobacillus acidophilus*). Stir this amount into the milk and pour it all at once into a wide-mouthed thermos jar. Cover it tightly and let it stand overnight. Upon uncapping the next morning, the yogurt will be thick and creamy. Refrigerate until served, and then enjoy.

B.
Function	Purpose
☑ Description	☑ To inform

UNIT 2: Memorable Moments

Practice 1
Answers will vary.

Practice 2
Crossword Puzzle

Across
1. counterparts
4. chiefly
6. adept
7. swap
8. start-up
10. catchy
11. tall tales
12. straightforward

Down
2. tucked away
3. thus
5. up and coming
9. set out

Practice 3
A, B. Answers will vary.

Practice 4
1. played or were playing
2. spent or was spending
3. was
4. left
5. picked or was picking
6. began
7. woke up
8. went
9. happened or was happening
10. was picking
11. had
12. was cutting
13. putting or was putting
14. was sleepwalking

Practice 5
B. Answers will vary.

Practice 6
1. When Christopher Columbus
   sailed
   ~~had sailed~~ across the Atlantic,
   was looking for
   he ~~looked for~~ the East Indies,
   but he landed in the Bahamas.

2. When Benjamin Franklin
   was flying   *discovered*
   ~~flew~~ a kite, he ~~was discovering~~
   that lightning was a form of
   electricity.

                        developed
3. Before they ~~were developing~~
   the first powered heavier-than-
   air aircraft, the Wright Brothers
   had flown gliders.

4. Scottish inventor Alexander
                was working
   Graham Bell ~~worked~~ on ways
   to improve the telegraph when
   he invented the telephone.

5. Sometime around 1450,
   while a German goldsmith
   named Johannes Gutenberg
   was studying
   ~~had studied~~ several key
   printing technologies, he
   created a hand-operated
   mechanical printing press.

Practice 7
A. 1. began
   2. accompanied
   3. fought or were fighting
   4. practiced or was practicing
   5. led or was leading
   6. fought/was fighting
   7. sank
   8. was appearing

Practice 8
B. 1. Jackie Robinson was born
      on January 31, 1919 in
      Cairo, Georgia.
   2. He played track and field,
      football, basketball, and
      baseball while in college.
   3. Jackie played for the Kansas
      City Monarchs in Kansas
      City, Missouri.
   4. Jackie was the first African
      American to play in the
      major leagues.
   5. Jackie Robinson showed
      courage by not responding
      to the insults and threats
      he received.
   6. He was Rookie of the Year
      in 1947 and Most Valuable
      Player in 1949.
   7. Jackie Robinson retired
      from baseball in 1956.

Practice 9
1. /d/
2. /ɪd/
3. /ɪd/
4. /ɪd/
5. /ɪd/
6. /t/
7. /ɪd/
8. /t/

Practice 10
Answers will vary.

Practice 11
1. Possible Essay Question:
   XYZ Company wants to
   build a new factory in your
   community. Do you believe
   they should be allowed?
   State your opinion and give
   specific reasons. (Accept
   similar questions.)
   Persuasive essay

2. Possible Essay Question:
   Do you believe that teenagers
   should be allowed to work
   while they attend school?
   State your opinion and give
   specific reasons. (Accept
   similar questions.)
   Persuasive essay

3. Possible Essay Question:
   People are living longer than
   they did fifty years ago.
   Why is this the case? State
   your reasons and support
   them with specific examples.
   (Accept similar questions.)
   Descriptive essay

UNIT 3: The Future of Film

Practice 1
Movie Directors—Country of Origin

Spike Lee — the United States
Ang Lee — Taiwan
Majid Majidi — Iran
George Lucas — the United States
Yimou Zhang — China
Roberto Benigni — Italy
Steven Spielberg — the United States
Carlos Saura — Spain
Jane Campion — New Zealand
Akira Kurosawa — Japan
Walter Salles — Brazil
Penny Marshall — the United States

Practice 2
1. spools
2. encrypted
3. hubs
4. deliver
5. screening
6. pristine

Practice 3
A, B. Answers will vary.

Practice 4
1. are doing or are going to do
2. 'm attending or 'm going to attend
3. will be

4. 'll call
5. is it starting
6. is it playing
7. 's starting
8. 'll check
9. 's playing
10. 'll go
11. are you getting
12. 'll hail
13. 'll see
14. 'll call

Practice 5

A. Hi !

<u>Are</u> we still <u>**going**</u> camping this weekend? I hope so. I watched the weather predictions on TV and they say <u>**it's going to be**</u> nice and fairly warm. That's good news! What <u>**are you bringing/taking**</u> with you for the weekend? I think <u>**I'll bring/take**</u> jeans and sweatshirts to wear at night and shorts and t-shirts to wear during the daytime. <u>**I'll bring/take**</u> my hiking boots, but no other shoes. What time <u>**are we leaving**</u> town? What time <u>**are you leaving**</u> work? <u>**Are you taking**</u> your car, for sure? I hope so, because mine needs to be taken to the garage before I drive very far. <u>**I'll wait**</u> for a message from you tomorrow. <u>**I'll talk**</u> to you soon!
Su Li

B. Answers will vary.

Practice 6

a. buying tickets   Conversation #5
b. making a   Conversation #4
   complaint
c. asking about   Conversation #1
   opening and
   closing times
d. getting infor-   Conversation #3
   mation about
   products
e. making a   Conversation #2
   reservation

Practice 7

B.

a. __4__ "North American directors are going to realize that they also need to change their mindset and have native dialogue in their films."
Support: Movie audiences are becoming more sophisticated. Seeing a movie set in a non-

English speaking country, but with everyone speaking English seems strange.

b. __2__ "We're going to discover more great Chinese directors, actors, and movies."

c. __3__ "More and more people are going to be open to viewing subtitled movies."

d. __1__ "I think we'll see a lot more films from other countries."

C. Answers will vary.

Practice 8

1. **pro**duce, pro**duce**
2. **ad**dress, ad**dress**
3. **con**tract, con**tract**
4. **des**ert, de**sert**
5. **ob**ject, ob**ject**
6. **prog**ress, pro**gress**

Practice 9

Answers will vary.

Practice 10

Answers will vary.

UNIT 4: I Beg to Differ

Practice 1

Answers will vary.

Practice 2

1. disguise
2. grievance
3. can't help
4. validate
5. empathize

Practice 3

A. Answers will vary.

Practice 4

A. 1. writing
2. having
3. to avoid
4. having
5. talking/to talk
6. ruining
7. having
8. to do
9. not saying
10. having
11. wearing
12. remembering
13. to be
14. overreacting

Practice 5

Answers will vary.

Practice 6

1. to speak   7. copying
2. to do   8. no error
3. no error   9. failing
4. to find   10. making
5. no error   11. to let
6. reading   12. to try

Practice 7

B. Conversation 1: WIN–LOSE
   Conversation 2: WIN–WIN
   Conversation 3: AVOIDANCE

Practice 8

1. No, I didn't say <u>you</u> had it. I said <u>Hugh</u> had it!
2. Was that <u>13</u> centimeters or <u>30</u> centimeters?
3. Not a complaint from a <u>resident</u>. It's a complaint from the <u>president</u>.
4. Do you think that was a win–<u>lose</u> or a win–<u>win</u> resolution?
5. No, it wasn't <u>last</u> night. It's <u>tomorrow</u> night.
6. She didn't buy a <u>sheep</u> farm. She bought a <u>cheap</u> farm and then had problems.
7. Did you say I could eat for <u>three</u> or for <u>free</u>?
8. No, the house wasn't <u>Ruby's</u>. It was <u>Rudy's</u>.

Practice 9

A. 1. P   5. P
   2. P   6. P
   3. I   7. I
   4. I   8. I

Practice 10

Answers will vary.

Practice 11

Topic Is Too Broad

Conflict Resolution

Understanding People from Different Cultures

Problems among Students

Topic Is Appropriate and Specific

The Most Effective Style of Conflict Resolution

My Personal Experience with a Cross-Cultural Conflict

Mediation as One Means of Conflict Resolution

UNIT 5: Odd Jobs

Practice 1
Answers will vary.

Practice 2
1. skydive
2. gear up
3. convenient
4. back out
5. get hooked
6. daredevil
7. under my belt

Practice 3
Answers will vary.

Practice 4
A. 1. is lost/has been lost
   2. be filled out
   3. must be given
   4. must be chosen
   5. are listed
   6. can be identified
   7. is checked
   8. is entered
   9. is prepared
   10. was sent/has been sent
   11. was checked in
   12. is handed
   13. is asked
   14. can be reached
   15. can be delivered
   16. is found

Practice 5
A. 1. The gestures and voice of the famous person are learned.
   2. Gifts and items are bought for busy people.
   3. Beautiful sculptures are made from simple balloons.
   4. Assistance and support are given to the gaffer in film work.
   5. Products are tested to make sure they work.
   6. Services are provided for people who don't have time to walk their dogs.
   7. The circus show is directed and the acts announced.
   8. The food at local restaurants is sampled and a review is written.

B. __2__ balloon artist
   __7__ restaurant critic
   __4__ product tester
   __5__ dog walker
   __6__ ringmaster
   __3__ best boy
   __1__ professional shopper

Practice 6
1. Certain kinds of people are attracted by dangerous jobs such as truck driver, forest firefighter, and construction worker.
2. The level of risk and injury on the job is increased by working outdoors.
3. Severe weather conditions will affect workers who have outdoor jobs.
4. For example, a higher rate of fishers drowning can be caused by bad weather.
5. The U.S. Labor Department has reported taxi driver as a dangerous job.
6. Are you excited by the thought of dangerous work?

Practice 7
B. Steps
1. Smell the water.
2. Swish the water around in your mouth.
3. Identify taste of the water, if any.
4. Compare tap water to bottled water.

C.
About Smell
Good tap water shouldn't have any smell.

Water samples that smell are rejected.

About Swallowing Water
Water tasters spit out the water after swishing it around in their mouths.

Water tasters don't swallow the water because they test a lot of it. Some of it is not very good.

About Taste
Ideally, water should have no taste.

Some tastes like chlorine or sulphur are pretty bad.

Water samples with a strong taste are eliminated.

Practice 8
1. I'd love to be a (restaurant critic). I love to eat!
2. Diane could never be a (wedding planner). Weddings always make her cry!
3. Steve could be a (mystery shopper). He says, "Shop till you drop!"
4. I wonder if a (perfume tester) needs strong skin or sensitive skin.
5. A (dog)walker has to be careful that the dog doesn't get away.
6. A (zoo)keeper has to get used to strong smells.
7. Every movie production has a (best)boy.
8. I'd be afraid to be a (lion)tamer. It seems like a very dangerous job!

Practice 9
1. P
2. C
3. P
4. C
5. A
6. C
7. P
8. A
9. P

Practice 10
Answers will vary.

UNIT 6: Beholding Beauty

Practice 1
Answers will vary.

Practice 2
Crossword Puzzle
Across
3. oval
5. auburn
7. opt
9. stocky
11. heart-shaped
13. athletic

Down
1. beard
2. moustache
4. cropped
6. blond
8. goatee
10. wavy
12. hazel

Practice 3
A, B. Answers will vary.

Practice 4
1. could change
2. would you change
3. would make
4. had
5. wouldn't need to
6. wanted
7. would need to

8. would have to
9. decided to
10. could take
11. got
12. would you want to
13. would like
14. did
15. would be
16. decided
17. would see
18. would consider

Practice 5

Answers will vary but this is the general structure.

b. **Q:** What would your father have done if your mother had taken a modeling course?

   A: If my mother had taken a modeling course, my father would have supported her.

c. **Q:** What would your best friend have done if you had cut your hair?

   A: If I had cut my hair, my best friend would have stopped speaking to me.

d. **Q:** What would you have done if your sister had gotten her teeth fixed?

   A: If my sister had gotten her teeth fixed, I would have helped her pay for it.

e. **Q:** What would you have done if your best friend had gained weight?

   A: If my best friend had gained weight, I would have put her on an exercise and diet plan.

f. **Q:** What would Philip have done if his father had shaved his head?

   A: If Philip's father had shaved his head, Philip would have bought him a wig.

Practice 6

Answers will vary.
Possible examples:

a. If I grow tall, I'll be a basketball player.
b. If I had lots of hair, I'd be more attractive.
c. If I hadn't cut my hair, I wouldn't be so unhappy now.
d. If I save enough money, I can go to the health spa.
e. If I would stop eating so much, I could lose weight.

f. If I practice my music, I could be a rock star.

Practice 7

1. in case *or* as long as
2. as long as
3. in case
4. in case
5. In case *or* As long as
6. in case
7. In case
8. in case *or* as long as

Practice 8

Answers will vary.

Practice 9

B. Name of the legendary figure discussed: Helen of Troy

Major historical event with which she is associated: The Trojan War

Parents according to legend: Zeus was supposedly Helen of Troy's father and Leda was her mother.

Husband chosen for her: Menelaus was chosen as Helen's husband.

Person she ran away with: Helen ran away with Paris.

Two contrasting views of the woman's character: Some people feel Helen was evil and indifferent to the suffering caused in her name. Others believe she was a beautiful human being, inside and out, and simply a victim of the gods.

Practice 10

1. **A:** Mom! *Surprise!* I got a new hairstyle.

   B: Oh *fantastic*!

   A: No, *really*! It's *awesome*!

   B: *Yeah, right.*

2. **A:** Look at *that*! Margot's got her head shaved!

   B: *What?*

   A: Yeah, *look!*

   B: *Awful!*

3. **A:** I saw Roseanne at the mall.

   B: *And?*

   A: She's lost sixty pounds.

   B: *No!*

   A: Exercise and dieting.

   B: That's *amazing*!

   A: *Yeah!*

Practice 11

Answers will vary.

Practice 12

Answers will vary.

UNIT 7: Feeling Left Out

Practice 1

Answers will vary.

Practice 2

1. reveal
2. bias
3. exemplary
4. embedded
5. rejected
6. synonymous
7. derive
8. dread

Practice 3

A, B. Answers will vary.

Practice 4

A. 1. D
  2. ND (Right-handed people, who are the majority, often don't realize . . .)
  3. D
  4. ND (That book, which came on the market last year, teaches your left-handed . . .)
  5. D
  6. ND (Roberto's sister, who is left-handed, is an excellent tennis player.)

Practice 5

1. A left-hand mouse makes it easier for a left hander to use the computer.
2. Left-handed piano players often find it easier to play bass clef parts.
3. Left handers have adapted to inconveniences despite being forgotten by product makers.
4. Only my right-handed friends forget to put me at the left end of the table.

Practice 6

A. 1. that/which
  2. who
  3. whose
  4. whom
  5. who
  6. who

Practice 7

1. Ken, whose desk is left-handed, uses it every day.
2. Mary, whose car is specially equipped, is left-handed.
3. That man, whose wife we interviewed, lent his pen to me.
4. Tomoko, whose pictures are beautiful, is a talented artist.
5. That company, whose left-hand scissors I bought, is very small.
6. Ms. Chekov, whose students are all left-handed, won a big teaching award.

Practice 8

Answers will vary.

Practice 9

B. Two people are talking about products for left-handed children that are available in the store.

C. 1. F   5. T
    2. F   6. F
    3. T   7. F
    4. T   8. T

Practice 10

1. They went to visit **La_nd's E_nd**.
2. **She's socially** acquainted with them.
3. **He's serious.**
4. That's the store where we **went to** find gloves.
5. She wore a **black cape.**
6. I **wa_shed** all the dishes.
7. **Let's eat** some **asparagus soup.**
8. They **coo_ked** a wonderful dinner.

Practice 11

A. 1. P   5. E
    2. E   6. E
    3. P   7. E
    4. P   8. P

Practice 12

A, B. Answers will vary.

UNIT 8: You're Not My Type

Practice 1

Answers will vary.

Practice 2

1. put on   4. open up
2. hold back   5. make up
3. carry out   6. look at

Practice 3

A, B. Answers will vary.

Practice 4

1. **b.** look up
2. **c.** gets over
3. **a.** goes for
4. **c.** gives up
5. **a.** put off
6. **b.** turn . . . down

Practice 5

Answers will vary.

Practice 6

1. on   5. over
2. into   6. out
3. off   7. back
4. up

Practice 7

A. 1. f   5. a
    2. g   6. b
    3. h   7. c
    4. e   8. d

Practice 8

1. check up on them
2. came to me
3. figure it out
4. hold her back
5. turned him down
6. Open it up
7. look into it

Practice 9

Answers will vary.

Practice 10

B. 1. F
    2. F
    3. T
    4. F
    5. F

C.

Person	Favorite Personality Theory	Reason
Margaret	Blood type	Interesting theory
William	Order of birth	More scientific and has a sociological basis
Elizabeth	Type A and Type B	Other theories are illogical, can apply Type A and B to everyone
Elton	Astrology	People fit their astrological descriptions

Practice 11

1. Ambitious people <u>look</u> for ways to advance.
2. People who are reserved hesitate to <u>ask</u> for things.
3. Bosses often like to <u>check up</u> on their employees.
4. He had an appointment, so he had to <u>turn down</u> Jeremy's invitation.
5. We might <u>run into</u> some bad weather today.
6. I'm <u>looking forward</u> to meeting your partner.
7. Let's <u>turn on</u> the news and <u>find out</u> what happened.
8. She had to <u>give up</u> tennis, because of her bad knee.

Practice 12

Answers will vary.

Practice 13

Answers will vary.

UNIT 9: Tech Trends

Practice 1

Answers will vary.

Practice 2

1. e
2. d
3. b
4. a
5. c

Practice 3

A, B. Answers will vary.

Practice 4

Answers will vary.

Practice 5

1. I need to find ~~the~~ *a* computer shop. There must be one near here.
2. He went to the computer shop on ~~a~~ *the* corner.
3. I'll go to the bank to get money to buy myself ~~the~~ *a* computer.
4. Do you have ~~the~~ *a* cell phone? I need to find one.
5. To open our garage you need to push ~~a~~ *the* remote control above the rearview mirror.
6. Do you heat your house with ~~the~~ solar power, ~~the~~ gas, or electricity?

7. Let's watch *the* ~~a~~ DVD video I gave you tonight. It's really good.

8. He has *a* ~~the~~ pressure-sensitive floor in his house.

Practice 6

A. Anya got **(1.) a** new computer last week, and she has been on it as much as possible ever since. She has sent **(2.)** e-mail messages and has spent a lot of time on **(3.) the** Internet. **(4.) The** Internet has opened up **(5.) a** whole new world for her! **(6.) The** other day, Anya discovered **(7.) the** *National Geographic* web site and stayed on it for hours. She "visited" **(8.)** Yellowstone Park, then jumped over to **(9.)** Lake Victoria, **(10.) the** second largest lake in **(11.) the** world, then went down **(12.) the** Nile River from Aswan to Cairo. Later she went to **(13.) the** United States and toured New York City along **(14.)** 5th Avenue all the way up to **(15.)** Central Park. Then she decided to go to **(16.)** Europe, starting with **(17.) the** Netherlands, as **(18.) a** grandmother had come from there. Anya loved **(19.) the** canals in Amsterdam and **(20.) the** beautiful flowers everywhere.

After all that surfing, Anya was so tired, she had to take **(21.) a** nap. She woke up **(22.) an** hour later and went right back on **(23.) the** computer. She decided she would like to see **(24.) the** news, so she opened **(25.) the/a** browser and typed in **(26.) the** name of her favorite newspaper. Right away, **(27.) the** news was on **(28.) the** screen. She quickly scanned **(29.) the** headlines and then decided to enter **(30.) the** name of her favorite sport: **(31.)** soccer. When Anya did that, she got **(32.) a** huge choice of teams, statistics, stadiums, and famous players. She even found **(33.) a** forum where she could write comments or ask questions and get responses from other fans. She found **(34.) a** chatroom site where she could talk online about her favorite team to **(35.)** other people.

(36.) The computer definitely had her fascinated. She hoped her fascination wouldn't become **(37.) a** computer addiction!

Practice 7

B. Summary of Advertisement 1: Buy a modern Cellex cell phone at PMC Electronics stores for $69.95.

Summary of Advertisement 2: Buy a DV-MAN DVD player at most electronics stores for $499.95.

C.

ADVERTISEMENT 1

Product	cell phone
Features	Access to Internet, get weather and traffic reports, listen to music, and send email and faxes
Name	Cellex
Price	$69.95
Where sold	PMC Electronics

ADVERTISEMENT 2

Product	DVD player
Features	Clear viewing screen, high-definition images, and state-of-the-art sound system.
Name	DV-MAN
Price	$499.95
Where sold	At most electronics stores

Practice 8

1. A: Did you say DVDs can hold up to <u>85 megabytes</u> of data?
   B: No, <u>8.5 gigabytes</u>.
2. A: Was that <u>four</u> hours of movies on a DVD?
   B: Yes, <u>four</u>.
3. A: DVDs come in two formats: DVD-<u>Video</u> and DVD-<u>ROM</u>.
   B: Did you say DVD-<u>RAM</u>?
   A: No, <u>ROM</u>!
4. A: The laser printer is based on technology used by <u>photographers</u>, right?
   B: No, not <u>photographers</u>, <u>photocopiers</u>!
   A: Oh, <u>photocopiers</u>!

5. A: So the optical scanner is a computer <u>output</u> device.
   B: No, it's an <u>input</u> device.

Practice 9

A.
1. B	4. B
2. B	5. M
3. M	6. M

B. Answers will vary.

Practice 10

A, B. Answers will vary.

UNIT 10: Space Exploration

Practice 1

Answers will vary.

Practice 2

1. prominent
2. shrink
3. deteriorate
4. would-be
5. second thoughts
6. commonplace
7. seasoned
8. grueling

Practice 3

A, B. Answers will vary.

Practice 4

1. will be
2. will begin
3. will be making
4. will have
5. will be getting
6. will make/will be making
7. will take
8. will develop/will be developing
9. will give
10. will be investing

Practice 5

Answers will vary.

Practice 6

1. It will take no more than twenty years to discover Planet X.
2. Time travel will not be achieved before the 22nd century.
3. People will next see Halley's comet before 2061.
4. A spaceship that high temperatures on Venus won't destroy will be ready in about ten years.

5. Before this century ends, there will be proof of the existence of extraterrestrial intelligence.

Practice 7

A. 1. will have designed
  2. will have experimented
  3. will have replaced
  4. will have provided
  5. will have proved/proven

Practice 8

Answers will vary.

Practice 9

B. 1. A black hole is a star that has run out of fuel and collapsed into itself. It has such a large concentration of mass that the gravitational pull is very strong.
  2. Escape velocity is the speed necessary to travel in order to escape the gravitational pull of the planet you are escaping.
  3. Escape velocity of the Earth is 25,000 miles per hour; escape velocity of the Moon is 5,300 miles per hour.
  4. Nothing can escape from a black hole—not even light.
  5. The existence of white holes is a theory, but there is no evidence to support it. The theory is that white holes are the opposite of black holes. They push everything out of their center instead of pulling it in.

Practice 10

1. A combination of a black hole

and a white hole is called a wormhole.
2. In theory, the black hole and a white hole could be

separated by vast distances.
3. A white hole could even be in

a different region of space time.
4. Entering a black hole and exiting a white hole would

essentially result in time travel.
5. Theoretically, wormholes could

connect two or more universes.

Practice 11

Answers will vary.

Practice 12

Answers will vary.

UNIT 11: Adventure Vacations

Practice 1

Answers will vary.

Practice 2

1. scenic   5. immersed
2. dig   6. donate
3. figurine   7. artifacts
4. stimulate   8. suspense

Practice 3

A, B. Answers will vary.

Practice 4

A. 1. Had Carrie not missed her flight to Tokyo, she wouldn't have had to wait 14 hours.
  2. Were Louis more careful, he wouldn't have lost his passport and traveler's checks.
  3. Should you go camping, you'll need water purification tablets.
  4. Had Jennifer stayed an extra day at the ski lodge, she would have been trapped there during the snowstorm.
  5. Were David wearing good hiking boots, he wouldn't have had to turn back.
  6. Should a shark swim by you, you'll want to stay as still as possible.

Practice 5

Possible answers:
1. She wishes she hadn't brought so many clothes.
2. He wishes he could go swimming. He wishes he hadn't broken his arm.
3. They wish they had brought more water.
4. She wishes she could go parasailing.
5. He wishes he could find his identification.
  He wishes he had remembered to bring his identification.
6. She wishes she had brought more film.

Practice 6

A. 1. hadn't gone
  2. had known
  3. would have stayed
  4. remember
  5. hadn't been
  6. would change
  7. had been
  8. hadn't fallen
  9. broken
  10. hadn't run

Practice 7

Possible answers:
1. If only Sue had remembered to bring film! She would have had great photos.
2. If only Vera had learned to drive! She would have been able to help on the safari.
3. If only Nick had saved money! He would have gone white water rafting.
4. If only Bill had kept a first aid kit! He would have handled the emergency.
5. If only Pat had been less shy! She would have had more fun on the vacation.
6. If only Maria had studied archeology! She would have led the archeological dig.

Practice 8

B. 1. Ellen went to the Dominican Republic.
  2. It was a shipwreck-diving trip.
  3. The trip lasted one week.
  4. She searched for buried artifacts from the ship.
  5. She liked the first sight of the very old ship underwater.
  6. Yoko visited her cousin in Philadelphia.

C. Ellen—excited
  Yoko—envious
  Bobby—curious

Practice 9

One of the most beautiful places | to explore caves | is in Belize. | In Cayo, | you can cross rivers | and hike through the jungle. | You will reach a site | where the ancient Mayan people | held ritual ceremonies | over 2000 years ago. | The cave was discovered | in 1989. | It holds ceremonial vessels | and other artifacts | that reveal much | about the Mayan civilization.

Practice 10

Answers will vary.

Practice 11

Answers will vary.

UNIT 12: A Way With Words

Practice 1

Answers will vary.

Practice 2

Crossword Puzzle

Across	Down
1. hilarious	2. ancestors
3. case	4. faced
6. pitfalls	5. label
7. bloopers	6. pastry
8. grave	

Practice 3

A, B. Answers will vary.

Practice 4

1. La Rochefoucauld said that it was more shameful to distrust your friends than to be deceived by them.
2. Eleanor Roosevelt said that no one could make you feel inferior without your consent.
3. Groucho Marx said that he had had a marvelous evening, but this wasn't it.

Practice 5

A. 1. My friend said that Colombian novelist Gabriel García Márquez had won the Nobel Prize for Literature in 1982.
   2. I asked her if (whether) she had read any translations of Gabriel García Márquez's books.

3. My friend replied that she was reading the English translation of *Love in the Time of Cholera*.
4. I added that I hear Gabo, as he is fondly called, is writing his memoirs.
5. My friend remarked that he would be publishing three volumes of memoirs in the near future.
6. I asked her if (whether) we could find more information about García Márquez on the Internet.

Practice 6

• Mr. Walker asked Ms. Chaplin where she wanted to eat today.
• Ms. Chaplin said that she loved the Sushi Palace. She said their sushi and sashimi were fabulous.
• Mr. Walker said that he agreed. And said that their prices were good, too.
• Ms. Chaplin asked how you translated sushi.
• Mr. Walker said that he didn't know, but that it was raw fish on top of rice.
• Ms. Chaplin asked if Mr. Walker had tried their tempura.
• Mr. Walker said no but that he would. He asked which one she recommended.
• Ms. Chaplin said that last time she had had the shrimp tempura. She said it was their specialty!

Practice 7

B. 1. T
   2. F
   3. F
   4. T
   5. T

C. 1. The friends were discussing embarrassing situations they had in foreign cultures.

2. The confusion about "pool" was because of the multiple meaning of some words.
3. The confusion about "cocoa" was because it sounded very similar to a Japanese phrase and cocoa wasn't a Japanese word.
4. The confusion about "groceries" was because Tom tried to make it into a Spanish word or what we call a cognate; however, it was a false cognate.
5. When words or expressions go into another language, the pronunciation may change, the meaning may change, or the spelling may change.

Practice 8

1. A: I got a raise!

   B: No!

   A: Yes! 350 dollars!
2. A: I'll get you a new computer when we can afford it.

   B: Sure!

   A: No, really!
3. A: Luther came in first!

   B: Right!

   A: I'm serious!

   B: Wow!

Practice 9

A. 1. M
   2. S
   3. S
   4. P
   5. M